A
LAYMAN'S
Take on
CHRISTIANITY

A
LAYMAN'S
Take on
CHRISTIANITY

EDWARD A. BISCHOFF

MILL CITY PRESS

Mill City Press, Inc.
2301 Lucien Way #415
Maitland, FL 32751
407.339.4217
www.millcitypress.net

Paperback ISBN-13: 978-1-6628-3009-9
Hard Cover ISBN-13: 978-1-6628-3010-5
Ebook ISBN-13: 978-1-6628-3011-2

PREFACE

I take issue with much of the basic thinking of Christianity. I believe Christianity is missing the central idea and key points about God's offer of a supportive relationship with each one of us.

This book, *A Layman's Take on Christianity*, begins with Genesis, the first book in the Bible. Genesis 1, a story of the beginning of life, as described by long-forgotten people. This story opens the Old Testament. Old Testament stories tell of the simple faith and trust in the God of the leader of the Hebrews, Abraham. That faith led to the Hebrews' relationship with God. The trust and respect God and Abraham had for each other resulted in a friendship between the two that remained strong even though Abraham tested God more than once. The Bible then tells how the Hebrews become the Israelites, who then become the Jews. We are told of the Jewish couple, Mary and Joseph, whose son Jesus lived with total commitment of his heart and soul to His spiritual leader, God.

After the death of Jesus, the followers of Jesus split into several groups, which collectively became known as Christianity. As Christianity grew from this auspicious beginning, choices were made that led Christians to be less than they could be. Christians lost their sense of direction and purpose in their quest to become a major force in the affairs of the world.

Some of these choices are described in this book. The leaders of Christianity lost track of God's offer that He would be mankind's God—if mankind would follow Him, that is, to live as God lived.

I have come to appreciate that early Christianity was not created in a vacuum. The early Christians were introducing a new concept into existing social and religious cultures. The existing cultures were well established and much stronger than Christianity. The early Christians, however, believed that their story about Jesus and His ministry would fill a void in the lives of the Jewish and Greek world; it was a void that the existing religions did not fill. They believed the existing religions simply were not meeting the spiritual needs of the people. It seemed to me that failure to meet the spiritual needs of people is true today for Christianity.

God did not and does not require perfection. He demonstrates this by continuing to work with such Hebrews and Jews as Abraham, Jacob, Moses, and David, and Christians—such as Paul and the various Catholic and Protestant leaders, despite their shortcomings.

Lost in all the Christian ritual, structure, and theology is God's simple message that He will be our God if we will make our relationship with Him the most important thing in our lives, a message that Jesus lived on to His death.

I thought I knew more about Jesus than I did about God, but have, over the years, become less sure of what I know about God *or Jesus*. The problem is not with God or Jesus but rather with what has become the relationship Christians have with God and Jesus, and the theological requirements that have been made a part of those relationships.

While I am not sure who or what God is, it does not seem reasonable to think that God, who cares about each person, requires one or more groups of Christians to have control over how all people relate to Him.

Writing this book has clarified my thinking about Jesus and His relationship with God and clarified my relationship with God. I recognize that there is much to learn about a relationship with God. I hope that reading this book will allow you to clarify your relationship with God.

The following books and magazines referenced or quoted in this book are listed alphabetically, with the abbreviations used in this book.

Ancient Christian Commentary on Scripture. General Editor Thomas C. Oden. Inter Varsity Press. Downers Grove, Illinois. ACCS. The following volumes are the ones referenced in this book.

Vol. I Edited by Andrew Louth
Vol. II Edited by Thomas C. Oder
Vol. VI Edited by Gerald Bray
Vol. XI Edited by Gerald Bray

Biblical Archaeology Review. Editor before 2018 Hershel Shanks. Starting in 2018 Robert Cargill.
Publisher Susan Laden. BAR

The Israelites B.S.J. Isserlin 1998 Thames and Hudson Ltd. The Israelites.

Man's Religion John B. Noss. Third Edition Eight Printing 1967. The Macmillan Limited, New York. Noss

The Oxford Annotated Bible, Revised Standard Version. Oxford University Press 1962. All biblical references in this book will be from the Revised Standard Version RSV.

Webster's New World Dictionary College Edition Copyright 1953 The World Publishing Company. Webster's Dictionary

Who's Who in the Bible, The Reader's Digest Association Inc. 1994. WWB

TABLE OF CONTENTS

Chapter 1

SETTING

THE BEGINNING

The first creation story in the Bible tells of the love God has for mankind. It was developed by an ancient people in a land called Mesopotamia, who perceived that a clear and spiritual relationship was available between an unknown entity— one we now call *God or Lord*— and mankind. It is a story that happened thousands of years before Christianity became a religion, but is central to the message that a spiritual relationship with God is available to each one of us (Gen. 1:1-31).

This story begins without fanfare or pronouncement of God's presence, but rather accepts that there is a God of gods who set to work creating the world, and then created mankind, male and female, in His image, and blessed them, and said to them, "Be fruitful and multiply, and fill the earth and subdue it; and have dominion over the fish of the sea and over the birds of the air and over every living thing that moves upon the earth." The story ends with God seeing all that He had made and observed that it was very good. God creates mankind and set mankind apart from all other living things by making mankind in God's image, which provides the spiritual basis for each person to have a close personal relationship with God.

The central message of this creation story is the ancient people's belief that there is a God, who, through His generosity and loving spirit made mankind in His image, gave mankind the gift of life in the setting of God's making that had everything mankind needed to enjoy His gift of life. It expresses the underlying theme of God's unconditional love for all mankind, which threads through both the Old and New Testaments of the Bible and is incorporated in Israelite's Judaism and Christianity.

Being made in the image of God means that He did not have any favorites. He did not create some to be different from others. It means that all mankind has everything it needs to live as God would in His world. These ancient people believed His spiritual relationship with mankind would not require any future action on His part. So, they thought of God as, "a laid back, hands-off God," willing to give mankind the freedom to live in His image without further instructions. It means that mankind has all the attributes of God. Think of it as being a copy of God without being the spiritual entity that is God.

This ancient story has served well as the foundation for the Israelite and Christian recognition of God and the relation with him that is available to them and all mankind.

LIVING IN THE LIKENESS OF GOD

So, God made mankind in His image, but not in his likeness. Instead of directing mankind to live in His likeness, He gave mankind everything humans need to live in His likeness and the freedom to choose to live in His likeness. He left it up to us to decide how we would use His gifts. Although the Bible describes times when mankind has stretched God's patience to the limit, God has never stopped loving us or stopped giving us grace for our mistakes and shortcomings, nor has He taken back His gifts.

So, what does it mean to live in the likeness of God, and how does that differ from being made in God's image?

This issue is described in the *Ancient Christian Commentary on Scripture* (ACCS), Book I, Genesis I-II, page 27.

Among the Greeks, there is generally a distinction drawn between the image and the likeness: man is created according to the image, and his destiny in freedom is to achieve likeness to God

(Origen, Diadochus).

The issue of image is further described:

As to what constitutes the Image of God in man, Irenaeus maintained that this included both the corporal and spiritual aspect of man.

Most, however, found it in man's soul or spiritual aspect (Origen, John, Cassian, Ambrose).

God freely gave us two great gifts, His creation, and the freedom to use His creation without restrictions or instructions, that is, He gave us the opportunity to live in the likeness of God. God will not tell us how to live in His world or how we are to use His gifts. It's up to each one of us to decide if he or she will live in the likeness of God, which includes giving all others the opportunity to live in His likeness. Each person can have a relationship with God that can guide that person to living in God's likeness.

Story Background

The main message of this story came from the ancient peoples' belief in God and the relationship that they believed they could have with God. These ancient people sensed an unknown quality in the rhythm of their lives and their surroundings that provided purpose and direction to them. They sensed that they were part of an undefinable existence that was much greater than they were. Their search for an explanation of how they could fit together all that they could see, feel, hear, and believe became the creation story of Genesis 1:1-31.

This creation story came from the ancient people's perception of how the earth came to be and their belief that God was a loving God, who believed in His creation and thought that it was very good. It does not limit God. It describes what God did without indicating that He could or could not do more.

This creation story began by indicating that God was not alone and ended with God being alone. It was developed well before the *single God* concept became an important part of the Israelite religion called Judaism and, the Christian religion. There does not seem to be much significance in having God in the company of other gods rather than being by Himself.

There is much we, like the originators of the first creation story, do not know about this higher spirit we call God. The originators of this creation story accepted God's creation as they found it without questioning why. We are indebted to these ancient people for the gift of their reasoning and insight that led them to this creation story.

Believing that mankind was made in the image of God was a radical idea when tribes and religions were structured along the lines of kings and servants, and of people being dependent on priests. Just as there is today, there were the *haves* and the *have nots*. Even with the evidence around them to the contrary, the originators of the creation story tell us that all mankind is equal in the eyes of God.

They did not form this creation story to start a religion. They reached beyond the limitations of their religion. They believed that there was an unseen entity called God who cared about and loved them, and they wanted to describe the relationship they believed they could have with God.

The loving and tolerant relationship described in this story was much different from the worshipful, and dutiful relationship people had toward the gods of the existing religions.

This story ends with God looking at His work as a finished product, one that He saw as being very good—otherwise, His work would not have been finished. The story has God being satisfied that He had given everything mankind needed to live in His likeness. This story is not about the first phase of a long and continuous creation process. God was satisfied and His creation was completed and needed nothing more.

This creation story is just that, a story, not a record of actual events. It was developed based on what they could gather from their surroundings, and their sense that there was more to their existence than what they could see, feel, and hear. Their sequence of events was not time sensitive. They had no idea of how much time had elapsed from when the world began to their time. The use of days to set the sequence of events could be as simple as being what they knew and could easily identify and could use to easily set the sequent of events. To stretch this story to tell more than its sole message serves no useful purpose and dilutes the message of the story.

This story most probably did not originate with the Hebrews. Although the Hebrews were in Mesopotamia at the time of Abraham, it is thought that this story originated long before the Hebrews arrived in Mesopotamia. The ancient people who originated this story had no inkling that their concept of their relationship with God would serve as the opening to the book that describes the beginning, development, and growth of faith in God, based on a spiritual relationship between God and the Israelites and Christians.

STRENGTH OF THE STORY

It is a testament to the power and clarity of this story that the Israelites made it the foundation of their relationship with God. Opening the Old Testament with this story sets the reference for the many ups and downs of the Israelites' relationship with God. The belief that they were made in the image of God, and that God loved them was, and remains, central to the Israelites' relationship with God and was the reason they returned to God after they'd wandered off in another direction. The

Old Testament tells of God's continuous tolerance, and love and support, of the Israelites.

Equally true, the Christians who assembled the New Testament also believed that this creation story belonged at the beginning of the Bible, which was used by both the Israelites and Christians. *The Ancient Christian Commentary on Scripture,* Old Testament I, Genesis I-II pg. xlviii", states:

> CREATION. The Father's sense of the fundamental place of creation in Christian doctrine was a consciously maintained theological premise. Athanasius, at the beginning of his treatise On the Incarnation asserts: "But as we proceed in our exposition of this (the incarnation of the Word), we must first speak about the creation of the universe and its creator, God, so that in this way we may consider as fitting that its renewal was effected by the Word who created the beginning."
>
> It is only against the background of a proper understanding of the doctrine of creation that we are able to grasp the significance of the incarnation of the Word.

This creation story provides the foundation for Christianity and our relationship with God. That the ancient people who originated this story did so in a non-religious, simple, and clear manner that made it available to all people, regardless of where they lived or live or who they were or are. Being made in the image of God, and with God wanting mankind to live in His likeness, is the basis for the relationship between man and God, supported by God's love and grace that threads through the Bible.

The ancient originators of this creation story had a spiritual connection with God that is available to each one of us. They became spiritually connected to God and lived in His blessing without His nature being well defined.

This story is critical for the belief in God of both the Israelites and Christians. The unfortunate adventures that have caused the Israelites and Christians to stray away from the simple message of the first story of creation has not changed the story's message of God's love for mankind and God's trust that mankind will eventually live in the likeness of God.

It is an unfortunate reality that the simple message of God's direct spiritual connection with mankind was and continues to be beyond the ability of mankind to accept as guidance for life.

The message of a loving God being available to all mankind begins with this creation story. It continues to thread the narrative through both the Old and New Testaments and is not changed by what mankind does.

Chapter 2

ABOUT THE BIBLE

INTRODUCTION

The Bible tells of the relationship with God that is available to Israelites, Jews, and Christians, and anyone else who believes in God and establishes a spiritual relationship with God. It is a collection of stories assembled from a vast number of manuscripts about the successes and failures of an ancient people, and early Israelites and early Christians in their relationships with God. The Old Testament was set in about AD 100 (RSV pg. xxii). The books of the New Testament were written in approximately less than one hundred years, although changes to the New Testament were made until it was set in AD 367 (RSV pgs. 1167 and 1170).

The stories in both the Old and New Testament tell of the belief in God's involvement with the Israelites and Christians and describe a caring and loving God, who has been supportive to those who have a spiritual relationship with Him.

The Bible tends to leave unanswered questions by telling stories without tying up loose ends. This highlights evidence that the Bible was not assembled to be a book of answers but rather a book of information given in pose, poems and parables, and other forms of literature, to be used by each person in building their own relationship with God.

When using a current translation of the Bible and other material for study and worship, it is helpful to realize that none of the material currently available is *original*. It has been translated and copied into versions several times removed from the original. The information available today may not be, and in all probability is not, an exact duplicate of the original. Having said that, I believe that the core message of God's love continues to be described in both the Old Testament and New Testament. The wide variety of beliefs in Christianity of today comes from different interpretations of the core message rather than the core message being wrong or inaccurate.

The Bible, with its many stories about Jewish and Christian relationships with God, does not offer concrete proof that one can use to show conclusively that there is a God, a point that atheists delight in making every chance they get. Conversely, the lack of definitive, indisputable evidence that there is a God does not preclude the existence of God. The Bible has much on which one can base his or her belief in God. God's existence does not depend on our belief that He exists. He is what He is regardless of our belief in whom or what He is or the form of His existence, or how we fit Him into our beliefs.

God's nature does not need to be well defined. God may be he, she, or it. A strong case can be made that God is gender neutral so "it" may be the appropriate designation. Historically, God has been identified as a male, as He is in this book. However, our lack of clearly knowing what pronoun to use has not decreased His acceptance of our spiritual relationship with Him. That God may be much different than the terms we use to identify our awareness of Him does not interfere with each person having a relationship with Him.

The following is from the *Ancient Christian Commentary on Scripture*.

> These texts assume some level of unity and continuity of
> ecumenical consensus in the mind of the believing church,
> a consensus more clearly grasped in the patristic period

than later. We would be less than true to the sacred text if we allowed modern assumptions to overrun these premises.

(ACCS, Vol. 1, pg. xix)

To summarize, God may have been unhappy with the Israelites' and Christians' failures and heartened by their successes but that did not mean that He changed His mind and wrote the Bible as instructions to be followed. To whatever extent God may have had a hand in preparing the Bible, the Bible came into being through the effort of many people who wanted to describe their perception of God's relationship with the Jews and Christians.

There are blank periods in Old Testament stories, as well as a limited ability to date the time or when the stories happened, or to verify the accuracy of the information in the stories. In like manner, there is very little non-biblical information about the first few hundred years of Christianity. Our inability to confirm a story should not be proof that there was no basis for the story. Also, while the Bible certainly includes information about historical events, it is not an accurate historical document.

Stories were included in the Bible in the context of that time, which is a much different context than when the stories are being read today.

The Bible tells us that we are blessed with His eternal spiritual support, forgiveness, and grace, and the eternal freedom to make our own futures.

OLD TESTAMENT

The people compiling the Old Testament accepted the two creation stories that tell of the beginning of mankind and the relationship God wanted to have with mankind. They thought enough of these stories to have the Old Testament begin with them. The remaining stories in the first eleven chapters of Genesis tell of Cain killing Abel, the birth of

Seth, the great flood with Gods relationship with Noah before, during, and after the flood, the Tower of Babel, and introduces Abram, later to be called Abraham.

The Old Testament stories are told from mankind's view rather than from the view of God. Without question, the Hebrews, not God, wrote the description in the Old Testament of the Hebrews' perception that, through Abraham, God chose to be involved with the Hebrews. This is central to the understanding of who Hebrews were and the Israelites understanding who they are.

The Israelites believed that God intervened from time to time, such as when Jacob fought the angel or God; and when God had Moses brought the Israelites out of Egypt; and then after the golden calf incident when the Israelites were in the desert, when Moses successfully appealed to God to give them another chance.

The stories were told in the context of people's experiences, beliefs, and understanding of their surroundings and their relationship with God. These stories became part of the Hebrew-Israel folklore, which supported their perception of their relationship with God. They were carried forward from one generation to the next until at some point, they became part of a written record. It was much later when several manuscripts, written by different people, that, in part or whole, were selected to be included in what is now the thirty-nine books of the Old Testament.

The *Introduction to the Old Testament* (RSV xxi) describes in many ways how the life of the Hebrews-Israel continued their belief that their God was a merciful God of justice and redemption over more than a thousand years covered in the Old Testament.

The Old Testament describes the difficulties the Israelites had keeping a God-centered relationship, and how their relationship grew from a simple one of close friendship and trust between God and Abraham to a more complex one between God and the Israelites. As this relationship became more complex and the pressure from the neighboring kingdoms increased, the Israelites had more difficulty maintaining their relationship with God. Even with Israelite difficulties, the underlying message of God's steadfast love and caring for the Israelites remained. God did not have trouble keeping His part of the relationships with the Israelites regardless of difficulties the Israelites had keeping their part of the relationship. Even when the Israelites failed to stay true to God, and of God getting mad at them, His love for them won out and He did not give up on them. He continued to bless and give them grace and forgiveness.

It is important to point out that much uncertainty exists about the accuracy and dating of the Hebrew-Israelite history in the Old Testament. The dating of archaeological findings is not always accurate. Equally true, the dating and the description of events in the Old Testament are not always accurate. Also, there often is no clear indication of how events in one location relate to events in another location. If that was not enough another source of problems arises when trying to match languages and dates in the Old Testament with the languages and dates from outside sources or archaeological findings.

These problems have caused much debate, and it does not seem likely that any resolution of these problems will be found in the foreseeable future.

That some books of the Old Testament were compiled long after the fact could have contributed to some of these problems. For example, there is some indication that much of the first five books of the Old Testament were put together during the time of the Israelites exile to Babylon, which was several centuries after the fact. If the first five were written while the Israelites were in Babylon, that could account for why some Persian ideas were included.

The Old Testament stories were primarily to make a point, not necessarily to describe an actual event. For example, without knowing what we know today about how the universe began or the world was formed, the originators of the first creation story described the beginning of the world and their place in the world as they perceived it. The accuracy of the details is not as important as the concept of the gods being involved in the process, as well as the idea of the relationship the ancient people had with God and their place in the story.

Critical to the story is the understanding that there was, and is, a power greater than mankind, which was involved in the formation of the world. And this entity has given each one of us the opportunity to establish a spiritual relationship with Him and to have His support and grace through good and bad times.

It seems the originators of the first creation story were interested in supporting the evidence of there being a great unknown power, one that they called God, who caused the rain and wind, and caused giant trees to grow from small seeds they could hold in their hand and caused events to happen that were unexplainable. Threading through the story is the loving relationship they believed God had with mankind.

The Old Testament tells of the Israelites early struggles to be a separate people. They were distinctly different from other tribes of the Semitic people. The lack of details in this story of the Israelites beginning does not make the story any less compelling or less important to the Israelites' strong belief that they have a continuing personal relationship with God, separate from other peoples' relationship with God, that has carried them through terrible times throughout the centuries.

During the many hundred years separating the earliest and the latest writings of the Old Testament, the Israelites used what was available at any given time. For example, a copy of the "book of law" was found in the temple in Jerusalem in 621 BC and was used as the basis for Josiah's reform.

Although the Israelites had copies of some of Old Testament writings, a *canon*, or authorized version of the Old Testament did not show up until about AD 100 and some of the manuscripts that did not make it into the Old Testament continued in use after the authorized version of the Old Testament was set.

The Dead Sea Scrolls have added to the knowledge of the Old Testament. The Dead Sea Scrolls are, in some instances, thought to be the oldest available source of information. While there have been some differences between the Scrolls version and Old Testament, by and large, there has been a general agreement between the two. (My conclusion from reading the "Dead Sea Scrolls" on the internet.)

The original manuscripts of both Testaments are long gone. In the case of the Old Testament, before the discovery of the Dead Sea Scrolls, there were two main texts used to evaluate the translations of the Old Testament. In the article in the July/August 2016 Biblical Archaeology Review by Emanuel Tov, titled, *Searching for the Original Bible,* Emanuel Tov writes about the search for original texts. Starting on page 48, he writes:

> Prior to their (Dead Sea Scrolls) discovery, scholars looked mainly to two texts ... They are the Masoretic Text, which was finalized by Jewish scholars in about 1000 C.E. and a Greek translation of the Hebrew text called the Septuagint (or LXX). This Greek translation of the Pentateuch (Torah) was made for the Jews of Alexandria in the beginning of the third century BCE. According to tradition, 72 or 70 wise men translated the Torah into Greek in 72 days seating in 36 separate cells, and lo and behold, produced identical Greek translations, supposedly testifying to the accuracy of their translation.

Emanuel Tov describes other sources that can be and are used, but there is no "right answer." He closes the article by writing, "In many instances that ideal that we are searching for—the original text—is unobtainable."

So, the Old Testament we read today provides the latest translation of a wide variety of stories that are an integral part of the Israelites story and identity. Using the RSV Bible as reference, the information on the first five books in the Old Testament comes from the Pentateuch section. Pentateuch is found at the beginning of the Old Testament. The information for the remaining books comes from the section at the beginning of each book.

The first five books of the Old Testament (Genesis, Exodus, Leviticus, Numbers, and Deuteronomy) are the Pentateuch (literally, the "five scrolls"). It comprises the so-called "five books of Moses," known in Jewish tradition as the *Law* or *Torah*. These books elaborate on basic themes of Israeli's traditions: the relationship to the patriarchs against the background of primeval history (Genesis), the exodus from Egypt (Exodus 1-18), the giving of the law in connection with the Sinai covenant (Exodus 19-40; Leviticus); and the Lord's guidance of his people through the wilderness toward the promised land (Numbers). The last book, Deuteronomy, which gives Moses' final address to Israel, represents a pause in the flow of the narratives toward the realization of the promise (Joshua).

The Pentateuch embraces a great diversity of material which reflects Israel's pilgrimage from the time of Abraham to the Exile... thus the Pentateuch took shape over a long period of time.

The books of the major prophets, Joshua, Judges, 1 and 2 Samuel, 1 and 2 Kings, Isaiah, Jeremiah, and Ezekiel, tell of the leaders' efforts to conquer the promised land (Joshua, and the first part of Judges) and tell of the actions of the other Judges. I and 2 Samuel, which originally were one book, tell about the Prophet Samuel, King Saul, and King David. 1 and 2 Kings which also originally were one book are a continuation of the books of Samuel, which provides a history from the beginning of the period of the Judges to the exile. Isaiah, Jeremiah, and Ezekiel were prophets who railed against Israel's failure to follow and worship God. Their predictions of the hard times that would and had to befall them came from their understanding that their troubles were from their failure to live a God-centered life.

The books of the twelve minor prophets, Micah, Nahum, Zephaniah, Haggai, Malachi, Habakkuk, Joel, Zechariah, Jonah, Hosea, Amos, and Obadiah are called minor prophets because they are shorter books. As with the major prophets, they tell about the failures of Israel to follow God and the need for the Israel people to turn back to God. See Internet for, "Old Testament Prophets."

The remaining books called the Writings, are Psalms, Esther, Job, Proverbs, Ecclesiastes, 1 and 2 Chronicles, Ezra, Nehemiah, Daniel, Lamentations, and Ruth.

The summary of these books of the Old Testament was taken from the introduction for each book.

The book of Psalms is a collection of hymns poems that praise God and ask God for guidance and forgiveness. David is given credit for writing many of them. One of the most famous Psalms credited to Dave is the 23rd Psalm, *The Lord is My Shepherd*.

The book of Esther. One thought is that this book was written in Maccabean times to celebrate Jewish triumph over the Seleucids (see "Survey of ... Bible Lands," 15). It is probably earlier and may have been written as propaganda for the observance in Palestine of a festival, called *Purim*. It was a legend to explain the origin and significance of Purim which was celebrated on the 14th and 15th of Adar (in February-March). It was brought back to Israel by Jews from the Dispersion.

The book of Job does not try to explain the mystery of suffering or "justify the ways of God with men." It aims at probing the depths of faith even when there is suffering. The ancient folklore of a patient Job (RSV 1:1-2.13; 42:7-17; Jas. 5:11) circulated orally among oriental sages in the second millennium BC and was probably written down in Hebrew at the time of David and Solomon or a century later (about 1000-800 BC)

The book of Proverbs is a compendium of moral and religious instruction as given to Jewish youth by professional sages in the post-exile period. It included much older material from the long tradition of such training in the wisdom deemed necessary for the good life.

The book of Ecclesiastes, or the Preacher, contains the reflections of a philosopher rather than a testimony of belief. The author seeks to understand, by the use of reason, the meaning of human existence and the good which man can find in life. He questions many of the accepted beliefs of Hebrew traditions. To him God is the inscrutable originator of the world and determiner of man's fate. As the natural world is in constant movement without real change, so man's expenditure of effort achieves nothing.

The books of 1 and 2 Chronicles were originally a single book. The purpose of 1 and 2 Chronicles, like 1 and 2 Kings, is theological and idealistic. There is practically no attempt to present history as we understand the word. The chronicler wishes to advocate a certain pattern of religious life.

The books of Ezra and Nehemiah were prepared by the chronicler as a supplement to Chronicles based on Hebrew and Aramaic documents, memoirs of Nehemiah, a memorial of Ezra, genealogies, and archives. This supplement, the first verses of which appear also at the end of Chronicles, was written to tell how some returning from captivity and labored at restoring religion at a restored temple in a refortified Jerusalem.

The book of Daniel's six stories and four dream visions make up the first great work of apocalyptic, later examples of which are 1 Enoch, Syriac Baruch, and the New Testament book of Revelations. These apocalypses come from times of national or community tribulations and are not actual history, but through symbols and signs, are interpretations of current history with its background and predictions of the future where tribulations and sorrow will give place to triumph and peace.

The book of Lamentations is a series of poems mourning over the desolation of Jerusalem and the suffering of her people, following the siege and destruction of the city and the burning of the temple by the Babylonians in 587(586) BC The poems have been ascribed traditionally to the prophet Jeremiah (2 Chron. 35.25), but their thought and diction are sufficiently different from his to make this improbable.

The book of Ruth. The quiet, idyllic mood of the book of Ruth and the charm of its gentle heroine has given it a special appeal to many generations of readers. Although the story is ostensibly set in the days of Judges, it has nothing in common with the sanguinary tales of international and inter-tribal warfare narrated in the preceding book. Since the woman Ruth is a Moabitess and not an Israelite, the effect of the book, if not its purpose, is to create a sympathetic feeling toward foreigners who put themselves under the protection of Israel's God.

Although the Old Testament was not authorized until 100 C.E., the manuscripts that comprise the Old Testament were in use long before that. We know that the Old Testament manuscripts were valuable to Jesus for he used them in His ministry. The Old Testament is the foundation for the New Testament.

The Old Testament was written for use by the Israelites of the time of it being written, not for the people in the twenty-first century. It was composed from oral and written traditions and rituals that were developed over centuries to explain the unexplainable and to affirm the Hebrews covenant with God.

NEW TESTAMENT

Unless stated, otherwise all biblical references in this section are RSV.

Three sources of information exist today for our knowledge of the text of the New Testament. They are Greek manuscripts, early translations into other languages (Primarily Syriac, Latin, and Coptic), and quotations from early ecclesiastical writers. The total number of Greek manuscripts of all or parts of the New Testament is close to five thousand. Of this number the most important are, in general, the oldest; more than three hundred, written on papyrus or parchment, which date from the second to the eighth century (Introduction to the New Testament pgs. 1168-1169).

When St. Athanasius, in his Festal Letter for AD 367, named the twenty-seven books of the New Testament as exclusively canonical (Introduction to The New Testament, 1170). Many of manuscripts that did not make it into the New Testament continued in use long after the canonization of the New Testament.

Christians' belief in God's love is well described in Christian writings and the New Testament. God's comment at Jesus' baptism (Matt. 4:17, Mark 1:11, Luke 3:22, and John 1:34) and the description of Jesus' transfiguration (Matt. 17:1-8, and Luke 9:28-36) are two examples of the trusting, respectful relationship Jesus demonstrated with His living in God's likeness during His three-year ministry.

The New Testament tells the story of the birth, ministry, and death of Jesus, His work to simplify and make personal the relationship the Israelites had with God and to have the Israelites live with the blessing of God. There is much in the New Testament one can use to define Jesus' ministry. There are many stories of Jesus' teachings and ministry that are relevant today.

Some of the original New Testament manuscripts were written as a continuation of the Old Testament stories that told of the Prophet Jesus and the Israelites, and their life and religious history, and not necessarily as a separate book. If the followers of Jesus had stayed tied to the Jewish religion, the manuscripts that became the New Testament could very well have become a continuation of what is the current Old Testament, rather than a separate set of books as the New Testament.

With the many changes and copying errors that were made to the New Testament before it was accepted around AD 367, the New Testament continues to describe Jesus' basic message of changing the Jews' thinking about themselves and their relationship with God, which was the central message of His ministry.

It should be remembered that Jesus was talking to Jews who were shepherds, carpenters, fishers, and farmers. While they were literate, they used the simple and direct language they needed for their daily work and lives. So, it is highly likely that current descriptions and interpretations of Jesus' message are much more complicated than Jesus used in His ministry. So much has been read into his simple messages that in some cases Jesus' real message may have become diluted or lost.

The Gospels of Matthew, Mark, Luke, and John were written by Israelites, as were some of the epistles (letters). The early writing was Israelite in nature and referred to Jesus as a prophet. A second idea that Jesus was divine came from the Pharisee Paul who converted to follow Jesus and decided that Jesus was divine.

Since both ideas, prophet Jesus and divine Jesus, were being discussed while the gospels were being written, and since the non-Jewish followers were growing in numbers and prominence, the thinking of the non-Jewish followers that Jesus was divine, become more prominent in the gospels as they were written. The Gospel of John, the last one written, is the most affected by Paul's thinking. The Gospel of Mark appears to be the least affected by the later additions.

There is available information that allows for some ability to distinguish original writings from later additions to the gospels, but the information is insufficient to totally separate original writing from the later additions to the gospels. The use of terms and style of writing can also be used, to a limited extent, to separate the old from the new writing.

Without question, taking from the vast number of manuscripts, the twenty-seven books that became the New Testament as being the most representative of Jesus' ministry after the death of Jesus is a magnificent feat. The inclusion of Paul's ideas regarding Jesus being divine surely was an important factor in the increased prominence of the Gentile Christians and with the decreased influence of the Jerusalem Christians.

Some of the stories in the New Testament also originated as oral stories that were recorded and later included as part of the New Testament. For example, it is generally accepted that the Gospel of Mark was written by Mark and based on what Apostle Peter told him.

It is also generally accepted that Mark was the first gospel, written between AD 30 and AD 62 when Mark died in Egypt. The early church widely regarded the author of Mark's gospel as the authentic voice and interpretation of the stories Peter gave to Mark. There was some debate among the church fathers as to Matthew having been written before Mark. Even with the issue still in debate, the consensus is that Mark was first (Introduction to Mark, ACCS, Vol. II, 1998).

The strongest reason for Mark being the first book is that Mark contains very little that is not also in Matthew or Luke. When Mark and Matthew differ as to the sequence of events Luke agrees with Mark, and when Mark and Luke differ as to their sequence of events, Matthew agrees with Mark; and Matthew and Luke never agree to sequence of events against Mark (Introduction to The New Testament, (pg. 1167-1168).

Each gospel starts telling the story of Jesus differently. Matthew starts with the genealogy from Abraham to Jesus. Mark starts with a quote from Isaiah fore telling the arrival of John the Baptist and has John the Baptist appearing first on the scene. Luke starts with an explanation of why he wrote his gospel and John starts with an explanation of the mystery of Jesus. Although they each tell the story of Jesus' ministry differently, they, each in their own way, give voice to Jesus as He went from town to town telling the people of God's Covenant and the new age He believed was on the horizon. Each gospel includes the information that the writers of that gospel considered important. So, even with their differences, the combination of the four gospels gives a more complete description of Jesus' ministry than each gospel does separately. Even though their stories do not always agree, their stories make the total story of His ministry much stronger than each writer could individually. Said another way, the level of activity and the profound things that Jesus said and did could not have been captured by one person, and even the four gospels did not fully capture Jesus' three-year ministry.

The Gospels of Matthew and Luke include some descriptions of events that are not included in Mark. The Gospel of John includes events that are not in any of the three synoptic gospels (Matthew, Mark, and Luke).

The timeline and sequence of events are not the same in any of the synoptic gospels. The only sequences on which the three Gospels agree is that after Jesus was baptized by John the Baptist and Jesus completed his forty days of temptations, He began his ministry, and about three years later, after a Passover meal He was captured and crucified, and He was resurrected.

Two gospels, Matthew, and Luke, describe some of the events surrounding Jesus' birth. Luke describes Jesus' experience in Jerusalem when he was twelve and all four gospels, Matthew, Mark, Luke, and John, describe some of the events of his ministry, and his crucifixion, resurrection, and final earthly visit to his disciples.

Since Jesus did not leave a written record of his ministry, and it does not appear that any of the disciples did while Jesus was alive, the experiences people had with Jesus were recorded after the fact from oral stories and some manuscripts written by others. Many of these stories were recorded primarily in the seventy years between AD 30 and AD 100. Although there is little doubt that the manuscripts that became the New Testament were written in the firm belief that writers were accurately describing Jesus' teachings and the events surrounding his ministry, it is reasonable to think some of the details in a story differ between the gospels because of how they were experienced and remembered. And then, as the original copies were lost, copies were made from copies, and translated from one language to another, until the gospels we use today retain these differences.

There are issues regarding when some material in the four Gospels was written. Based on Jesus being a Jew whose purpose was to address the Jews' relationship with God, some of the entries in the gospels probably were made based on after His crucifixion understanding of Jesus' ministry. For example, in Matthew 10:5-6, Jesus' instructions to the twelve disciples were, "Go nowhere among the Gentiles, and enter no town of the Samaritans, but go rather to the lost sheep of the house of Israel." And in Matthew 15:24, Jesus responds to a Canaanite woman, "I was sent only to the lost sheep of the house of Israel." On the other hand, in Matthew 28:19, Jesus' final instructions to His disciples, just prior to his ascension, tells them to, "Go therefore and make disciples of all nations, baptizing them in the name of the Father and of the Son and of the Holy Spirit." Similar verses are found in Mark 16:15 and Luke 24:47. This contradiction to earlier statements made by Jesus is most surely a late addition to Matthew. However, it has been treated with the same validity as the rest of the Book of Matthew. It also includes the Trinity—Father, Son, and Holy Spirit, which did not come into usage until sometime after Paul become involved.

Another simple example of this issue is in Mark 8:35, which states, "For whoever would save his life will lose it; and whoever loses his life for my sake and the gospel's will save it." Since Matthew 10.39, Luke 17.33 and John 12.25 do not include, "the gospels" and only Matthew includes, "for my sake," these may be later additions to the verse. John's version of the verse is quite a bit different.

Regardless of what Jesus did and did not do and say, these gospels are an integral part of what Christianity is today. The differences in how his ministry was described in the gospels do not detract from Jesus' core message of living in a spiritual relationship with God.

It is evident that there were several sources of material available to the writers of the four gospels. It is also evident that some of the material that was available when the New Testament was being assembled was not included for one or more reasons. The four gospels and the other books and letters that were included in the New Testament provide, from several different perceptions, a common purpose and meaning of Jesus' ministry.

Recent finds of lost gospels have raised questions about why the Bible only has the four gospels. The Gospel of Thomas is one that has received much comment. The dating of these books in relationship with the four gospels has primarily been educated guesses, so how they fit into the writing of the four gospels is unknown. Their widely different views of Jesus and his teaching were also detrimental to their acceptance as part of the New Testament.

There is no consensus about whether Mark used other sources. Matthew and Luke have included information from other sources. The Gospel of John also uses other sources as well as John's own interpretation of the events. John goes farther than the synoptic gospels in declaring Jesus' divinity by have Andrew telling his brother Simon (Peter), "We have found the Messiah (which means Christ)" (John 1:41).

The following description of each gospel is based on the introduction to each of the four gospels in the RSV.

The Gospel of Matthew is a manual of Christian teachings in which Jesus Christ, Lord of the new-yet-old community, the church, is described particularly as the fulfiller and fulfillment of God's will disclosed in the Old Testament. The unknown teacher who wrote the Gospel of Matthew used Mark and other sources, including the writings of the apostle Matthew, which resulted in the gospel being named Matthew.

The Gospel of Mark is largely a collection of narratives that depict Jesus as being almost constantly active (a favorite word in Mark is "immediately," which occurs about forty times in sixteen chapters). On the other hand, Mark records fewer words of Jesus than any of the other gospels. It contains one collection of sayings in the form of a discourse (Ch. 13) and a few parables.

We do not have the original copy of Mark or the other three gospels, so there is no way to separate the memories of the actual happenings from later additions. Having said that, the lack of the actual account of Jesus' activities during his ministry does not detract from message of hope and God's love Jesus brought to the Jewish people and was later passed on to the Christians.

The Gospel of Luke sets forth the words and works of Jesus as the divine Savior, whose compassion and tenderness extended to all who were needy. The universal mission of Jesus is emphasized (a) by tracing his genealogy back to Adam, the father of the race (3.38; contrast Matt. 1:1-2); (b) by including references which commend members of a despised people, the Samaritans (10:30-37; 17:11-19; see Acts 8:5n);

(c) by indicating that women have a new place of importance among the followers of Jesus (7:36-50; 8:3; 10:38-42); and (d) by promising that the Gentiles would have an opportunity to accept the gospel (2:32; 3:6; 24:47; compare 15:4n) The unknown writer used Mark and other Christian sources and is generally thought to be a physician named Luke.

The purpose of the Gospel of John is to support the strength of the teachings of Jesus in his description of man's need to adhere to the will of God. The Gospel of John explains the mystery of Jesus. Like other men he is yet unlike them, standing above them in unique, solitary grandeur. John gives more details of his instructions to his disciples as well as his own interpretation of the events.

The Gospel of John goes beyond describing the events by giving meaning to them. His opening verses, Jn.1:1-18, is a poetic statement of God's creation as personified in Jesus. John wrote more of the glory of Jesus than the other three gospels. John's gospel was written later than the synoptic gospels which may have given him the opportunity to strengthen the spiritual message of the synoptic gospels.

Tradition says it was the apostle, John. Many scholars, however, think that it was composed by a disciple of John who recorded his preaching as Mark did that of Peter. In any case, when the gospel was published toward the close of the first century, the church accepted it as authentic and apostolic testimony to Jesus (Jn. 21:24), written that men might "believe that Jesus is the Christ, the Son of God," and thus "have life in his name" (20:31). (Introduction to the Book of John)

The Gospel of John strongly supports Paul's determination that Jesus was divine. The Gentiles could relate much better to Jesus' ministry with the divine Jesus being elevated to the same level as the gods in the pagan mythology.

The book of Acts of the Apostles, which is thought to be written by Luke as a continuation of the Gospel of Luke, tells the story of the early Christians through the time of Paul's ministry. The first half covers the Jerusalem church, and the second half primarily covers Paul's missionary travels.

The remainder of the New Testament includes the epistles written by the Apostle Paul and other Christian leaders that tells about the followers of Jesus working to grasp Jesus' message and spread it outside the land of Israel. The epistles are letters that were written to provide guidance and direction to the churches, rather than to be included in the Bible. The last New Testament book is the Revelation to John.

Paul was a Pharisee who worked to eliminate the followers of Jesus until he converted to follow Jesus. He traveled through the area outside of Palestine supporting existing churches and starting new churches where there was a need. During his travels, he wrote letters (epistles), as did other Christian leaders, to the Christian churches scattered through the Roman Empire to provide them with insight and instruction. In the early time before the gospels were written and distributed, these letters were used as guidance for the churches. There was little else available.

It is generally accepted that his thirteen letters that are included in the Bible are only a portion of the Pauline letters, the others having been lost. Paul's letter to the church in Roman was probably written in AD 55-57. The importance of this letter is described in, "ACCS, Vol. VI, pg. xvii, Introduction to Romans," as follows.

> This epistle is important because of what it tells us about the early days of the Roman church. Paul had not yet visited Rome when he wrote the epistle, to some extent the epistle was a letter introducing him to the leaders of the church at Rome. Who these leaders were is not clear, although a number of names are given to us in the final chapter. This is a matter of considerable historical interest, because for hundreds of years Western tradition have maintained that the apostle Peter was the first bishop of Rome. Why does Paul nowhere mention him? And if Peter had already brought the Christian gospel to the city, why

was it necessary for Paul to write such a letter. Until the fourth century there is little mention of Peter in any of the commentaries or remarks on the epistles that have come down to us. In any case Paul's epistle is the earliest evidence for the Christian community in the capital of the Roman Empire. (ACCS Vol VI, pg. xvii-xviii.)

The Introduction to Romans goes on to describe the difficulties that the Jewish Christians and Greek-speaking Christians were having with respect to the Covenant with God. The Gentile group, thought the Jews, were being arrogant and unreasonable in their strong support for following the legal and ceremonial systems that were part of what the Jewish Christians thought was necessary to stay in God's favor. The Gentile group, with little or no understanding of the Old Testament, saw no reason for adhering to these requirements. Paul said that each side was partially right and partially wrong. He said that Faith was the key theological principle that unites both Jews and Gentiles to be right with God. (ACCS Vol. VI. page xviii.)

Paul's letters to the Corinthians were probably written between AD 52 and AD 56.

The epistles are important because of what they tell us about the difficulties encountered by one of the most important churches planted by Paul. Many of these difficulties focused on the vexing questions of authority and leadership. Uncertainty about the leadership at Corinth had produced a situation in which the church was in danger of dissolving into competing factions based on personalities, some of whom were teaching false doctrine as well. (ACCS Vol. VII pages xvii-xviii.)

One of the passages from Paul's letters that receive much attention is 1 Corinthian 13:1-13, which closes with, "So faith, hope, love abide, these three; but the greatest of these is love." Paul believed that this strong statement of the primary Christian theology was needed to pull the members of the church back to Jesus' core message.

The ten shorter Pauline letters relate to the issues that are specific to the church or person to which the letter was addressed. Many of the issues among these churches were likened to the ones that Paul covered in his Roman and Corinthian letters.

The authorship of five of the seven general letters (Catholic Epistles) is in doubt while two, I John and I Peter, are generally regarded as the authentic writings of the apostles of the same name. The authors of each of the other five letters may be the apostles or more probably are someone who knew the apostle or had the same name as the apostle of each letter. The *Ancient Christian Commentary* states:

> The importance of the Catholic Epistles lies primarily in the fact that They offer a non-Pauline witness to the beliefs and practices of the first Christian communities. It is true that they are not the only non-Pauline voice in the New Testament, but they are the only group of Letters that has never been associated in any way with the great apostle to the Gentiles. Letters, by their very nature, have an immediacy that is lacking in more formal documents, and it has long been held that in them we get a truer picture of early church life than is available to us in the Gospels or Acts of the Apostles. (ACCS Vol. XI pg. xxi.)

The introduction to the Hebrew Epistle states that:

> This anonymous treatise contains the longest sustained argument of any book in the Bible. With a careful and closely-knit discussion, the unknown author moves with confidence step by step through an elaborate proof of the pre-eminence of Christianity over Judaism. (RVS pg. 1453)

The final book in the Bible, The Revelation to John (or Apocalypse), is a story of John's vision regarding the confusion and turmoil of the times. The John of these revelations is thought not to be the apostle John. This is a good example of stories that were not intended for general reading. The meaning of words and sentences would have the intended meaning to the intended audience but not the general population. The introduction to the Revelation to John, explains prophetic happenings.

This book contains many symbols involving numbers, strange beasts, and other Apocalyptic figures. Though the key for understanding some of these symbols has been lost, in other cases a comparison with the prophetic symbolism in the Old Testament, especially Daniel and Ezekiel, sheds light upon the author's meaning.

For example, John did not say the Romans are going to start persecutions in plain language, but rather described the pending persecution allegorically. The Romans could read it without knowing its actual message. In like manner, John described his vision throughout Revelations. Unfortunately, we have not been able to fully grasp his vision because of the lost meaning of some of the symbols.

The book, Revelation to John, was probably written in the middle AD 80 which is a time when Christians had grown in numbers enough that the Roman Emperor was getting concerned about these people who meet secretly, ate, and spent time together, follow a dead Jew who they claim to be the Son of the supreme God, who is greater than their pagan gods.

The article, *Laodicea's 'Lukewarm' Legacy* by Mark R. Fairchild in the March/April 2017 Biblical Archaeology Review describes a connection between the City of Laodicea and, "The Revelation to John,". Taken from the article:

> The church at Laodicea was addressed in the last letter to the seven churches of the apocalypse one of the seven churches of the apocalypse (Revelation 3:14-22}, where it is described as lukewarm-neither hot or cold. Moreover, the church is noted as being wealthy. This corresponds with what is known about the city during this period. The letter evidently quotes the views of some of the Laodicean Christians.

The book of Revelation to John was written near the end of the first century during the reign of the Roman emperor Domitian, who was the first emperor openly to proclaim himself a living god. ... Emperor worship was common in the Roman Empire, but it was believed that the emperors became gods only at their death. (page 37)

The Romans had a cult of emperor worship. The Jews were exempt from participating in emperor worship, and the church was included in this exemption until its membership included many more Gentiles than Jews. When the exemption was removed for the Christian church, those who refused to worship the emperor were killed. Christians were no longer permitted to buy or sell goods unless they obtain a mark of worship. All seven churches were confronted with these same difficulties.

John warns the churches to stop the practice of worshiping local gods and rituals and return to God. He calls all Christians to be among those who will be chosen to be with God when the world comes to an end. The early Christians continued the belief of the Jews, that the time was short before God would come down and collect the righteous to be with Him at the end of the world.

While there are differences in the books of the New Testament, they come from the differences the writers had in coming to the common purpose of describing Jesus' ministry. The *Ancient Christian Commentary on Scripture* makes this point:

> Note how scrupulously the disciples refuse to record those things that might have given the impression of their fame. ... How can believers of such character ascribe falsely to their own Lord things he never did? This is why I think it has been rightly said that "One must put complete confidence in the disciples of Jesus, or none at all." For if we are to distrust those of such unimpeachable character, we reasonably must also distrust all ancient writers on the same principle. (ACCS, Vol. II pg. xxiv.)

Thoughts On The Use Of The Bible

The one underlying fact about Hebrew-Israelite history and early Christian history is that there is much more we do not know than we do know. While, from the archaeological excavations and historical research and study, we continue to increase our knowledge and understanding of the civilizations and their cultures in and around the east end of the Mediterranean Sea during the time of the stories in the Bible, it is unlikely that all the unanswered questions will even be answered.

The Bible was written by many different people in support of their relationship with God. The Bible gives the writers' own perspective of the relationship that was available to people who were in a God-centered relationship. These stories of the Jews and early Christians' relationship with God, provides current readers information they can use for their own relationship with God.

The Bible opens with the first of two creation stories. It is a story of how the world and man came into being and describes the relationship between mankind and God. The core message of this creation story continues through the Bible. Having a God-centered spiritual relationship gives strength and purpose to all that mankind does and can do.

The Bible is not about specific answers. It gives information about the relationship between God and the Israelites and Christians. Even when there are conflicting passages in the Bible, the writers of the conflicting passages were equally true to their beliefs. The Bible provides a wealth of information a person can use to develop and live in his or her spiritual relationship with God.

Certain passages in the New Testament refer to Jesus as *the Christ* or a god. These passages conflict with other passages. While one can pick and choose Bible verses out of both Testaments to make his or her argument about Jesus, it is well to recognize that the Bible is not intended to solve arguments. A person's reading of the Bible is true to that person, and his or her reading of the Bible certainly can be central to his or her life. The full value of the Bible comes with recognizing that the writers were true to their beliefs as each one of us should be true to his or her beliefs.

What purpose is served by arguing over different interpretations of Bible verses? One person's interpretation of Bible verses is his or her alone and no good purpose served when that person requires other people to interpret the Bible verses the same as he or she does.

Remember that the Bible was not written for the twenty-first century. It was written to tell of the issues and events of the time when it was written. The Old Testament was written over several centuries before Jesus' birth and the New Testament was basically written within a hundred years after Jesus' death, but was not assembled as an authorized, "canon" book until AD 367. Both Testaments were written for the people of that time in the language and culture of that time. Any major modifications and amendments to the Old Testament after it was accepted in AD 100 and of the New Testament in AD 367 were often due to the language and culture of that time.

One has only to look at the wide variety of Jewish groups and Christian denominations to see the many interruptions of God's message and Jesus' restatement of God's message, even when both are seemingly clear and straightforward. That, however, does not mean they are easy to understand or follow.

What a Bible story meant to people in Jesus' time is different than what it means today. For example, take a trip from one town to another town that are forty miles apart. In Jesus' time, it was a long journey that required decisions, such as how to schedule the trip so as not be on the road after dark, and to decide how much food to take. The possibility of running into thieves was enough of a concern that inquiring about joining a group of people going in the same direction could have been an important part of preparing for the trip. An alternate may have been to hire guards for the trip. So, it is a trip that may take two or more days and certainly contained danger and uncertainty. And then similar preparations would be needed for the return trip.

Today it is not a big problem to get in a car and drive the 40 miles in, depending on the road conditions and traffic, 40 to 120 minutes. The two towns have not moved but going the 40 miles that separates them is much less difficult today than it was in the time of Jesus. So, walking or riding a donkey 40 miles represented a much greater problem in Jesus' time than traveling by car or bus does today.

Another hindrance to fully appreciate the writing in the Bible is the lack of understanding of the apocalyptic nature of the writing in the manuscripts that became the Bible. While Daniel and Ezekiel in the Old Testament and Revelations in the New Testament are clearly apocalyptic other books of the Bible also contain apocalyptic verses. The Webster Dictionary defines apocalypse as,

> One of the Jewish and Christian writings of 200 BC to AD 150 marked by pseudosymmetry, symbolic imagery, and the expectation of an imminent cosmic cataclysm in which God destroys the powers of evil and raises the righteous to life in a messianic kingdom.

Much of what we know to be true today was well beyond the imagination of the writers of the books in the Bible. For example, it was centuries after the Bible was completed that the fact became known and generally accepted that the earth rotated around the sun instead of the earth being the center of creation. It is still not well understood that our solar system is on the fringe of a galaxy that is not close to the center of the universe. If by some strange event the writers had known these things, would they have changed the message of their writings? The terms and words used by the writers certainly could have been different, but the core messages of God would have been similar. While their concept of God may have been different, God would not have been different.

A second difference between today and when the events in the Bible occurred is the vastly greater ability to cure diseases and provide health care today than existed in biblical times. Simple things that we take for granted today were non-existent in Jesus, time and earlier. Vaccinations, antibiotic medicines, and cleanliness were unimagined and would have been declared miracles if someone had stumbled across such medicines and concepts. Appling the stories in the Bible to lifestyles of today without adjustments for the different circumstances can lead to false conclusions.

Is reading and knowing the Bible a must for Israelites and Christians? And if that is true, did all the Israelites and Christians who lived before the Bible was finally assembled fall short because, at best, all they had were oral stories or copies of manuscripts that only told some of the story? And the manuscript they had may not have been one that ended up in the Bible.

Reading the Bible is not a requirement to have faith in God, although reading the Bible can certainly help. The faith in God that the early Hebrews had before the Old Testament was available, and the early Christians had before the New Testament was available, is what the Bible is about. It tells the stories of their belief in God and the relationship they had with God. The Bible is the result of their work to put together these stories in one book a collection of the many stories the early Jewish leaders and Christian fathers believed best portrayed the basis for faith in God.

The Bible is the one source of information that tells the story of God's love starting with an ancient people's story about their feeling of there being a bond between mankind and the unknown entity we call God and continues with stories of how the Semitic people of the Hebrew Tribe became the Jews of today, and stories of the of development Jewish religion, Judaism, and the story of the beginning and development of early Christianity. It tells this story through the stories of people who, through their trials and tribulations, and their continuing failure to keep their end of their Covenant with God, continue to receive God's steadfast and enduring love and God's continuing grace and forgiveness.

Although early Jewish and Christian scholars put together the structure of the Bible, the current Bible we use today was not assembled until must later. The King James Version was published in 1611; however, it was found to have some serious defects. Since then, several versions of the Bible have been used and these versions have also been revised. For example, the forerunner of todays' "Oxford Annotated Bible, Revised Standard Version", was published in 1901. The copy I use was printed in 1962 and is based on a 1952 revision.

While there have been additions, deletions, and revisions to some passages and more than one interpretation of words and passages, I believe that the basic contexts of the original writings have survived. The Old Testament continues to tell the stories of the Israelites and the combination of the Old and New Testaments is the Bible that tells the story of the Christians' efforts to live in the blessing of God. An example of the success of the writers and the early fathers in telling their story is the opening book of Genesis, and more particularly, the creation story as the first story in the Bible, Genesis 1:1-31. With various stories available, it is significate that the Israelites began telling their story of their relationship with God with this creation story, a decision which was accepted by the Christians assembling the New Testaments. I can think of no better opening to the Bible and its stories of our relationship to God than this creation story.

So, even though different Jewish and Christian denominations use different versions, the Bible we know today is the result of compiling and sorting through Jewish and Christian manuscripts that were written in various languages, and under a variety of cultural, social, religious, and governmental conditions, to come up with the manuscripts that best describe the basis for our relationship with God. Despite the difficulty of translating manuscripts from one language to another, when the same words don't mean the same, or when some words don't exist in both languages, it seems that, as near as it can be determined, the stories in the Bible well describe the Jews and Christians struggles to fulfill their Covenant with God.

With all the telling and writing, and copying and translating, the stories from their beginning to their ending, have retained the core message of God's will. The people giving the stories to the next generation were intent on telling its core message. So, even though we do not have the original copies of any stories, I think that the original messages have been saved.

Another issue is the lack of details that surround the events described in the Bible. The scope of the stories was limited to providing the information necessary to tell the point of the stories. There often is little or no information to identify the location, time or circumstances surrounding a story. Some of these limitations are caused by readers of today being unfamiliar with the terms, names and description of things or activities, or the locations and land areas used in the stories. Some of the information that was part of the original stories may have been lost while being coped or translated. Some of the limitations may also have been caused by the person telling or writing the story simply not including enough information to completely describe the location, time or circumstances surrounding the story.

And finally, the person telling the story may have thought the purpose of the story had been accomplished without providing more details. For example, the crowds that followed Jesus during Holy Week were probably a mixed group of the Galilean people, some of whom went with Jesus to Jerusalem, the people who joined Jesus' group as he traveled to Jerusalem simply for company and safety, and the curious and the mildly interested people who were in Jerusalem for the Passover week. People came into Jerusalem from all over the Mediterranean and Arabic lands for Passover week. It was a chaotic week of religious activity. The purpose of telling the story of Jesus' last trip to Jerusalem did not require information about who the people were or how many people were in Jerusalem for Holy week. Said another way, if a story was about the spiritual awaking a man experienced on his trip from Jericho to Gaza, then describing the details of his trip were not important to the story.

The purpose of the story of Jesus' last couple of weeks, which is told differently in the four gospels, was to describe Jesus' activities before, during, and after his crucifixion. It was not necessary to know the details such as, size of the crowds in Jerusalem, the number of witnesses to Jesus' crucifixion, or who were in the crowd that told Pontus Pilot to crucify him, to describe Jesus' painful death.

The writers of both the Old and New Testaments took liberties with the stories as they wrote them, which in that day and age was permissible. An example in the Old Testament is the story of the destruction of Sodom and Gomorrah. It may have happened just as the Bible tells us, but probably not. First, if such a major event as the destruction of two towns at one time happened It would have shown up in the records of the neighboring towns and countries. While no such entries have been found, there are indications that earthquakes may have caused massive destruction in that part of Palestine during the time of Abraham; however, I am not aware of any connection having been made to the destruction of Sodom and Gomorrah and an earthquake.

Even with not knowing the details of the destruction of Sodom and Gomorrah, the fact that the two towns were destroyed was all that was necessary for the story. And even if someday it is discovered that the massive destruction was caused by an earthquake or fire or volcano eruption or other worldly forces, who can say that God did not have a hand in the destruction of two towns?

Equally true, there is little information regarding the actual events in support of the story of Moses and the Israelites escape from Egypt as written in Exodus. Some event or events happen that became the basis of this story. The story is an integral part of the Israelites history, and it has been given its rightful place, along with stories about Abraham, David, and the Israelite exile in Babylon, in defining the Israelites and their relationship with God.

Regardless of the differences that have existed in the various copies over the past many centuries, the basic story of God's caring relationship with the Israelites in the Old Testament and the followers of Jesus, or Christians, in the New Testament has remained.

The Bible is not an accurate, time-sensitive record, nor is it a complete record of deeds or events during the periods of the biblical stories.

Much happened that affected the lives of the people in the centuries from the time of the first creation story to the time of the early Christians is not included in the Bible. The stories and events in the Bible are the ones that well described the relationship the Israelites and Christians had or could have with God, and the continuing grace and forgiveness God freely gives to mankind.

Reading the Bible in the context of the time of the writing of each book is difficult but can give better meaning to the messages in the Bible. The stories in the Bible were written in times and situations that are much different than exist today when the Bible is being read. Some of the words had different meanings and connotations when they were written from when they have today. Even though it is next to impossible to know how to accurately interpret the stories, allowing the stories to remain in the context of their time provides the reader a better chance of having insight into the purpose of the stories, and, in the case of Jesus, the simplicity and power of His three-year ministry.

When all is said and done, the Bible, with all its unanswered issues, provides a compelling message of God's belief in the goodness of mankind, His all-encompassing grace, and His faith that we will eventually get it right.

Jesus' life and ministry were about helping the Jews in their daily life. Making the Bible and its stories holy makes them less useful.

When all is said and done, the Bible was written primarily by Hebrew-Jewish people expressing his or her feelings and understanding of the relationship that is available to people who accept God's offer to guide them through their lives.

Chapter 3

EARLY RELIGION

F rom the beginning, early man felt that he was not alone, that a great unseen entity, or entities, were also involved with the world. Stories about the relationship between early man and these unseen entities, were developed thousands of years ago by the ancient people throughout the world. The ancient stories that were developed in and around Mesopotamia included the two creation stories, the story of Adam and Eve and their three sons, Cain, Abel and Seth, and the stories of Noah and the flood, the tower of Babel, and the genealogies from Adam of the second creation story to Abram or Abraham.

Well before writing was developed, each tribe or group developed an idea of who and what their gods were, they worked to establish and maintain a good relationship that they believed would put them in good standing with their gods. Even though they knew not from whence their belief in gods came or how it became part of who they were, their awareness of their gods was an integral part of who they were.

The explanations and measures taken by each group or tribe to relate well with their gods were passed down orally until, at some point, they were written down to be passed from one generation to the next. These manuscripts were revised as needed to better describe their relationship with their gods as new situations arose. Each group or tribe established a relationship with their gods. These relationships become part of the history of the group or tribe.

Man has had religious beliefs since very early in prehistoric times, well before there were Hebrews or Christians. There is evidence of religion in the graves of the Neanderthals, who lived between 25,000 to 100,000 years ago (Noss pg.5). Much of the basic religious concepts, such as worshiping gods, have been with mankind from early in the history of mankind. The basic ingredient of the various religious beliefs centers on believing that a good relationship between mankind and the gods is possible and necessary.

It was believed that the religious structures and theologies developed by early man were necessary to keep good relationships with the gods. So much of the life of early man was based on the unknown and unexplainable. Myths, mysteries, and magics were integral parts of their relationship with the gods and remain so in today's religion. From early times the continuing wide variety in structures and theologies of the various religions shows the creativity of the human mind and the unlimited options available for developing and maintaining a positive relationship between mankind and the gods.

Early Man, Its Gods And World

The world of our early man with its many dangers, such as dangerous animals, unpredictable weather, and events that they did not understand and could not control, provided the issues for which early man looked to their gods for relief. From the very beginning, early man did not just count on help from his gods. It had to initiate actions with the hope that the gods would support and provide guidance.

Early man was among the smallest and least equipped mammals to survive among the hazards and difficulties of its surroundings. Just to survive it had to continually be innovative and creative and to learn quickly how to work together in teams.

Teamwork is not a new concept. Our ancestors learned that hunting in teams and working together gathering eatable food from their surroundings, greatly improved their chances of survival. It has been said that our ancestors were more creative and innovative than we are today. They developed new and profound ways of living that we take for granted. They started out with nothing but themselves, and from scratch, learned to make tools from rocks and stones that were lying around, to fashion shelter and clothing from wood, grass, and animal skins, to master fire, and to develop communication skills and language that gave them a survival advantages over other life forms.

Even with their innovativeness, creativity, and they're successfully working together, our ancestors accepted that many of the things going on around them were out of their control and could not be explained by their hard, smart work. Over time they slowly put names and human-like qualities and characteristics to the unseen gods that they believed controlled the things that were beyond their control.

They separated the unknown into specific areas, so they could better relate. It made no sense to worship the god that controlled the growth of plants and trees if their survival depended upon the sea. And it made no sense to worship the sea god if their survival depended upon the animals, plants, and trees. Of course, if they needed both the land and the sea for survival, they had more gods to respect and worship. If they lived close to a mountain, then the god of the mountain was one of the gods they respected and worshiped, for they had seen what happens when the god of the mountain was unhappy.

The gods were not seen, and their next move could not be predicted. So, our ancestors did what they thought would make the gods happy, or what seemed to work the last time. They regularly asked for forgiveness from the gods and acceptance of their gifts by the gods.

Before long there were good gods and bad gods or demons, there were rituals to the rain god when it was too dry and rituals to the sun god when it was too wet. The god that protected the trees was good because the trees provided shade, shelter, and firewood, and quieted the wind and the surrounding sounds. On the other hand, the forest could be a dark and forbidding place with dangerous animals, where bad things happened so, the god of the forests may be a different god than the tree god, and each needed to be worshiped differently, and the forest god may even be considered a demon. So, mixed in with the worship of the wind, rain, sun, rivers, animals, birds, fish, etc., were the worship of gods that could cause good and evil.

As the worship of gods became more complex and dominant, a person or persons were chosen to be the intermediaries between the gods and the people. So, if the hunters were coming home empty-handed the people would go to their intermediary that worked with the god of hunting to find out how to get back in the good graces with that god. This could mean a sacrifice to the god or some other solution like going through a ritual process to find a new hunting ground.

There were many names for the intermediaries but the names all eventually came to common words, as priest or minister.

With our ancestors living on what they could gather and catch, and later, on what their primitive agriculture could produce, minor changes in their environment could have a catastrophic effect. So many things had the potential of going wrong that keeping the gods happy was a major and continuous effort. Their religious activities were an integral part of their daily lives and came to control their daily lives. Most if not all decisions were weighted against how they thought the gods would react.

They kept their relationship with their gods sacred and they developed and practiced rituals in response to their anxiety and in the hope that the gods would be favorably impressed and act on their behalf. There was magic in the rituals and their belief was that the ritual would be successful. And a tradition or myth developed of the ability of the intermediary or priest to identify signs of the success of a ritual that would relieve anxiety and bring comfort to the group members.

Our ancestors built their basic concept of gods from their own experience. Early on our ancestors lived in small family groups with everyone doing, as best they could, what was needed to stay alive. Over time family groups would work together and became a tribe. At some point, it began to make sense to consolidate the gods of the families into tribal gods, with, over time, one god became the most powerful of all the gods, which lead to the combination of all gods into one god. To go from specific gods for specific issues to one god for everything would certainly have been accomplished, over time, with much trepidation and conflict. The worship of more than one God continues today in some religions.

There are many stories of the creation of life and the world, and the relationship between mankind and the unseen entities that affected daily life. The most important gods of a group, be it a tribal or clan, were depicted as a variety of things, such as the sun, moon, and various animals, or monuments or structures. Each group came up with their own explanation of the beginning of life, and how the world worked, and their relationship with their gods. In general, the relationship between a group and their gods was tied to the relationship between the group leader or king, who was often considered to be a god, and his subjects.

In addition to tribal or group gods, families would also have had household gods that followed the families as they move from place to place. The household gods were independent of the tribal gods, so, when tribal gods were consolidated the household gods remained a part of the family. There was great reluctance to give up these household gods, especially if the family believed that its gods had been successfully meeting their needs. The household gods were often not given up for a long time after the tribal gods were being worshiped, and some household gods are still used today.

This issue is highlighted by the story of Jacob's wife, Rachel, stealing the household gods of her father, Laban, when Jacob, along with his family and livestock, left Laban. Even after the relationship between God and the Hebrews had been established, the evidence of the important of household gods is shown in Rachel taking her father's household gods as part of her inheritance, and Laban chasing after Jacob in a failed attempt to get back his household gods. According to ancient custom the possession of household gods insured a man's leadership of the family and his claim on the property (Gen. 31:17-21).

To show respect and to honor a group's gods, things that mark its existence are worship, glorious buildings and monuments are constructed, and paintings, poetry and prose are completed, all in hope and belief that the gods will enjoy and appreciate the high regard they are held. In like manner, Israelites and Christians build monuments and glorious buildings, paint paintings and write poetry and prose about God and to glorify God in hope and belief that God will appreciate the work and look kindly upon the Jews and Christians.

This section is my summary of what I have read over the years regarding how man has gone from early man to what we are today. My thinking about man's development has come from the articles, books, and other written material I have read, and my own experiences over the years. The sequence of events I have describe certainly is not the only way mankind may have developed.

Pre-Judaism

Of interest to Jewish and Christian religions are the people in the area north and east of Canaan known as Mesopotamia. It is generally accepted that the two creation stories that begin the Old Testament, as well as much of the first eleven chapters of Genesis, are based on stories that came out of Mesopotamia, an area that is generally defined as the area around the Tigris and Euphrates rivers and is where an ancient civilization began. While the date of when these stories originated is unknown it is general accepted that the creation stories originated well before 2000 BC. There are signs of people living in Mesopotamia earlier than 5,000 BC.

Two main groups of people lived in ancient Mesopotamia at that time. The people who lived mainly in cities along the two rivers were

Sumerians, who developed an early writing system. The religion of the Sumerians had many gods and goddesses. The second group of people called the Semitic people had come from the Arabian Desert and wandered into the outlying areas of Mesopotamia. It was not until sometime prior to the time of Abraham that they became a major factor in Mesopotamia. Interestingly, the civilization and language that began in Mesopotamia with the Sumerians were not the basis for the languages of the world. It was the Semitic language that served as the dialect from which came the Arabic and Hebrew languages. Arabic and Hebrew languages came from the Semitic Akkadian language. (Summarized from Internet articles on Sumerian Language and Akkadian Language.)

Why did the Bible open with two creation stories? While we may never know the answer to that question, it is apparent that the Israelites who put together the Old Testament and the Christians who put together the New Testament thought enough of both stories to start their stories about who they were and their place in their world with these two stories. Also, it seems that they did not have a problem with having two different creation stories.

There is some thought that the creation stories were written to support the relationship between God and Abraham. While the Bible has the two creation stories leading into the story of Abraham and his relationship with God, there is no evidence of the God of Abraham telling the people who originated the two creation stories to develop and tell the creation stories. There are strong indications that the creation stories predate Abraham by at least 1000 years and there is no evidence of any connection between the creation stories and Abraham.

Each story describes creation differently. The first creation story describes the ancient people's belief that mankind was made in God's image and had the opportunity to manage the world and to be fruitful and multiply.

The second creation story describes how God created a woman, Eve, from a rib of Adam, although doubts have been raised about a rib being the part of Adam used by God. It has God giving Adam and Eve the

Garden of Eden, with everything they needed to live, with only the instruction to stay away from the tree of knowledge of good and evil. Apparently, the wise use of judgment was as much of a problem back then as it is today. The story also tells how Adam and Eve quickly got into trouble with God, by allowing a snake to convince them to partake of the forbidden fruit (not an apple) from the tree of knowledge of good and evil. This is the first case in the Bible of, "the devil made me do it."

God had to intervene to straighten out the mess Adam and Eve had made. God was not pleased, and He drove them out of the garden. They would continue to live; however, instead of living as God intended, their lives would be filled with hardship, toil, and pain. Only by staying connected to God could they mitigate the continuing disappointments and hardships they had created for themselves.

This is the first case of God intervening in the affairs of mankind. His intervention was direct, clear, single-purposed, and fully understood by Adam and Eve. As would be the case time and time again, it was not God or the animals or the world that caused God to intervene, but rather mankind itself that caused trouble for mankind.

Why did God put the tree of knowledge of good and evil in the Garden of Eden, if He did not want Adam and Eve to learn from it? Was it an oversight by God or did He want to see how Adam and Eve would do without the benefit of learning the difference between good and evil from the fruit of the tree or was it a test to see if Adam and Eve could be trusted? Adam and Eve had a fifty percent chance of making the right decision, and they did not. So, they had experienced good and were about to experience evil.

God may have wanted to keep mankind from having to decide what was good and what was evil. Of all the gifts God gave mankind why, was knowing the difference between good and evil the one that gave Him the great concern?

God's gift of judgment has been the most difficult gift for mankind to use. When one looks at the history of mankind, the gift God did not want mankind to use is the one gift that has consumed much of history with the strife and conflict that comes from the poor use of judgment by mankind.

If God wanted Adam and Eve to learn about using judgment, the learning curve has been a very long and flat, with little sign of any learning taking place.

After being driven out of the Garden of Eden, the story continues with Adam and Eve having two sons, Cain, the first born, and Abel. Cain was a farmer and Abel was a shepherd. Both made an offering to God. As written in the Bible, "And the Lord had regard for Abel and his offering, but for Cain and his offering He had no regard" (Gen. 4:4-5).

It is well to realize that in the time of this story the first-born son was normally the privileged son. So, the rejection by God of Cain's offering was a double rejection, one of being the deserving first son and the second of rejecting his work.

As one might expect, Cain was disappointed and angry with God's judgement, and ended up killing Abel. The Lord banished Cain from his land and made him a fugitive and a wanderer. However, the Lord protected Cain with a mark that is not described. (It would need to be something that would be universally known to indicate divine protection.) So, Cain leaves home and goes away from the presence of the Lord to dwell in the land of Nod east of Eden. Nod means Wandering. Cain settled down, married and his wife bore a son, Enoch, and built a city named after his son Enoch. (Gen.4:6-17 and accompanying footnotes.)

I think the originator of this story recognized the problem mankind was having with judgment and that God realized that mankind was a long way from being ready to handle the ability to make judgments. If Cain's action was why God did not want Adam and Eve eating from the tree of knowledge of good and evil, mankind has certainly validated

God's concern. Beginning with Cain's poor judgment resulting in poor results for both Cain and Abel, mankind has demonstrated, over many thousands of years, how disastrous the misuse of judgment has been.

This story leaves unanswered questions. Why was it necessary for the Lord to use His prerogative of choosing either Cain's or Abel's offering in the first place? Up to this point, there was no order of value or priority placed on God's gifts to mankind. And why was Cain's offering not acceptable? From the opposite viewpoint, why wouldn't God have the freedom to decide what he did and did not like?

Why God would choose Abel's offering over Cain's was not important to the purpose of the story. *What* God did, not *why* He did it, was germane to the story. God made a choice, as He certainly is permitted to do, and punished Cain for overreacting.

Shepherds and farmers have been at odds over the use of land since the beginning of when there were shepherds and farmers, and this certainly could have been the case at the time of this story. If this is the case, one can suppose that the storyteller was allied with the shepherds and that the conflict was enough of a problem that it needed to be dealt with in the context of worshiping God.

Continuing with other questions raised by the story, if Adam and Eve are the first people on earth and Eve is the "mother of all living," where did Cain's wife come from? (Genesis 3:20) Did the storyteller miss Adam and Eve having a daughter who Cain married or were Adam and Eve not the only people on earth? Did God under a different guise create other Adams and Eves in parts of the world that were unknown to the Adam and Eve storyteller?

Israelite's idea of Eve being the mother of all things may have meant that Eve was the mother of all Israelites, and Cain going away from God and taking a wife could have meant that Cain went to a neighboring kingdom with a different god. The modern-day reading of the Bible gives stories like these a very broad meaning that may have exceeded the scope of the writer's vision of his or her world.

Equally confusing is Cain going away from the presence of the Lord. Did he come into the presence of another god, which means there is more than one God, or were there portions of the world that had no presence of a god? Which would mean that the god or gods who, "... saw that what he (or they) had made was good" missed something.

With the world the Israelites knew being a portion of the area that encompassed Mesopotamia and the eastern and southern end of the Mediterranean Sea, their continuing struggle to keep the land they believed God had given them may have colored their interpretation of what the word *world* meant so that their idea of their world may have only included the local area they knew rather than the world that we know.

The few verses about Adam and Eve and their sons, Cain and Abel leave more questions than answers. As is true throughout the Bible, it often provides information without providing answers. Apparently, the writers of the stories wanted the readers of their stories to make up their own minds about how the stories should end.

When the story of Abraham and later stories in Genesis were recorded there were tribes of people in and around the Palestine area, each having their own religion and god(s). For example, the kingdoms of Ammon, Moabite, and Edom, which were tribal kingdoms with their own kings, were all on the east side of the Jordan River next to Israel. The Israelites continued to have trouble with the surrounding tribal kingdoms, some of which were Semitic, as described to some extent in Genesis, Deuteronomy, Joshua, Judges, I Kings, II Kings, and Jeremiah.

Continuing with the story of Adam and Eve, they had another son, Seth, who was the beginning of the generations that lead to Noah and from Noah to the Hebrews, Abraham, the Jews, and Christianity.

It seems that, like Adam and Eve, mankind was proving to be easily swayed off course and was not living as God had intended. God was not happy and was thinking about getting rid of mankind and starting over; however, He looked with favor on a man named Noah. Genesis 5:1-32 gives the genealogy from Seth to Noah.

The Lord instructed Noah to build an Ark and to collect a male and female of every living thing and load them into the Ark, along with his wives and sons and families. God's instructions to Noah in Genesis 6:5-22 differs from His instructions in Genesis 7:1-5. Noah did as God commanded, and it rained forty days and nights to flood all the earth and destroy all that was not in the Ark. So, the Bible describes all mankind, from that day forward, are descendants of Noah.

Noah had three sons, Shem, Ham, and Japheth. The Bible gives the generation of Noah's three sons. When the flood subsided enough that Noah found land dry enough Noah release the animals. The Lord establish a covenant with Noah and his descendants that follows the message in the first creation story with the added restraint against murder and the restraint from eating, "the flesh with its life, that is, its blood." The Lord's sign of the covenant was to be his bow in the clouds, which has been taken to be the rainbows. It is also interesting that this covenant with Noah covers all the people in the world not just the Hebrews. This story, in Genesis 6:5-8:22 comes from both the Babylonian and the Priestly writings.

This story of the world, as people knew it, being destroyed, including all mankind, animals, and plants except for Noah and his family and the animals in the Ark, would have certainly been a rude awaking to the people of God's power and His willingness to use it.

The story may have been to explain that a disastrous flood that the ancient people in the Mesopotamia area had experienced was the action of God in response to the actions of the ancient people that were intolerable to God. How God makes His point is not the issue, that God forcibility reacted to unacceptable actions of the ancient people is the point of the story.

The event that led up to the story had to be of such magnitude that it could be equated to a massive flood of the world. How else could the religious leaders or the king of the region explain the misfortune that had befallen the land? Not only did they look to God for help they looked to God to explain things they did not understand, as we do today. Writing stories to identify the seriousness of an event or situation in a manner that the people could understand was the purpose of the biblical stories.

I have often speculated about the condition and smell of the Ark when the flood had retreated enough for the Ark to land on a mountain top and the animals were released. I speculate that all the people and animals were very eager to leave the Ark.

In the middle of giving the generation of Noah's three sons, the Bible tells the story of the Tower of Babel. The next major event in the Genesis is the construction of the tower of Babel. This story tells us that at one time all people in the world spoke the same language and a group of men thought they could build a tower to the heavens. The Lord looked at the tower and, seeing the potential for what they could do, confused their language so that they could not understand each other and scattered them throughout the world (Gen. 11:1-9).

This story may have come from the idea expressed in the first creation story, that God placed a firmament in the waters that separated the waters under the firmament from the waters above the firmament, and the waters above the firmament were called heaven (Gen. 1:6-8). So, the people thought that the heavens were a finite thing that they could see and, therefore, they could touch, if only they could reach it.

Whatever the reasoning was, building a tower to reach the heavens seemed possible, and surely would have looked like a great accomplishment if completed. So, what happened? While there is no evidence that a tower was ever built, or that it was even started, the story of the Tower of Babel could have come out of the idea that heaven was a place that could be reached if they knew how. Closely allied with this idea is the belief that heaven was a place, somewhere, the people can go after they die.

A second origin for the story could have been that as the tribes of Mesopotamia and the surrounding area interacted with each other, the lack of a common language inhabited trade and commerce. In looking for an explanation for the different languages, the story of the tower of Babel came into being.

VALUE OF THESE STORIES

What can these stories tell us? If it is necessary for these stories to have been written by God, and therefore, they are word for word true to what happened, making sense out of them can be difficult, for there are many loose ends and there are no ancient records that describe events in the manner they are described in the Genesis. Records indicate that these stories originated well before Abraham was born and were used by people living in and around Mesopotamia before the idea of there being a single God had been developed.

If, however, they are stories written by people to make sense of their world as they saw it, and the storms and floods that devastated their area; and to provide plausible explanations of the family or tribal history of such things, and how different people speak different languages, then they became part of the family or tribe's culture and help define each family or tribe to other families or tribes as they move from one place to another. The stories served as a foundation for the culture of the people and to support their belief that there was a god.

People today, at great expense and time, have looked for the remains of the ancient structures and sites mentioned in these stories without success. The message of these stories is about the relationship early people had with their God or gods. These early relationships were not dependent on people in the twenty-first century finding evidence of the Ark or the tower or a location called Nod, or any other things mentioned in the Bible.

These stories were told long before anyone thought about collecting them and assembling them into a book called the Bible. They were part of the tribal culture that gave the people guidance and direction for living from one day to the next.

Also, it is impossible to know how much these stories in the current book of Genesis differ from the original oral story. In any case, the stories were told in the language of the people and would have become part of the belief structure of these people, and the reason for the stories would have been understood and accepted at the time of the telling.

The people of that time lacked almost everything we consider basic to our existence today. Much of what happened appeared to be coming from the gods as mythical or mysterious and magical happenings. For them, the gods controlled the rain and sun and the success in hunting and farming. The person who came up with a way of improving the lifestyle of a tribe was considered blessed by a god.

Many things happened that could not be easily explained. Coming up with plausible explanations did not have to explain all the issues, just the main issues. Some of the side issues, like wondering where Cain's wife had come from, could be overlooked. All that was necessary for the people to accept the story was for the main part of the story to make sense and to be believable. These early stories and religious beliefs were used to start the most important book of the Hebrew tribe and its descendants, the Old Testament.

These stories are the Hebrew adaptations of stories that originated in Mesopotamia. Without a clue as to the time span between these stories, and without any knowledge of exactly where and when they originated, little can be gained by being more accurate regarding their origination than to say that they came from the Mesopotamia area a long time before a group of Semitic people were identified as Hebrews and, the writing of the Old Testament.

The relationship our ancestors had with their gods was a group relationship rather than a personal one. The members of a group related to the god of the group, as a member of the group not as an individual. When someone joined a new group, he or she would adopt the religious rituals and sacred beliefs of the new group and discard the religious beliefs and rituals of their previous group.

The major break from the concept of tribal or group gods was the idea of having a personal relationship with a god, such as what God and Abraham had, a relationship based on mutual trust, respect, and friendship.

One final thought, assuming a piece of Noah's ark, or some other biblical artifact is found and positively identified as an actual true artifact, how would that change the message of the story? Is our relationship with God so fragile that proving the actual existence of an artifact would change the message of the story? Would finding a piece of Noah's Ark mean that the message of God's anger with mankind caused Him to use Noah and his ark to start over, would need to be changed to something else?

The stories and their messages did not require proving that the event happened as described in the stories. The stories are about God's spiritual relationship with mankind and the messages about God's spiritual relationship with mankind do not need finding some physical evidence of an artifact from the story.

SEMITIC PEOPLE

The generations continue from Adam through Noah to the Semitic people, who were descendants of Noah's son, *Shem*. They were ethnic or cultural people who spoke the Semitic languages. They included the Arabs, Akkadians, Canaanites, and Aramaeans. Abram (Abraham), the son of Terah was the leader of the Hebrew Tribe of the Semitic people.

The Semitic people were organized into tribes, which was common in the land east of the Mediterranean Sea during that period, as it remains in many areas today. Each tribe was primarily a self-contained unit with a ruling elder or patriarch setting the routine and order for that tribe (Noss pg.495).

Developing the Semitic religion was not a simple, clean, uniform process. There was a long process of adopting and removing religious elements. They looked at the religions they encountered and included some of the practices of these religions.

Many religions of that period ran through the ruling king, emperor, or other power center. Whatever the ruler of a county or nation was called, he or she was often considered a god or a personification of a god. As the Semitic people traveling from the Arabian Desert to Mesopotamia through the land of different groups of people, who had their own gods, customs, and cultures, the Semitic people were developing their own relationship to their gods, which set them apart from the other religions they encountered in their wanderings. While we do not know how big a part the Hebrews played in developing the Semitic's relationship with their god's, this relationship was the foundation for the Hebrew's relationship with God.

We now come to the Hebrew Tribe of the Semitic people.

As we will see in chapter 4, from this point on the Old Testament follows the Hebrew tribe and its descendants to the birth of Christ.

THE HEBREW-JEWISH PEOPLE

THE HEBREW TRIBE

It may be said that one great theme dominates the course of Jewish religion; this is the theme that a single righteous God is at work in the social and natural order. This theme was not immediately arrived at, but somehow it seems implicit from the beginning. Only morally and socially sensitive minds could conceive of history in such terms or develop a group consciousness of such a god (Noss, pg. 494).

The Israelites are descendants of Abraham's tribe of Hebrews. Throughout the stories in the Bible, Hebrew, Israelite, and Jew all have names for the same people, during different times in their history.

The Hebrews were a tribe of the Semitic people who wandered the Arabian Desert for many years before migrated into Mesopotamia. Their story is a remarkable story about a people developing a personal relationship with their god.

The early Hebrew tribe started out with many spirits (or gods); however, over time some spirits became more important than others. The spirits that were thought to have special powers were given the name El (sing.), or Elim or Elohim.

Although there were similarities in living standards between the Hebrews and other Semitic tribes, the Hebrews arrived at a distinctly different relationship with their gods, one that opened a wealth of possibilities in their relationship with their gods. Developing their own relationship with their gods did not prohibit the inclusion of some Persian ideas into their religious thinking.

Rather than being subservient to the master, the relationship was more akin to a caring father looking after his children. The Hebrews had the sense of being *chosen* and of choosing. In other words, their relationship with their god(s) was personal and direct, and they developed a sense of having some say in the choosing process. The combination of being chosen and having a direct connection with their gods eliminated having the ruling leader being a god.

The Hebrew direct relationship with their gods as a chosen people was a major accomplishment. This sense of being chosen continued with the Hebrews and on through the Jewish and Christian religions.

Being chosen by a god and choosing to have a personal relationship with that god carries the expectation of much more than blindly following a set of rules and regulations, as would a person that is subservient to a god. It is a relationship that has the *give and take* that requires personal instead of group commitment, and it has surprises.

The Bible tells stories of the chosen people living in direct relationship with their god. They try things that sometimes fail and sometimes work. The god forgave their failures, sometimes with punishment, and accepts and supports their successes. The one constant, above all else, was the requirement to be respectful of the god and having their lives centered on their god.

The idea of one god may have started with the Semitic people; however, when it started is unknown. Regardless of when it started or when other people switched to one god, the leap in faith to one god had to be enormous. Try to imagine the turmoil this would have caused in an existing religious establishment. The supporter of each god would not willingly give up his or her god.

The relationship the Hebrews established with their God reflects their unusual insight into the world around them. The story of this relationship is a story that was told and written in the confidence that a unique relationship existed between the Hebrews and an unseen entity they called God, who was willing to look after and guide them through life. Their relationship was not master and servant, but rather a relationship between respected and close friends.

ABRAHAM

The story of Abraham begins when Abraham's forefathers migrated out of the desert to the Mesopotamia area. Abraham's father, Terah, settled with his extended family in Ur of the Chaldeans. While they were in Ur Abraham married Sarah. Terah next took his extended family to Haran and that is where Terah died (Gen. 11:27-32).

There is a debate about whether Abraham was a single person or a combination of Hebrew leaders. Regardless of where one is in that debate, the story is an amazing story. It describes the Hebrews developing a special relationship with God.

The Hebrew-Jewish relationship with God began with Abraham being called by God to pull up stakes and move south. It was Abraham's decision to put his full faith and trust in God Almighty (El Shaddai), meaning "God, the One, of the Mountains" (Gen. 17:1 footnote). Abraham accepted God's simple promise that He will make Abraham a great nation if Abraham would migrate south to the land of Canaan. God ends His promise by stating that "...and by you all the families of the earth shall bless themselves." There is an alternate translation to this ending that states, "...in you all the families of the earth shall be blessed" (Gen. 12:1-3). In Genesis 15:18-21, God spells out the boundaries of the land He gave to Abraham and his descendants, which were the boundaries of David's empire.

Originally Abraham's name was Abram; however, God changed his name to Abraham in Genesis 17:5, which was taken to mean *father of a multitude*. In Genesis 17:15, God changes Sarai's name to Sarah meaning *princess*. The more familiar names of Abraham and Sarah have been used throughout this book.

Continuing the story of Abraham's migration, His migration appears to be a part of a general migration of Semitic people to the south. The Semitic tribes were migrating south out of Mesopotamia in response to the pressure from the tribes migrating south from the areas north and east of Mesopotamia.

If Abraham was having second thoughts about migrating south. It was God's encouragement and Abraham's strong faith in God that led him to join the migration and travel south with all his household and stock into an unknown future in the land of Canaan.

Abraham's relationship with God centered on Abraham's acceptance that his life was a gift from God, and his willingness to be guided by God. God's relationship with Abraham centered on His decision to be Abraham's God and to accept Abraham as he was, strengths and weakness included.

Abraham's acceptance of God's promise was central to their relationship. Their relationship was based on the choices both God and Abraham made. It worked because of the respect, trust, and love each had for the other.

The Hebrews' special role began with Abraham's personal and direct relationship with God. See Gen 12:1-3, and Gen 17:1, and footnotes. The word, *choosing*, comes from the word, *chosen*, which was translated from the Hebrew word for *known*.

God Almighty went with Abraham when he traveled to Canaan. At this point, God was more than a regional god of the mountain.

God's relationship with Abraham was different from the relationship other people had with their god or gods. The mutually supportive spiritual friendship between God and Abraham was unique. The depth and richness of this relationship can be difficult to understand; however, it is a relationship that has remained a key part of the Jewish and Christian relationship with God. Without Abraham's relationship, the Jewish and Christian religions could not have survived as they have.

Abraham's break from having tribal gods to having a personal relationship with God was based on mutual trust, respect, and love. It was a major change in the way he related to the idea that there were spiritual entities. The idea to rely on only one god, that is God, was a different way of thinking about the supernatural beings.

The Hebrews also had to make a conscious decision to give up their tribal gods to have a spiritual relationship with God. It was not a foregone conclusion that the Hebrews would change from worshiping their old gods to this new relationship with God. By choosing God and God choosing them, a mutually supportive spiritual relationship was established. Rather than worshiping a tribal god, the Hebrews had this new personal relationship with God.

However, the Hebrews did not give up their house gods. The Bible gives the impression that the house gods were easily replaced with one god; however, it is questionable if house gods ever were completely given up.

The Bible does describe the continued importance of house gods, long after Abraham chose God. Gen. 31:17-55 describes Jacob's wife Rachel stealing the house gods of her father, Laban. When Jacob left Laban with his family, and his cattle and other livestock. The footnote for verse 19 states that possession of the house gods ensured a man's leadership of the family and his claim on the property. It would have been hard to change the household gods from being of such importance as to not being necessary at all. In some areas of the world worshiping house gods is still practiced.

Although the Covenant in Genesis 12:1-3 covers everyone, not just the Hebrews, later texts are more centered on the Hebrews. Genesis 17:1-14 states that Abraham will be the father of a multitude of nations and extends His Covenant to include Abraham's descendants, "… throughout their generations for an everlasting covenant," and gave the land of Canaan to Abraham's descendants and would be their God. Although God included giving the land to Abraham's descendants, it is God agreeing to be their God that set the identity of the Hebrews.

The Covenant gave subsistence and direction to the Hebrews' relationship with God. See Genesis 17:1-4. Abraham, with all his shortcomings, set the example for his descendants to follow by choosing God and living in the blessing of God's guidance and His forgiveness, which Abraham received more than once. With the Hebrews' acceptance of the Covenant between God and Abraham, his descendants received God's commitment to be their God for all time.

The relationship between God and Abraham may have been getting shaky. Genesis 17:1-27 establishes that God required the sign of the Covenant to be that all men who were born in or becomes a part of the Hebrew tribe would be circumcised. While circumcision may not have been unique to the Hebrews, it still was confirmation to the Hebrews that they were God's special people.

The circumcision requirement came from a priestly tradition. The priests may have been the ones needing assurance of who was to be counted as being Hebrew. With Genesis being written long after Abraham died, and this priestly requirement was not originally included in the Covenant, it may have been included to solve a problem at the time Genesis was written.

The Jewish religion, Judaism, that grew out of the Covenant was not the intent of either God or Abraham. The Covenant established the relationship the Hebrews could have with God. It was only later when the Israelites did not believe God's simple and direct commitment to them that it was deemed the Israelites needed more information. It was not because of God, but rather, because of the Israelites' failure to hold up their end of the Covenant that Judaism was developed.

Abraham's faith in God wavered and God questioned Abraham's trust in Him from time to time. For example, there was a famine in Canaan and rather than waiting on God to take care of him, Abraham pulled up stakes and went to Egypt. Abraham told his wife, Sarah, to say that she was his sister because he was afraid that he would be killed so someone could have her. Apparently, Sarah was Abraham's half-sister (Gen. 20:12).

In Genesis 12:10-13:1, the Egyptian Pharaoh, thinking that Sara was Abraham's sister, took Sara as his wife until God told the Pharaoh that Sara was Abraham's wife, although she was also Abraham's half-sister. When the Pharaoh found out about Abraham's lie, he ordered Abraham to leave with Sarah and all his belongings. Genesis 12:10-20 was not one of Abrahams' finest moments. God was in the mode of picking up after His wayward son.

As time passed and Abraham and Sarah were still childless, Abraham was concerned about God's promise to him that he would be a great nation, but God affirmed His promise to Abraham (Gen. 15:1-6, 17:1-14). Next, since Sarah had not given Abraham a child, she convinced Abraham to have a child with her maid Hagar, which he did. The boy was named Ishmael. The birth of Ishmael created friction between Sarah and Hagar, which became serious enough that God intervened and restored calm (Gen. 16:1-10).

One day, Abraham was resting at his tent when three men came into his camp. When Abraham saw them, he immediately invited them to stay, which was the courtesy and hospitality of his time. The three men are recognized as being the Lord in a manner that is not described. The Lord tells Abraham that He will return in the spring and Sarah will have a son.

Since Abraham and Sarah were both well past the childbearing age, Sarah who was quietly listening, laughed to herself. Sarah expressed her doubts, and the Lord asked, "Is anything too hard for the Lord?" He then repeated that in the spring she would have a son (Gen. 18:1-15). This highlights the thinking in the time of Abraham, people believed that God was in control of the miracle of birth.

Genesis next describes that Abraham did have a special relationship with God in telling the story of the destruction of Sodom and Gomorrah (Gen. 18:16-33, 19:1-38). First, God wonders about telling Abraham that He was going to destroy Sodom and Gomorrah because of their wickedness; however, because Abraham was chosen, God tells Abraham of his plan. Abraham talked with his friend God about His plan. Abraham starts out asking if God would spare Sodom if there were fifty righteous men in Sodom, to which God agrees. Through a series of similar questions Abraham works God down agreeing that if there were ten righteous men, He would not destroy Sodom and Gomorrah.

I have always found this discussion intriguing. The two are talking about a major issue as friends, rather as strong and weak parties of a Covenant. God allowed his friend, Abraham, to change His mind about what He had already decided to do.

There apparently were not even ten righteous people in Sodom and Gomorrah, for starting with verse Genesis 19:1, the destruction of the two towns began with angels coming to Lot, Abraham's nephew, warning him of the impending destruction. Lot left with his wife and two daughters. On the way out, Lot's wife looked back at the destruction and was turned into a pillar of salt.

This story of the destruction of Sodom and Gomorrah had at least two lasting effects on the Israelite people. The first is that it impressed itself deeply upon later generations as an example of God's total judgment against appalling wickedness. (See footnote to Genesis 19:1-38.) It also reaffirmed that the God of Abraham was not some distant deity sitting on high but rather, demonstrated that a caring personal relationship could be established with God based on God's love for the Hebrews.

After the destruction of Sodom and Gomorrah, Genesis 20:1-18 tells of Abraham traveling to the Gerar, a town in southern Canaan, and repeated his instructions for Sarah to say she is his sister. Once again, God intervened with Abimelech, the ruler of Gerar, when, Abimelech took Abraham's wife, Sarah, under the misconception that Sarah was Abraham's sister. God came to Abimelech in a dream and told him that Sara was Abraham's wife.

The outcome of Abraham's lie in this case followed the outcome of his lie described in Genesis 12:10-20 when he was in Egypt. Again, God cleans up after Abraham.

Today it is hard to understand why Abraham made the same decision twice forcing God to respond as He did. In the context of that time, it may have been the overall power rulers had over all within their kingdom was too much for Abraham to take. This being the case the two stories confirm the extensive reach and power of God.

In the spring, Sarah gives Abraham a son, Isaac, who begins the linage of Abraham to the people of Israel. God apparently still had concerns about Abraham's loyalty to their Covenant. As the final test of Abraham, God instructed Abraham to take his son, Isaac, to a mountain of God's choosing—as a sacrifice. Abraham did so and when he had built the wood altar and was about to kill Isaac on the altar when God stopped him saying that He, God, knew that Abraham feared God. At that point God provided a ram to be sacrificed (Gen. 22:1-14).

I think that God had an inkling of what He was getting when He made His covenant with Abraham. Abraham was a flawed person who could be impatient and deceitful. While the Covenant between God and Abraham was the foundation of their relationship, the relationship was a work in progress until Abraham put aside his worries and doubts and embrace his spiritual connection with God and the resulting peace of mind. The process Abraham went through demonstrated God's patience in allowing Abraham to fully accept God's love and support at his own pace, in his own time.

The story of Abraham is important for several reasons. I think a particular reason that is most important is that the story shows that God does not require perfection. God only requires each person to have a God-centered spiritual relationship with Him. Just like Abraham, each one of us, with all our flaws and shortcomings, can live in God's blessing simply by having a spiritual relationship with God.

The core value of the relationship between God and Abraham was the love each had for the other. Grace was always present within their relationship.

The relationship between God and Abraham's descendants continued across centuries with the Hebrew-Israelite believing that they were God's people, and the Israelites reestablishing their relationship with God after each time they fell away from their Covenant with God. The Israelites believe today, as they have always, that they are God's people.

JACOB/ISRAEL

Abraham's son Isaac married Rebekah, the daughter of Abraham's nephew, Bethu'el. They had two sons, Jacob, and Esau. While Esau was the oldest, and therefore, should have received Isaac's blessing, Jacob tricked Isaac into blessing him rather Esau. After receiving Isaac's blessing and seeing the anger of Esau, Rebekah decided that Jacob should go live with her brother Laban. Rebekah told Isaac that she was afraid that Jacob would marry a Canaanite woman. Isaac called Jacob blessed Jacob again, charged him not to marry a Canaanite and sent him to household of Laban, Rebekah's brother to marry one of his daughters (Gen. 27-28:22).

The issue of receiving a blessing was extremely important to the Hebrews. A verbal blessing released power that could not be retrieved. When people of that time spoke of being blessed it made the person being blessed special and important to the person giving the blessing. While being blessed may not mean nearly as must today as it did them, it still has a positive meaning.

As night came while Jacob was on the way to Laban's house, Jacob went to sleep. He dreamed that he saw the presence of the God of Abraham and of Isaac who gave that same promise to Jacob. God affirmed that Jacob's descendants will spread throughout the world.

When Jacob arrived at Laban's farm he met and fell in love with Laban's daughter, Rachel. Jacob was to work for Laban for seven years to marry Rachel; however, due to trickery by Laban, at the end of seven years Jacob married Leah instead. It was becoming apparent that that Laban and Jacob deserved each other.

So, Jacob began working another seven years to marry Rachel; however, Jacob married Rachel after only two years, but continued to work for Laban. Jacob fathered six sons and a daughter with Leah, and four sons with Leah's and Rachel's maids, but Rachel was barren. After years of having no sons, Rachel finally conceived a son named Joseph. Later after Jacob had left Laban, Rachel died in childbirth giving birth to one more son, Benjamin. The twelve sons of Jacob became the twelve tribes of Israel.

Jacob decided to part from Laban. They agreed on how Jacob could separate his sheep and goats to take with him; however, Laban tricked Jacob by making the sheep that Jacob had chosen unavailable. Jacob countered with a trick of his own which gained him sheep to replace the sheep Laban had taken. Jacob then gathered up his family and animals and left without giving Laban a chance to dispute his latest trick. Since both were untrustworthy it seemed prudent to Jacob to leave while Laban was away shearing sheep.

Laban was upset that Jacob unceremoniously left without giving him a chance to say goodbye. Laban chased after Jacob. When he caught up with Jacob in Gilead, he complained about Jacob's poor manners. Laban also complained that Jacob had taken his house gods. Jacob denied doing so, unaware that Rachel had taken the house gods. When Laban looked in Rachel's tent, she told him she could not move because, as the Bible explains, "the way of women is upon me." Laban headed back to his farm empty-handed. Jacob remained in Gilead. As earlier described, the house gods were important to ensuring Laban's leadership of the family and his claim on the property. (See Genesis 29.1-31.55 for Jacob's time with Laban.)

Jacob decided to reconnect with Esau and sent a friendly message with gifts to Esau. When Jacob learned that Esau was coming toward him Jacob basically panicked and sent his family and livestock away across the Jabbok stream and stayed where he was alone. That night Jacob found himself wrestling with a man and was winning when the man touched Jacob's thigh (misplaced or broke it?) but Jacob held on. At this point it seems that the man was God or an angel from God who said, "Let me go, for the day is breaking." Jacob would not let him go without receiving a blessing. The angel gave Jacob the new name of Israel (Gen. 32:24-30). The name *Israel* means, "one who has striven with God and with man and have prevailed." Jacob's new name, Israel, became the name of his descendants, "the Israelites."

Jacob had twelve sons who became the leaders of the twelve tribes of Israel. One of the sons was Joseph, Jacob's favorite. His eleven brothers were jealous and sold him to a merchant, who sold him into slavery in Egypt. After being imprisoned, Joseph interpreted a dream that was troubling the Pharaoh. The dream predicted seven years of plentiful harvest followed by seven years of famine. Joseph successfully collected and stored enough grain during the good year to provide enough grain for the bad years. This led to him becoming an important leader of the Egyptian people.

Because the famine was also in Canaan, Jacob sent his sons to Egypt to buy grain. When Joseph's brothers first met him in Egypt, they did not recognize him; however, over time they did. Joseph's meetings with his brothers were joyous occasions. Joseph told the brothers to bring Jacob and his family to Egypt, which they did. The reunion between Jacob and Joseph was another joyous occasion. Jacob and his family settled in the part of Egypt called Goshen (Gen. 49:29-50:26). The Bible tells us that Jacob died when he was 147 years old and was buried in Machpelah, with his parents and grandparents. Joseph lived to be 110 years old and was probably buried in Egypt.

Jacob's death ends a period that some call a Patriarch period. Some think the stories in the Biblical account of this period are based on historical events, while others think they are based on stories that were told many years after the Patriarch period to provide a beginning for the Israelites. In either case, the importance of the stories is that they established a beginning that has been accepted and woven into the fabric of understanding the history and life of the Israel people.

Once again God chose to work with a flawed person. One idea is that in the case of both Abraham and Jacob, it was the will of God, rather than the skill and competence of Abraham and Jacob, that things would work out as they did. Another idea is that God did not intervene until it was obvious that Abraham and Jacob were in over their heads and absolutely needed God's help. The stories about God's interactions with Abraham and Jacob represent a small part of the total lives of Abraham and Jacob, both of whom lives long lives and prospered. Apparently, God did not need to intervene during the remainder of their lives. God must have thought they were living close enough to His likeness without His intervention.

This idea that God is a hands-on God, who continuously intervenes in our daily lives negates the basic idea of the first creation story. Having a hands-on God controlling the outcomes of people's effort presents a much different perception of God than is presented in the first creation story. The God who created us in His image and was happy with his creation was not a hands-on God.

God continues to treat us as being made in His image and welcomes our spiritual connection with Him, for it allows Him to provide guidance, support, and encouragement, rather than direction and control. Having been created in His image means that He gave us everything we need to live in His likeness. His occasional intervention to save us from ourselves is the exception rather than the rule. This does not rule out the occasions when a person receives a spiritual message that God recognizes that a person is living in His likeness. And while that is what He wants for us, He has also given us His forgiveness and grace when we fail to do so.

The message one gets from these stories will depend in large measure on how one views his or her relationship with God, as well as what that person believes the relationship is that Israelite and Christian people had and have with God.

Continuing the history of the Israelites begins with the twelve sons of Jacob taking on the leadership roles of the twelve tribes of the Israelites. While we already know how important Joseph was to Israel's history, his brother Judah was also important in Israel's history. Judah was the one who said to sell Joseph to the merchant rather than kill him. The linage of Joseph, the adoptive father of Jesus, goes back to David and continues back to Judah.

Jacob's family lived in the favor of the Pharaoh; however, over time and as God had directed starting with Abraham, the sons of Jacob families increased in numbers and strength. A new pharaoh came to power who did not know or ignored the history of Joseph and the Israelites and became concerned about the number and strength of the Israelites. He decided to place overseers over the Israelites and turn them into slaves. The hardships imposed on the Israelites by the Egyptians caused the Israelites to complain to God about their situation and God heard their complaint and sent Moses to take them out of Egypt and return them to Canaan, their promised land.

MOSES

Who was Moses and where did he come from? The book of Exodus tells the story of Moses' birth and his taking the Israelites out of Egypt. Moses was an Israelite born in Egypt to Yocheved. At the time of his birth, the pharaoh had decreed that all Israelite male babies would be killed. After Yocheved gave birth to Moses, she hid him for three months. She then took him in a basket and set the basket in the Nile River where the Pharaoh's daughter found him and took him in. Moses' sister Miriam watched Moses being picked up by the Pharaoh's daughter.

Moses was raised and lived as an Egyptian noble until he was about forty when he killed an Egyptian for beating an Israelite. The Pharaoh ordered that Moses be killed but Moses escaped to Midian where he married the daughter of the priest, Jethro, and settled into the life of a shepherd. This is where God found him. (Exod. 2:1-25 and Moses on the Internet).

Pause for a moment to consider the story behind the dry description of Moses' birth in the Bible. He was born in Egypt to Israelite slaves. Knowing the danger involved, his mother, certainly with her husband's agreement, protected him from being killed by the Egyptians. When she could no long do that, certainly with fear and a heavy heart, she put Moses in a basket in the Nile River to an uncertain fate. That had to be the worst day of her life. Even with the relief of hearing from Miriam that Moses was safe in the Pharaoh's household, her sadness still had to be great because she would not be able to nurture and raise him.

The slavery of the Israelites in Egypt had become so bad that they cried out to God for relief. God, hearing their cries, looked to Moses to go to Egypt to relieve the Israelites of their slavery.

Moses was a contented man happy in his life as a shepherd, apparently with little thought of religious or worldly affairs when God came calling. Moses was a reluctant servant of God.

God talked to Moses through a burning bush, telling him to go to Egypt and take the Israelites out of Egypt. One would think that having a bush catch on fire, on its own, would get Moses' attention. However, even with the burning bush, Moses was still reluctant to do as God directed. Moses asked God what he should say when the Israelites asked, "What is his name?" God said to Moses, "I AM WHO I AM." The footnote in the Bible states that I AM is etymology of the Israelites name for God, YHWH. (Exod. 3:2-15). Moses' question also suggests a polytheistic environment.

Finally convinced to do as God directed, Moses goes to Egypt, has a reunion with his family, and goes to the Pharaoh to ask him to release the Israelites from their bondage. After the Pharaoh refused to release the Israelites, God caused ten plagues to befall the Egyptians. Moses asked for the release of the Israelites after each plague. Moses was not having success convincing the Egyptian Pharaoh to release the Israelites with God's first nine plagues; however, the tenth plague did the trick. The tenth plague caused the death of the first born of all of Egypt, except for the Israelites' firstborn. The loss of the first born in all of Egypt caused the Pharaoh to relent and release the Israelites.

Exodus 12:1-7 describes God's instructions to the Israelites for preparing the sacrificial lamb to protect the firstborn from the tenth plague. The Israelites households were identified by having the blood of the sacrificial lamb put on the doorpost and lintel of their houses. Exodus 12:12-13 states, "For I will pass through the land of Egypt that night and I will smite all the first-born in the land of Egypt, both man and beast; and all the gods of Egypt I will execute judgment. The blood shall be a sign for you, upon the house where you are; and when I see the blood, I will pass over you, and no plague shall fall upon you to destroy you, when I smite the land of Egypt."

God instructed the Israelites to roast the lamb and eat it with unleavened bread on the night of the Passover and to burn all leftovers in the morning.

God explains in Exodus 12:14-15, "This day shall be for you a Memorial Day, and you shall keep to as a feast to the Lord; throughout your generations you shall observe it as an ordinance for even. Seven days you shall eat unleavened bread; The importance of this event to the Jewish people cannot be overstated. Each year on the same day every year, as determined by the Israelite calendar, the Israelites celebrate and recognize this critical event and renew their faith in their spiritual relationship with God.

The footnote in Exodus 12:14 tells that the feast of unleavened bread was originally an agricultural festival held at the time of the barley harvest and was converted into a historical commemoration closely connected to Passover.

71

The Passover also began the process of establishing the Israel Nation and is also the start of the Israelite calendar.

The Lord performed the plagues, not an angel of death. While it is considered a punishment to Egypt it was also a message to the Israelites that they were never to forget. The Lord was their Lord, and they were His people.

Noss tells us that against all odds Moses got the Israelites out of Egypt:

> The high place which Moses has held in Hebrew- Jewish devotions is richly deserved. Recent scholarship, while denying to him the authorship of the Pentateuch and the extremely complicated legal provisions of the Law (Torah), has vindicated his place of highest honor in the early history of Israel. He was a creative personality of the first order. Unfortunately, the exact details of his work are shrouded from us in tradition. The story of Moses has come down to us in the narratives (known to scholars as J and E) intertwined in Exodus and Numbers. The written form of these traditions dates from three or four hundred years after his time. (Noss pg. 500-501)

It is while the Israelites were in Egypt and Moses was being called by God to lead them that the name of God changed from El Shaddai, Gen. 17:1, to YHWH or Yahweh, Jehovah – Lord, Exodus 6:3. Abraham's God was one who moved with Abraham and Abraham's Covenant with God was central to his life. God was a personal God with whom Abraham could argue and have discussions. Under God's new name He continued His covenant with Abraham to include all the Israelites and to look after them as individuals in their quest to become the Israel nation rather than as a group of similar individuals. His realm comprised everything needed for the Israelites to have a good existence. All they needed to do was abide by their end of the covenant.

After the Israelites left Egypt, the Pharaoh changed his mind and sent the army after them. The Israelites escaped when the sea parted for them and closed back in when the Egyptian army tried to follow them.

Interestingly there is no record of the exodus in Egyptian or other non-biblical writing. This may very well be due to the escape of the Israelites and the loss of an army was not somethings the Egyptian scribes would advertise or report in stories of Egyptian conquests and glory.

While the Egyptian records have no mention of the Israelites mass exodus from Egypt or the loss of an army, there is no doubt that the Israelite traditions of Moses and the exodus were created from something that had a profound effect on the Israelites.

Regardless of what happened and who the people were that were involved with Moses, it all became an integral part of the Israelites identity. The event or events were significant enough that they are the tradition that began a new chapter in the lives of the Israelites.

The date of the exodus has not been well established. If the exodus happened during the reign of Ramses II, the exodus would be around 1300BC. However, if we use the I Kings 6:1 statement that the exodus was 480 years before the fourth year of the reign of Solomon, we have the exodus happening in 1446 BC. Some scholars arrive at a different date using the dates of other non-biblical events. The 1300 BC date is the date used for this chapter.

The story of Moses and the exodus of the Israelites from Egypt is a good example of the stories of the history of the Israelites. Although the Exodus story was not put in written form until long after the exodus and the forty-some years the Israelites wandered in the desert, something or a series of things happen to cause the story to be told, revered, and later put into written form.

The story reaffirmed the close relationship the Israelites had with God. That is, by following God's instructions and leaving Egypt the Israelites were confirming their commitment to God being their one and only God. The story tells of the new beginning for the Israelites and start of the process of becoming an Israel Nation.

The story of Moses' leadership begins with him accepting God's direction to free the Israelites. He was then able to take a disorganized group of beaten down, dispirited Israelites and convincing them to pick up and leave what they knew, and to follow him out of Egypt into the desert and the unknown. Having gotten them safely out of Egypt, he then "only" had to provide food and water for them and defend them from enemy tribes while getting them organized and establishing their own army.

Regardless of the number of Israelites that left Egypt, either in small groups or many people, the accomplishments of Moses getting the Israelites out of Egypt and then leading them through the desert over the next forty-some years is amazing. He truly deserves to be held in high esteem. He was a major game-changer for the Israelites.

Exodus 6:3 explains that God and the Lord are one and the same; however, when Moses and the Israelites entered the desert, the reach of Abraham's Covenant with the Lord, or the total commitment the Lord had to the Covenant, was not immediately evident to the Israelites.

At some point, the Israelites were getting desperate for water. They came to Moses complaining about Moses taking them away from what they'd known to a desert with no water. The Lord tells Moses, in Exodus 17:1-7, to hit a rock with his staff and water will come out. Moses hit the rock and water came out. The version of this story in Numbers 20:1-12 has God telling Moses to talk to the rock, but Moses hit it instead. Water came out, but the Lord was mad that Moses did not believe in Him and made it look like Moses instead of the Lord caused the water to come out of the rock, so God told Moses that he would not see the promised land. This story gives some insight into the struggle Moses was having defining God's commitment to himself and the Israelites.

The Bible indicates that the Israelites continually strayed from holding up their end of the covenant. An example of this problem is the golden calf incident. The difficulty in adhering to their Covenant with Yahweh was great while they were in the desert.

The golden calf incident occurred while the Israelites were in the desert. This event was not their finest hour. The incident begins in Exodus 24 and continues through Exodus 31, with the Lord directed Moses to go up on Mt. Sinai to receive the Ten Commandments. The Lord also gave Moses instructions on making a sanctuary, that is a tabernacle or tent, for the Lord, and making an Ark and other instructions for the Israelites to follow. When Moses was gone a long time, the Israelites became nervous and in Exodus 32 asked Aaron, Moses' older brother and a Levi Priest, to make them a visible symbol of a god they could see and follow in their travels in the desert, as was common in pagan religions. Aaron complied and came up with the golden calf, which in pagan religions was a symbol of fertility. Finally, Moses came down the mountain with the tablets containing the Ten Commandments. When he saw what the Israelites had done, he threw down the tablets, breaking them into pieces (Exod. 32:1-35).

This is a dry description of events that do not do justice to them. Exodus 24:18 states he was gone forty days and nights; however, that is not so much a count of days, but rather an indication that Moses was gone a long time. Moses was gone long enough that the Israelites became worried and fearful enough that they lost faith in the Lord and prodded Aaron into picking a new god, which resulted in the golden calf. They were upset enough to give up the jewelry and wealth, and to work hard to make the calf and cover it with gold.

These were people who believed Moses enough to pick up on short notice and leave what they knew to follow Moses into the desert. The perils of this adventure were evident when the Israelites realized the Egyptian army was coming after them and they were trapped between the army and the sea. When Moses raised his hand, the Lord opened the sea, so they could cross, and then Moses again raised his hand the

Lord closed the sea destroying the army. The Lord, through Moses, had saved them.

Their reliance on Moses as their connection to the Lord continued while they were in the desert. After three days they complained about there being no water so, the Lord had Moses get them water, but then there was no food, so the Lord provided them with bread, which they did not recognize until Moses told them what it was. And when an army came to fight the Israelites Moses had Joshua select men to go out and fight the enemy. Moses told Joshua that he would stand on a hill and raise his hand with the rod of God in it. When his hand was up the Israelites were winning, but when it was tired and down the Israelites were losing. Aaron and Hur had gone up on the hill with Moses. (Hur was a trusted associate of Moses). So, when Moses could no long hold his arms up Aaron and Hur each held up an arm and the Israelites won the battle (Exod. 17:13).

With all that, the Israelites attention span was still short enough, and their faith in the Lord weak enough, that their relationship with the Lord, as being chosen by God, wasn't strong enough to withstand the long absence of Moses.

The problem was that the Lord's support of the Israelites had come through Moses and although Moses continued to tell them that the Lord was supporting and protect them, it was hard for them to see that without Moses to guide them. The Lord's commitment to the Covenant with the Israelites was forever; however, the Israelites' commitment to the Covenant had an expiration date. This problem continued to exist long after the Israelites entered Canaan, and troubled Jesus during his ministry.

The Lord's Covenant had been broken and the Lord was full of wrath and was ready to destroy the Israelites. Moses intervened and convinced the Lord to give the Israelites another chance. The Lord relented, and Moses went back up Mt. Sinai. When Moses came down from Mt. Sinai with the renewed Ten Commandment stone tablets, it is written that his face shone from talking with the Lord. This time, the Lord granted the Ten Commandments and renewed the Covenant, which included some guidance and assurance that he would accompany them and not forsake them, despite their failure to hold up their end of the Covenant. The Ten Commandments are recorded in Exodus 20:1-17 and Deuteronomy 5:4-21. See Exodus 34:1-35 for the renewal of the Covenant. Throughout the entire episode, the Lord treated Moses as a trusted friend who, as He had with Abraham allowed Moses to change His mind.

It is important to recognize the Lord's great disappointment in Abraham's descendant's failure to keep their faith in Him. The Lord's frustration was so great that, in Exodus 33:5, He told Moses to tell the Israelites that they were, "Stiff-necked people; if for a single moment I should go up among you, I would consume you..." The Lord did not trust being with the Israelites and, instead, sent an angel, although the Lord would continue to guide them and vanquish their enemies. The Lord's love for the Israelites exceeded all things.

While the Israelites were in the wilderness, they were renewing their sense of connection to their Lord and their relationship with the Lord became more clearly defined, with the renewal of the Covenant, with the Ten Commandments, which were belatedly ratified by the Israelites. The Israelites were also developing an organizational and administrative system that led to establishing an effective army and developing the religious and social laws that later became the first five books of the Bible (the Pentateuch). These processes were anything but well planned and smoothly implemented.

Ten Commandments

Let us look at the Ten Commandments to see what they say—without looking at who wrote them (Exod. 20:1-17). There are two parts to this story. The first part is the story of Moses going up Mt. Sinai and receiving the Ten Commandments, the Israelites failure to wait on Moses to return with the ten Commandments, and then their final acceptance of the Ten Commandments. Without the Israelites seeing the error of their ways but then accepting the Ten Commandments, the story of the Ten Commandments and the Israelites would have been much different.

The second story is the message in the Ten Commandments and the prime importance the Ten Commandments have in both Judaism and Christianity. While the Ten Commandments were for the Israelites, they have been taken to apply equally to Christians.

Beginning with the first commandment, "I am the Lord your God. You should have no other gods before me." This simply states that the spiritual relationship each Israelite has with God must make God first in all that he or she each does. This highlights the problem of there being many gods the Israelites can choose to follow and often did choose to follow while in the desert. Each tribe the Israelites encountered had one or more gods. The problem of Israelites wandering away from God was ever-present and did not decrease with their arrival to the promised land.

The second commandment prohibits making graven images or any likeness of anything in heaven, or on or under earth or sea. This means not having house gods or shrines or having anything be a substitute or of equal or more important than God. Taken literally, such actions as praying to angels, objects, or symbols rather than to God was not making God first. The footnote for this commandment states that, "Imageless worship of the Lord made Israel's faith unique in the ancient world."

The third commandment prohibits taking the Lord's name in vain. The Lord will hold anyone guilty who does so. For the Israelites, and as it should be today, there was no crime worse than being found guilty by God. Closely following the idea in the third commandment, the fourth requires that the sabbath should be kept holy. No one should do any work on the sabbath that Lord has made hallowed. Whether the sabbath is a Saturday or a Sunday, this commandment is violated on a continuing basis. Today's society, without more than a passing thought, simply requires some people to work in the Sabbath.

The fifth commandment is to honor your father and mother, for they have given you your life to live in the blessing of God. Unfortunately, all too often the relationship between parents and children is not based on there being honor between parents and children, to the detriment of both the children and the parents.

The sixth commandment command is that you should not kill. Several commentaries on this commandment take it to mean murder and did not include the authorized killing, such as for war and capital punishment. This comes from a very old law against murder which is validated by man being made in God's image. This commandment continues to generate debate and discussion.

The seventh commandment requires that you shall not commit adultery. Jesus provided a definition of adultery in Matthew 5:27-32. Jesus' definition is stricter than how the Jews defined adultery and is stricter than the standard used today.

The eighth commandment, not to steal and the ninth commandment instructs us not to bear false witness are self-evident.

The tenth commandment, to not covet your neighbor's house his wife, or his things is also self-evident. Unfortunately, it is broken more often that one would suspect. The desire to have what someone else has continues to lead to many difficult and destructive situations. Even small transgression of this commandment seldom turned out well.

The Ten Commandments were instructions to the Israelites to give them guidance in their daily lives. They are simple, straight-forward requirements that fall well within the meaning of living in the likeness of God. Following them would eliminate the cause of the strife the Israelites continued to experience. In like manner they can serve the same purpose in Christian communities and are central to Judaism and Christianity. Today's Christians would do well to commit to abiding with the Ten Commandments.

ISRAELITES

When Jacob's family went to Egypt, the Bible narrows its coverage of events to Israel (Jacob) and his descendants. It seems improbable that all the Hebrews living in Canaan went to Egypt with Jacob (Israel). So, what happened to the Hebrews that stayed behind in Canaan? Indications reveal that the Hebrews and other tribes settled in the hill country. In truth, very little is known about them. What little we do know comes mostly from archaeological findings.

That there were Hill People may have been a result of the pressure from the stronger and better organized Canaanites and Philistines. And in fact, archaeological excavations indicate that the stronger Canaanites were in control of the main portion, and the stronger Philistines were in control of the coastal area of the land promised to the Hebrews. Either the Canaanites or Philistines also controlled the town centers.

Surely the people, regardless of who they were, settled in the hill county because that was the only available land area. While it seems likely that there was some trade between the hill people and the stronger Canaanite and Philistines, they probably were keeping their heads down and not making waves. Most likely, some Hebrews among them had adopted some of the Canaanite religious gods and beliefs, and ways of life.

At this point in their history, neither the Hebrews nor Israelites were a nation, but rather a people of common ancestry and heritage. Jacob's descendants were the Israelites in Egypt, most if not all of whom left Egypt with Moses. This is the main group covered in the Bible.

It is reasonable to think that there were Hebrews who went to Egypt and settled in Egypt before Jacob's family did. The Hebrews that were in Egypt when Jacob and his family came to Egypt were not Israelites, and the Hebrews that never left Canaan with Jacob and his family were not Israelites. All Israelites were Hebrews. Only the descendants of Jacob were Israelites. Each group was basically doing its own thing, with varying amounts of structure and organization, and apparently very little communication between any of these groups.

The story in Genesis about how Jacob was given the name *Israel* would indicate that Israel's descendants would be identified as Israelites; however, it was not that simple. There have been different ideas about when the descendants of Israel became the Israelite people. In other words, the issue is, when did the people we call the Israelites become separate and distantly different enough from other groups of people that they could clearly identify themselves by saying that they were Israelites? There are different ideas about when the name Israelite was sufficient to identify them as separate people.

How strong were the ties between the Hebrews in Canaan and the Israelites from Egypt? We can only guess, but they were all descendants of Abraham, and the Hebrews in Canaan may have had similar customs and religious beliefs as the Israelites in Egypt. Regardless, the worship of the Lord by the Israelites coming out of the wilderness, with the Ten Commandments and a Tabernacle with the Ark of the Covenant, had to appear strange to the Hebrews who had remained in Canaan. The cultural differences of the two groups and the disruption caused by the entrance of the Israelites from the desert, who were on the mission of recalling the land given to Abraham by God, would undoubtedly have presented some impediments for the two groups to join forces for the common purpose of obtaining control of the Promised Land.

Return To The Promised Land

It is something of a paradox that the land God gave to the Hebrews was not free for the taking. The Bible does not tell us that God told the Hebrews the land He had picked out for them was already occupied and they would have to fight to get it and fight to keep it. Why would God not tell Abraham this key bit of information? One thought is that God forgot. This is highly unlikely. There had to be more to it than that. It could be that God expected the Israelites to be assimilated peacefully at the land since this was the land that Abraham had settled when he moved south under pressure from northern tribes moving south. Or it may simply be that God intended for the Israelites to settle in Canaan regardless of what it would take for them to do so. Whatever the reason, occupy and retaining the land of Canaan has been a long and violent process, and has only been partially successful.

It may never have been God's intent for the Israelites' promised land to be worry free. If the Israelites were to be God's blessing to all mankind, then they would need to learn how to fulfill this responsibility under all conditions and circumstances. What better place to learn these lessons than in the center of activities that affect people of many cultures, lifestyles, and religions; and to learn how to preserver under adverse conditions, and when times and conditions appear hopeless.

If God had given the Israelites land that was off the beaten path, in an area of little interest to anyone, the Israelites may not have had such an intense struggle to keep their land or their faith in God. While it is true that in such a different location, the Israelites may not have tested God's patience as much as they did in Canaan, it is also true that the opportunity for the Israelites to have a close relationship with God may have been less critical to them.

It is well to point out that the land that God promised to the Israelites was in the commerce corridor for transporting goods between eastern, northern, southern, and western parts of the civilized world of that time. In short, it was at the crossroads of the civilized world; therefore, it was highly desired land, which meant that the Israelites were always going to have someone wanting to take it away from them. In truth, the land along the eastern end, the Mediterranean Sea has been fought over more than any other land on earth.

From when the Israelites entered the land of Canaan under the leadership of Joshua, Moses had died before they entered Canaan, and the Israelites accomplish two things. They won the fight to gain control of much of the land given to them by God and they formed a central government.

There is more than one theory on how the Israelites settled in southern Canaan. One theory, and the one that follows the story told in the book of Joshua, has the Israelites came out of the desert and crossed the Jordan River around the town of Jericho to begin the conquest of their Holy Land, the Land of Canaan. Another theory has unhappy Canaanites escaping from their overlords south into the hill country mixing with some Israelites who escaped from Egypt. This second theory, which seems to be a variation of the Joshua story, has received some acceptance as being more socially acceptable.

Regardless of which theory is followed, there would have been stirring and mixing of the new arrivals and the existing people in the area. The leadership, administrative and organizational skills the new arrivals brought with them may have gone a long way toward the successful mixing of the two groups.

The result seems to be that the hill people joined with the people from Egypt in the fight for land that God had given to their common ancestor, Abraham. In doing so the two groups, regardless of their historical background, became as one and were the beginning of what would become Israel people. One indication of this is that many of the settlements in the hill country were abandoned and not resettled. (See the article by Avraham Faust is in the Nov/Dec. 2009 BAR pg. 62-69, "How Did Israel Become A People?") There continue to be new discoveries that shed more light on this period. Unfortunately, as often is the case, as questions are answered, more are raised.

One of the barriers to forming a central government was the basic governing structure of the Israelites, which was the tribe, clan, and family. As the land was conquered, the twelve Israelite tribes were given a section of the land to govern. The leader of each tribe determined how the land under his control would be governed. Suffice it to say that the leader of each of the twelve tribes were not always in agreement on what needed to be accomplished or how things were to be done. To be successful any central government must have the blessing of the tribal leaders.

After Joshua entered the Land of Canaan there was a period of conquest, which led to a period of judges, or leaders and prophets, which led to the start of the monarchy. The *period of Judges* was a troubling time of chaos. The people who the Israelites drove out of their land wanted it back. The Philistines' who settled the coastal area were also looking for a chance to get rid of the Israelites. It boils down to, Israel as the aggressor did not have many friends.

The Rise And Fall Of Israelite Control Of The Promised Land

The period from when Joshua invaded Canaan through the time of the Judges to the start of the monarchy is not well defined. The dates given for events during this period vary by 100 years or more.

Conquering the promised land turned out to be extremely difficult. Joshua successfully obtained a foothold for the Israelites, but much remained to be done after he died. The judges were leaders of the Israelites for about 400 years after Joshua died. There is a long list of judges who were able to stave off total disaster but were not able to gain control of the different Israelite tribes.

Finally, the tribal leaders agreed that they needed a leader; however, they worried that there would not be a worthy replacement without having a king appointed. Some of the leaders were pressing Samuel, a judge and prophet, to appoint a king, but Samuel was against having a king. He worried that a king would take advantage of his position and be oppressive to the people. His other concern was that the king would be taking the place of God. It seems that although Samuel was elderly, he was highly respected be the other judges. Samuel received a message from God to appoint a king, so Samuel proceeded to do so.

Samuel selected Saul to be king. Saul was a reluctant king who began his reign well with several accomplishments. However, Saul did some things that upset Samuel which led Samuel to declare that Saul had lost favor with God. Saul was not able to retain the support of the tribal leaders and after losing in battle to the Philistines he fell on his sword, which opened the way for David to become King. The reign of King Saul lasted about twenty-five years.

David was a young man when he became king. David had supported Saul; however, Saul became paranoid and believed that David had turned against him. David escaped Saul's attempts to have him killed and went into hiding. David formed his own army and joined forces with the Philistines. However, David did not participate in the battle between Saul and the Philistines that led to Saul's death.

Before Saul's death, Samuel had anointed David as the future king of Israel some twenty years before he was anointed king, which certainly could account for Saul's belief that David had turned against him. After Saul's death, there was a period of struggle. They fought over Israel, with Saul's powerful commander, Abner, appointing a puppet king and claiming the northern part of Israel with David claiming the southern part. The ensuing battle led to Abner's defeat which paved the way for David being anointed king in Hebron. The book, The *Israelites*, places David becoming king at about 1005 BC (*Israelites* pg. 70).

David was another less than perfect person who has a special place in the history of the Israelites and a special relationship with God. The prophet Samuel had started David out with having a good relationship with God, which was demonstrated when David slew Goliath to keep Israel from being a puppet of the Philistine. He continued receiving God's blessing as the first leader to overcome tribal jealousies and join the southern and northern Israelite tribes into the United Monarchy. Finally, the Israelites were a nation. He captured the small farming center of Jerusalem and made it his capital and transferred the monarchy into an empire. There are differing opinions about how much of Israel and surrounding lands that David conquered.

While David brought all the tribes under central control, it was a tentative arrangement that David and his son Solomon maintained; however, it was not long (about forty years after Solomon died) before the breakup of Israel, with the northern tribes splitting from the southern tribes to create the kingdom of Israel and the southern tribes became the kingdom of Judah. Both nations continued to have conflict with each other and surrounding nations including Egypt, as well as a marked lack of faithfulness to God.

David did not always follow God; however, when he did his accomplishments were great. For example, after David made Jerusalem his capital, David decided to bring the Ark of the Covenant to Jerusalem from a small shrine in Kiriathjearim. The first attempt to move the Ark failed; however, the second attempt was successful. David erected a new tent for it. David now had the symbol of God in his new capital.

David fell out of favor with God when he stole Bathsheba, the wife of one of his soldiers. He took her for his own. From this point, there were tribal disputes and rebellions and infighting between his children. David's family and kingdom were not in good shape when David died.

His oldest surviving son, Adonijah, was preparing to replace David; however, the Prophet Nathan preferred Bathsheba's son, Solomon, to succeed David.

Solomon was known as being, "beloved of the Lord... and his life story indicates that God, indeed, favored him. Ever during his lifetime, King Solomon was internationally revered as being exceptionally wise and just. Today, his four-decade reign in the tenth century BC is considered Israel's golden age and one of unprecedented stability, prosperity, and national unity. Yet, in the long run, his rule proved disastrous because of its oppression of the people and tolerance of pagan worship, which fatally undermined Israel's hope for continued national unity. (Solomon in "Who's Who in the Bible".)

The book, *The Israelites*, pg. 71 describes two results of David's kingdom, "... two developments in David's reign have retained their importance to this day: Jerusalem began its transformation from a petty Canaanite capital to a holy city of international significance, while the promise that there would be a never-ending line of kings from David's family was, after the end of the rule of the dynasty, an important factor in the hope for a Messiah from the House of David."

At no time, even during the reign of David and Solomon, were the Israelites a large majority of the population of Israel. The mere fact that the Kingdom of Israel had been created does not mean that all the people who lived in region before the Israelite arrival left the area upon the Israelites arrival. The diverse population and religions certainly contributed to the Israelites unfaithfulness to God.

Of the two kingdoms, Israel was the first kingdom to be conquered. The Assyrians conquered Israel in 721 BC. The capital of Israel was Samaria, which was also the name of the area around the city. The Assyrians displaced some Israelites with settlers from Assyria who brought their own gods, including Baal, with them. With the backing of Assyria, the settlers had some success imposing their culture and religion on the remaining Israelites.

After the Assyrians lost control of Israel, Samaria was not able to lose the influence of the Assyrian conquest. The Israelites' religious leaders in Judah viewed the Samarian religion as being corrupt and the Samarians were looked on with displeasure. The sharp disagreement between the Israelites and the Samarians continued through and beyond the time of Jesus.

There are various descriptions of the events leading up to the demise of Judah, the last vestige of Israelite-Hebrew sovereignty. Assyria was in decline and Babylon was the new up-and-coming power in the region. This led to a struggle for control between Babylon and Egypt with Judah in the middle. Judah's king was Josiah, a well-respected king. That Josiah was held in high did not keep his kingdom from being the center of intrigue, with agents from both powers busy explaining the merits of siding with one power or the other.

Egypt was having some success in working to bring Judah on its side when, in 609 BC, a battle between the Egyptian army and the Judah army led to Josiah being killed. Josiah's son, Jehoahaz, became king of

Judah; however, after three months he was replaced by Pharaoh Neco with his older brother, Jehoiakim.

Judah paid tribute to Egypt until the Egyptian army was defeated by the Babylon Army of King Nebuchadnezzar. With the defeat of the Egyptian Army, Babylon was the power and Judah switched from paying tribute to Egypt to paying tribute to Babylon.

The intrigue continued with the pro-Egyptian party urging King Jehoiakim to withhold the tribute to Babylon, which he did in 597. King Nebuchadnezzar quickly marched on Jerusalem. After a three-month siege King Jehoiachin, who became king when Jehoiakim died during the siege, surrendered Jerusalem to avoid its destruction. Nebuchadnezzar looted the Temple and carried away to Babylon, as captives, the king and ten thousand of the citizens, or, as 2 Kings describes them, "all the nobles, and all the renowned warriors, and all the craftsmen, and all the smiths" as well as "all the strong men fit for war." The king was thrown into prison and the people were settled as colonists on the River Chebar. Those left behind were placed under the rule of Zedekiah. (Noss pg.535.)

After nine years Zedekiah rebelled, and this time Jerusalem was not spared. In 586 BC, the Babylonians systematically destroyed Jerusalem. The destruction of Jerusalem included the destruction of the Temple, and the Holy Ark was never heard of again. Before being led away Zedekiah was forced to watch the execution of his sons and then was blinded and led into exile where he died.

Some portion of the Israelite population fled to Egypt and settled along the Nile River. Any people who did not flee Jerusalem and surrounding communities were rounded up and taken away, except for the prophet Jeremiah and the poorest of the poor that stayed behind. These people were no longer called Hebrews or Israelites and hereinafter were called Jews. (Noss makes this point; however, other sources have the term *Jew* coming from other activities.)

Thus, the independence of the Israelites ended with all they had achieved laid to waste. They were in dire need of reestablishing their relationship with God.

Prophets

From the Israelite conquest of the land of Canaan through the time of Jesus and on to today, there have been other religions that worshiped other gods in competition with God. The Canaan god Baal was the main competition in the time of Judges, but not the only competition. The contests between competing gods for the Israelites to worship gave rise to prophets, who began to appear during the time of the biblical Judges and continued from that time to the time before Jesus.

The prophets, that were God's representatives to the Israelites, did not come suddenly on the scene but rather developed during the time of Judges and continued through the destruction of David's kingdom and the temple, and the times of turmoil up to the mid-400s BC. Some think that the last prophet is thought to have been Malachi living in the 500-450 BC; however, others list prophets through the time of Jesus and John the Baptist. The names of prophets and the number of prophets on the lists of prophets differ from one list to another.

The prophets decried the unfaithfulness of the Israelites and foretold the hardship and destruction of the Israelites people because of it. The prophets were not so much foretelling the future as predicting the future based on the Israelites' actions in response to the developments in the area east of the Mediterranean. They were able to see that the failure of the Israelites to unite in their belief in God and living in union with God was going to lead to the destruction of their nation and hardships in their daily lives.

Noss describes the early prophets on the bottom of page 515 and top of page 516 as, "they were ecstatics, who felt that when they were excited with religious frenzy, they were full of the spirit of Yahweh and had access to his truth." There arose along with those who were ecstatic were men of a cooler spirit who were the real predecessors of the later prophets.

Samuel was the last of the judges and first of the prophets with less fervor, who guided David before becoming king until Samuel's death. Samuel was the predecessor to later prophets such as Nathan, who become the prophet to David after Samuel's death, and Prophet Alijah during the time of Solomon. These were the prophets who spoke out about the destruction of the Israelites because of their failure to follow God.

It did not take much for the prophets to see the precarious position Israel was in. With Babylon, the strong land grabbing kingdom on one side and Egypt, beaten but still a strong land-grabbing kingdom on the other side, Israel had no hope for control of their nation if they did not unite under God's guidance.

There was great difficulty in keeping the Israelite peoples focus on God alone. They were exposed to a multitude of gods during their bondage in Egypt, through their wandering in the desert, and through the period of conquest and settling in their homeland. The Israelite people had many opportunities for their focus to wander to other gods. It was a constant struggle for them to stay true to God. From page 234 of *The Israelites*, "Israelites were, almost throughout their history, inclined to serve other gods. Israelites worshipped Baal, Ashtaroth (Astartes), and Asherah."

One source of religious competition came from Israel being on the crossroad of the civilized world. There was a continuous stream of foreigners passing through Israel with different lifestyles and less restrictive religions. While the commerce activity helped sustain a prosperous economy it also created opportunities for Israelites to weaken, and in some cases, lose their dedication to their God.

The competition for the heart and soul of the Israelites by the prophets of God and the prophets of other gods was ongoing. The Israelites were particularly venerable during the difficult times describe in 1 and

2 Kings. The Prophet Elijah was an important and powerful prophet during these times.

An example of Elijah's work to renew the Jew's trust and belief in God is the story we read about in I Kings 18:1-48. It tells of a contest between Elijah, the servant of God, and the worshipers of the Canaan god, Baal. The contest consisted of making two altars of wood and putting pieces of a butchered bull on the wood and having Elijah and the prophets of Baal call down fire from God and Baal. Elijah let the Baal prophets go first. They started in the morning and went through the evening with their rituals without success.

Then Elijah started his turn by first laying twelve stones down to make an altar, then having a trench dug around the altar, then putting wood on the stones and laying pieces of the second bull on the wood. He then had jars of water poured on the offering and altar three times, so the water ran off into the trench. Elijah then prayed to God. Elijah's result is recorded in 1 Kings 18:38. "Then the fire of the Lord fell, and consumed the burnt offering, and the wood, and the stones, and the dust, and licked up the water that was in the trench." The story goes on to say the people fell and proclaimed that God is Lord. Elijah continued his work for the Lord, and, in the end, he did not die but rather was taken up in a whirlwind to heaven. The Prophet Malachi has Elijah coming down before the coming of the Lord (Mal. 4:5).

Jeremiah was another important prophet born sometime after 650 BC and was called to be a prophet as a child. His reluctance to be a prophet was overcome by God and he served as God's prophet in Judah during the most unsettled time when Judah was under the control of Assyria and then Babylon. He acutely predicted or foretold disastrous results that befell Judah because the Kings and their leaders did not follow God.

What is God looking for in the Covenant? I believe that the prophet Micah stated it well in the period just before the capture of the kingdom of Judah by the Assyrians. Micah was a younger contemporary of Isaiah—but unlike Isaiah, Micah was neither of noble descent nor of the capital. Rather, he came from the common people, being a citizen of the small village of Moresheth in the Judean foothills southeast of Jerusalem. Therefore, from the introduction to the book of Micah, Micah looked upon the corruption and pretensions of the capital through different eyes. Micah 6:6-8 states:

> 6. With what shall I come before the Lord, and bow myself before God on high? Shall I come before him with burnt offerings, with calves a year old? 7. Will the Lord be pleased with thousands of rams, with ten thousands of rivers of oil? Shall I give my first born for my transgression, the fruit of my body for the sin of my soul?" 8.He has shown you, O man, what is good: and what does the Lord require of you, but to do justice, and love kindness, and to walk humbly with your God.

This is one of my favorite passages in the Old Testament. While Micah has clearly and simply stated God's requirements, history has shown that the simple relationship that Abraham had with God has been hard to copy. Micah had also clearly separated himself from the Judaism rules and instructions, and sacrifices, although all three remained in use.

THE CONTINUED STRUGGLES OF THE JEWS

In 538 BC, the Israelites could return from exile. Some returned, and some stayed in Babylonian and Egypt. Once again, there were two groups of Israelites, the exiles and the ones who'd stayed behind. Both groups came back together, but with different customs, religious materials, and rituals. Also, the returning Israelites wanted to reclaim the land and possessions they had left behind. The Israelites that remained in and around Jerusalem, now called the Jews, did not want to give up what they had claimed. It seems that once again the two groups overcame the difficulties and reunited and worked in concert.

As is often the case, some good came out of a bad situation. Much of the oral and written Hebrew history of Israelites relationship with God was gathered and consolidated into the beginnings of the biblical Old Testament by the exiled Israelites. Most certainly that was when some of the Persian religion (Zoroastrianism) and stories were incorporated in these writings.

To continue the covenant between God and the Israelites, it was critical to the strength of the Israelites faith that the message of God's willingness to have and maintain a close and personal relationship with the Israelites threaded through the material that became the Old Testament. Before the time of Moses, such a relationship came without rituals or rules except requiring each Israelite to keep God central in his or her life. At the request of God, Moses established the Tabernacle (tent, place of dwelling) and the Ark of the Covenant for God. This was also when the Torah began to be written.

Going from shepherds, wanderers, and slaves to a people with a land to conquer and occupy changed how living with a personal relationship with God could be retained. It seems that the golden calf incident showed both God and Moses the need for God's presence with the Israelites to be more real and visible.

And now at the time of the destruction of Jerusalem and the temple the Israelites again find themselves at loose ends. With the Temple gone and being exiled into Babylonian, the Israelites had to solve the problem of not having the one place where they could present sacrifices to God. This was a major test for the relationship between Yahweh and the Israelites. Basically, with the central place of Judaism gone, some Israelites lost faith in Yahweh and turn to local gods. Others began meeting in homes on the Sabbath and reading from the scrolls of law and the prophets that were available to them. From this grew the Synagogues.

The third long-term significant outcome of the exile to Babylon was the development of a core group of Israelites who, when they returned to Jerusalem and the surrounding area, rebuilt the city, and established a government.

The temple and city were rebuilt to some extent, and the relationship between the Jews and God was reestablished. This relationship and associated writings became known as Judaism. Seeking the spiritual renewal of the community led to the establishment of a theocratic state for the Jews with the power vested in the priests. (This was a major change in the approach to governing the Jews. There was no separation of religion and government.) Over time the religious leadership gained more control over the people, which seems to have been easily given.

As conditions changed, Judaism came under new outside influences. In 332 BC, the Greek influence was brought in by Alexander the Great. As he built new cities and placed the Jews living in these new cities under a municipal government with its governmental processes, their ties to the theocratic nation were less strong and their ties to the local Synagogue and local rabbi become stronger. Alexander's desire to spread the Hellenistic influence put strong pressure on the Jews to incorporate Hellenistic ideals into Judaism, and some did.

The pressure to change Judaism was slowed down by the area being continually overrun by a succession of armies until the Jews had had enough and revolted. The increasingly heavy oppression of the Jews and endangering of Judaism caused them to revolt. The Maccabees were the leaders of the revolt against Seleucid, king of Palestine and Syria. They were surprisingly successful, and the Jews enjoyed independence from about 165 BC to 63 BC.

The Jewish religion and rituals, from the time of Abraham to the time of Jesus continued to incorporate gods and rituals from other religions. As non-Jews were incorporated into the Jewish community through marriage and commerce, they brought their religion with them. The book "The Israelites," on page 236 tells that, "Biblical evidence thus confronts us with a bewildering variety of beliefs and practices." Also, from, "The Israelites," page 260, "From what has been said it will be clear that Israelite religion had, from beginning to end, much in common with Canaanite religion or even depended on Canaanite models."

With all the difficulties the Jews encountered, it was during the Greek and Maccabean periods that they continue writing about they religion and God. Many of the Old Testament books were being written such as Proverbs, Job and Ecclesiastes, and the books of Ruth, Esther, Jonah, and the books of Psalms, and Daniel appeared. Some of these books had existed before this period; however, the writing during this period shows definite Hellenistic influence. Another effect of the Greek influence was the Septuagint, the translation of the Old Testament into Greek by some scholars, said to be seventy or seventy-two; however, the Septuagint translation that began in this period was not completed until near the time of Christ.

The revisions to the Hebrew Bible continued. The concept of demons and hell, which in ancient Hebrew belief were of minor importance, now became much stronger and the demons were now organized and had a leader, usually called Satan. This seems to have come from the Israelites observations of Zoroastrianism while they were in Babylon. This is when Satan was included in Israel's history, including Satan being in the Garden of Eden.

This period is also when the predictions of the old prophet about there being a Day of Yahweh when the Israel enemies would be sent to doom and a new Israel kingdom would be established with a Messianic king of Davidic lineage on the throne went through a major change. This change may not have come from Zoroastrian and may have simply come from the realization that the old prediction was not going to happen. The new prediction was that an agent of deliverance from God would come from heaven at the end of the world. It looks like the idea of a final judgment, which was like Zoroastrian, was becoming part of Jewish writing.

As the pressure on the Jews continued from non-Jewish cultures, the Jewish high priests became more powerful as both the religious and civic leaders, with some slight checks by the Jewish elders in the Sanhedrin. New ideas, not found in the Torah, were not well received, but some cultural innovations that improved foreign relations and living conditions and standards were welcomed. Two new parties arose, the Sadducees and Pharisees. They vied for dominance, with the Pharisees coming out on top.

It was during the Maccabean period that the Jews were able to overthrow the yoke of the non-Jewish pressure for change and reaffirm their identity and their relationship with God. As the Maccabean leaders became more controlling and demanding; however, the Jews revolted. The ensuing civil war was with open violence and bloodshed. The situation resulted in a stalemate. The Romans, who were in neighboring Syria were called to arbitrate the situation. They resolved the situation by taking over the country and making it a Roman province.

The Roman control surpassed anything the Jews had seen, with the singular exception that the Romans did not interfere with Judaism. That single exception did not lessen the burden of the strict and unforgiving civilian control, taxes, and demands of the Romans.

The Messianic expectations increased with the Roman occupation. The central belief became that God would intervene and collect "His own," both living and dead and then live with them in blessedness forever. At the last moment, the Messiah would appear in the clouds, with all the heavenly angels. He would be a supernatural personage to be called the Son of Man, or other titles, such as the Christ, the Lord's Anointed, the Righteous Judge, and the Prince of Peace.

The Jewish people had not been able to escape the heavy influence of other nations and tribes except during the reign of David and Solomon and the Maccabees. The idea of a single god with whom they had a special relationship, plus the added rituals and requirements that were developed to live up to their Covenant with God, was receiving stiff competition from other religions in and around Israel. The Jewish people's concept of one god was not generally followed by other religions and some Jews were following other religions and still had household gods. It was well after the death of Jesus and the beginning of Christianity that a single God was more broadly accepted. Household gods may have never been totally removed.

Looking at the Jewish nation from the time it became a nation under David to the birth of Jesus, the Jews were continually beset with outside forces trying to gain control of their land and their religion. Their location gave them easy access to trade and commerce and when they believed in God their religious beliefs gave them the support in weathering the storms they endured.

The Old Testament tells of the unique, close, and stormy relationship the Israelites had with God throughout their history. The Old Testament has stories of God's continued effort to have the Israelites understand His relationship with them and their inability to sustain their relationship with God.

The competing religions were always close at hand and certain aspects of the Canaanite and Persian religions can be found in some of the Jewish religious rituals and in some of the later additions to the Old Testament. The more powerful neighboring nations that overran the Jewish land (Palestine) continued to take away more of the Jews control of their own future to the point that what little control they had was in the hands of the religious leaders, which left the great majority of Jews desperately looking for a savior, a Messiah, a son of God as described in the prophecy of Isaiah. At the time of the birth and teachings of Jesus, the Roman army was the major foreign presence that caused the Jews the most despair.

SUMMARY

I have always thought that the respect that Abraham and God had for each other, which was the cornerstone of their relationship, was what God wanted for all of us. The discussion God and Abraham had prior to the destruction of Sodom and Gomorrah, clearly shows this respect. (Genesis 17:22-33)

The Old Testament does not sugar-coat the difficulty the Israelites had living up to God's expectations. Regardless of the Israelites failures, God's expectations for the Israelites never changed. Abraham and his descendants did not always hold up their end of the Covenant, but God remained steadfast in his belief in them and welcomed them back, with His forgiveness, when they returned from straying from their belief and trust in Him.

Our review of the Israelites and their history stops with the birth of Jesus, although the Israelites' struggles and persecution continue today. The Jewish people were well versed in their history. It was their history that defined them and set them apart from other Semitic tribes, as well as other people they encountered throughout their history.

Their struggles to understand their relationship with God were central to their history. The history of these struggles and successes that the Israelites had in their relationship with God over some 2000 years prior to the birth of Jesus is the foundation on which Jesus built His faith in God, and on which he developed his spiritual relationship with God. Jesus' belief in the relationship with God that each one of us can have been the basis for early Christianity.

It is an amazing part of this story that the Hebrew descendants continued to be so confident in their relationship with God that they continue today to claim it without reservation. They continue to trust in God's intervention on their behalf, as He has done in the past.

Chapter 5

THE WORLD OF JESUS' MINISTRY

INTRODUCTION

Two men were born that would give new direction and meaning to the relationship the Israelites had with God. One was John the Baptist, who established himself as a prophet, who railed at the Israelites failure to live in accordance with their covenant with God. The second man was John's cousin, Jesus, who brought a new approach to the relationship the Israelites could have with God. John recognized that Jesus' understanding of the Israelites covenant with God was greater than his. It was Jesus being baptized by John that got Jesus' ministry off to a good start.

JESUS THE MAN

Before we get into a description of who Jesus was let us answer the question, did a person named Jesus exist? The bone box with the inscription, "James's brother to Jesus" that was discovered several years ago does not help much. Aside from the long and tortuous process of determining if it is a forgery, both Jesus and James were common enough names to make it difficult to narrow the box down to being for James the brother of Jesus of Nazareth, called Christ. It is worth noting that the

Israel Judge ruled the prosecution had failed to prove the ossuary was not authentic.

There are two sources outside the Bible that add credence to Jesus being a real person, rather than a composite of several people or a figment of someone's imagination. The article in the January/ February 2015 Biblical Archaeology Review, Did Jesus Exist?, written by Lawrence Mykytiuk, covers this issue well. The two non-biblical sources are a Roman named Tacitus and a Jew named Josephus. Tacitus hated the Christians, and the Jews hate Josephus, so neither one had a reason to support a non-existent Jesus.

Tacitus, who lived from about AD 55 to AD 118, was a Roman senator, orator, and ethnographer, and arguably the best of Roman historians. Tacitus mentions Jesus, who he despised, in connection with Nero being suspected of burning Roman. Quoting Lawrence Mykytiuk, Tacitus wrote—-the following excerpt is translation from Latin by Robert Van Voorst:

> [N]either human effort nor the emperor's generosity nor placating of the gods ended the scandalous belief that the fire had been ordered [by Nero]. Therefore to put down the rumor, Nero substituted as culprits and punished in the most unusual ways those hated for their shameful acts ... whom the crowd called "Chrestians." The founder of this name, Christ [Christus in Latin], had been executed in the reign of Tiberius by the procurator Pontius Pilate ...Suppressed for a time, the deadly superstition erupted again not only in Judea, the origin of this evil, but also in the City [Rome], where all things horrible and shameful from everywhere come together and become popular. (See pg. 46, BAR Jan./Feb 2015.) Interestingly, Tacitus states that Pilate, not the Jews crucified Jesus.

The other strong evidence comes from Josephus. Josephus was a Jewish priest who grew up as an aristocrat and was an army commander who was captured by the Romans, to be freed when Vespasian became emperor as Josephus had predicted. Josephus lived in Rome under the patronage of a succession of Emperors. By aligning himself with the Jew's worst enemies, the Roman Emperors, Josephus was considered a despised traitor by the Jews. So, from his vantage point in Rome Josephus could write of his pride in his Jewish heritage and write his view of the Jewish history for Roman reading, which was much different from the Jewish leaders' view. Quoting further from Lawrence's article, Did Jesus Exist? ...In the temporary absence of a Roman governor between Festus's death and governor Albinus's arrival in 62 C.E. the high priest Ananus instigated James's execution. Josephus described it:

Being therefore this kind of person [i.e., a heartless Sadducee], Ananus thinking that he had a favorable opportunity because Festus had died and Albinus was still on his way, called a meeting [literally, "Sanhedrin"] of the judges and brought into it the brother of Jesus- who-is-called-Messiah ...James by name, and some others. He made the accusation that they had transgressed the law, and he handed them over to be stoned. (pgs. 47-48, BAR, Jan/Feb 2015.)

Because both names were common, both writers ruled out mistaken identity by referring to Jesus as the Christ or the Messiah. Since both writers were outside the influence of the Jewish leadership or the followers of Jesus, and there was no love lost between either writer and the Jewish religious leaders or the followers of Jesus, neither writer had anything to gain by inventing a religious leader named Jesus. Therefore, the writings of Tacitus and Josephus regarding Jesus can be taken as having accurately identified Jesus as an actual person of the four gospels in the New Testament.

MARY AND JOSEPH

The circumstances surrounding the marriage of Mary and Joseph, Jesus' parents, and Jesus' birth are explained in Matthew 1:18-2:12 and Luke

1:26-2:40. While the Bible tells us that both Joseph and Mary had some indication that Jesus was special, there is little to indicate that Joseph or Mary said anything to the people of Nazareth about their experiences with angels.

We know little of Mary and her husband Joseph prior to the story of the birth of Jesus. We lack information on how they met and became betrothed, although from Luke and Matthew we gather that they both had lived in Nazareth both before and after their marriage. Matthew has the genealogy of Joseph going back to the house and lineage of David of the Judah Tribe and of Abraham. Luke ties Mary to priest Aaron through her cousin Elizabeth.

Mary and Joseph were betrothed when Mary was found to be with child. Being betrothed was a very serious commitment. It required more devotion to each other than is required in today's engagement of young couples. For a Jew to violate the betrothal vow was to go against the concept of the family—the bedrock of the Jewish tribal organization—and to break religious law which carried severe penalties up to death.

Through all the trials and tribulations, the Jewish people had experienced, the one strong point was their sense of family. Family had been the core organization of the Hebrews since before the time of Abraham and has remained so throughout the history of the Jewish people.

One can only imagine how upset and worried Mary must have been. However, in Luke 1:30, the angel Gabriel told Mary, "Do not be afraid, Mary, for you have found favor with God. And behold, you will conceive in your womb and bear a son, and you shall call his name Jesus."

Joseph had also been put in an untenable position. When Joseph found out that Mary was with child, he had to quickly make a choice. His first thought was to quietly break the betrothal and send her off to another area. However, the Lord told Joseph, "Joseph, son of David, do not fear to take Mary your wife, for that which is conceived in her is of the Holy Spirit" (Matt. 1:20).

So, how did Joseph know that Mary was with child if he was not the father of the child? The Bible does not tell how he found out, but once he found out, he had to do something quickly.

Very quickly, things got confusing. Matthew makes Jesus a descendent of David through Joseph. If Joseph is not Jesus' biological father how can Jesus be a descendant from David? As the Bible does, from time to time, it does not tie up loose ends when telling a story.

In the world of today, it is difficult to know how serious and precarious Joseph's position was. The relationship the Jews had with God was much different than the relationship Christians have with God today. The thinking of people today is based on decreased importance of family, and more knowledge of the biology of a child's birth, and the world in general.

In the time of Jesus, conceiving was a three-part process that included the man, woman, and God. For example, Genesis 4:1 records that, "Now Adam knew Eve his wife, and she conceived and bore Cain saying, 'I have gotten a man with the help of the Lord.'" Later, in Genesis 21:1-3, God visited Sara and Sara conceived and bore Abraham a son and Abraham named him Isaac. And in Genesis 30:1-24, Rachel told Jacob, "Give me children or I shall die!" Jacob angrily replied, "Am I in the place of God, who has withheld from you the fruit of the womb?" God heard Rachel and opened her womb. She conceived a son and named him Joseph. Even with Elizabeth being well past the childbearing age she credited God with her having a son, John the Baptist. The Jews regarded a woman being barren as a sign of being out of favor with God.

God was thought of as being a spiritual part of the Jewish family and an integral part of their life. They thought of their relationship with God as being like the relationship that Abraham had with God, rather than the Jews being subservient to God as a superior being. Apparently, the early Christian Jews followed this line of thinking when they did not seem to be concerned with the conflict of having God involved in the birth of Jesus and naming Joseph as his father.

Because Joseph and Mary were not married, including God in Jesus' birth would not help Joseph solve his dilemma. It was all well and good for the angel to tell Joseph that Mary's child was of God, but that information is of no value to Joseph in his relationship with his friends, neighbors, and Jewish religious leaders, because God was thought to be part of the birth of every child.

It was also highly likely that bringing God into the discussion of Mary's condition would have been detrimental to Joseph. It would have been unthinkable to have God involved in an action that conflicted with the strong position of the family, the foundation of the Jewish culture and religion. Joseph was on his own to quickly decide what he was going to do. Joseph made the brave choice to marry Mary and to be a father to Mary's son as He grew up.

By choosing to marry Mary, even though he was not the birth father of the child she carried, he was risking his good standing in the religious community and the respect of the Nazareth community. He was joining his future with Mary and her child. In the eyes of his friends and neighbors, he was violating the basic concept of family which could adversely affect him in all that he did.

Joseph is not mentioned again until he and Mary are on the way to Bethlehem for the birth of Jesus. Luke tells us that Jesus was born in Bethlehem because Joseph and Mary went there to register in a Roman census since Joseph was of the house of David. However, there is no Roman record of such an event. Matthew simply states that Jesus was born in Bethlehem.

Joseph is the forgotten man who was an important part of Jesus' life as he grew into a man. By marrying Mary, Joseph showed to be a man of strong character, with high moral values, and to be very compassionate. He went against the strong cultural and religious prohibition against an out-of-wedlock pregnancy. As Jesus' human father, he was Jesus' model as he grew into manhood. Certainly, many of Jesus' ideas and his approach to life came from Joseph.

Jesus' Birth

During the reign of Herod the Great, two things happen that had a profound effect on the Jewish people. The first was the birth of a boy to Elizabeth, named John, who became John the Baptist. Elizabeth was the wife of the priest Zechariah and a cousin to Mary, the mother of Jesus. A few months later Jesus was born. It seems paradoxical to say it, but Jesus was born in 4 BC or a year or two earlier (Noss pg. 593).

The birth of Jesus was an unpromising beginning for a worldwide organization that today is of unimaginable strength and wealth. The story begins with Elizabeth being with child as foretold to her husband, the priest Zechariah, by an angel of the Lord. Now while Elizabeth was with child, her cousin Mary, who was also with child, came to see Elizabeth. From this point the story has John being born and circumcised and, as Luke states, "And the child grew and became strong in spirit" (Luke 1:18-80).

Matthew has Jesus being born in a house, Luke in a manger. Matthew has three wise men and Luke has shepherds coming to see the newborn Jesus. Matthew also has Joseph taking Mary and Jesus to Egypt to protect Jesus from King Herod. When Herod dies, Joseph returns to Israel and returns to their home in the village of Nazareth. The summary of the events surrounding the birth of Jesus comes from Matthew 1:18-2:23 and Luke 1:26-2:40.

The lack of information regarding Jesus' birth and His first thirty years is understandable based on what we know of the world at the time of His birth and growing up. The world of Jesus was not a nice place. The moneyed upper class did little to nothing to help the poor simply exist. The burden of the conquering Romans and the vast number of rules the Jewish religious leaders required of the Jews added to the misery of the poor Jews. The wisemen were later additions to the story of Jesus' birth, as was the reason given for Joseph taking his family to Egypt. The reason for the trip to Egypt given in Matthew 2:13-23, that upon hearing that a king had been born, Herod had all the male children in Bethlehem killed has not been verified. There is no record of Herod have babies killed after the birth of Jesus. Even as small as Bethlehem may have been, such events as described in Matthew and Luke would have been remembered and later recorded.

If the Jews thought that Jesus was born the Son of God, there would have been much more written about His birth than the small entries in Matthew and Luke.

His birth was as inconspicuous as any other birth in a poor working family, excepting the issue of the time between Jesus' birth and the marriage of His parents. Joseph's handling of the situation, by spending some time in Egypt, would have decreased its adverse impact but not completely removed it.

Although Jesus was born in Bethlehem, He grew up with His parents and His siblings in the village of Nazareth, a small town in Galilee in an out-of-the-way area of Israel. Although Joseph was not Jesus' birth father, he was the father of Jesus' household. Jesus, as the eldest son, would have spent time with Joseph learning the carpentry trade as well as learning how Joseph lived. A story appeared in the second century that stated that Joseph had sons from a previous marriage; however, this idea does not have much support.

JOHN THE BAPTIST'S BIRTH

John's mother, Elizabeth, was a kinswoman to Jesus' mother, Mary. Besides being related, they were close enough that upon hearing that both she and Elizabeth were pregnant with sons, Mary went with haste to see Elizabeth, the mother of John the Baptist, in a town in Judea (Luke 1:18-40). This would have been a difficult journey. It would have been more than a one-day long trip. It would have included traveling through Samaria. It would also have been dangerous because of the bandits who generally were not nice people. The Bible does not tell us if she traveled alone or in the company of other travelers.

If this story does nothing else, it describes the very close relationship the two women had. It is reasonable to believe that the two families got together from time to time, and that John's family may have been part of the group that went to Jerusalem for the Passover each year. In any case the reaction of Mary upon the news that she and Elizabeth were pregnant supports the idea that John and Jesus grew up aware of each other's thinking and ideas about God's Covenant with the Jews.

JESUS AND COUSIN JOHN THE BAPTIST

The Bible does not make a close connection between the ministries of John the Baptist and Jesus. It seems reasonable, however, to think that both were told of the special blessing from God both received prior to their birth. The two families may have traveled together each year for the Passover Feast which would have given Jesus and John the Baptist time to talk about their understanding of the Covenant and how to represent God to the Jews. They could also have coordinated the beginning of their ministries.

Both Jesus and John were thirty-ish when they began their ministries. Being thirty years old in Jesus' time was being, at best, middle-aged, well past the time when men were married and pursued their future. The life expectancy, particularly among the poor Jewish people, was much shorter then than it is today. They may have been feeling that their own age was pushing them to get on with their ministries, while they still could.

Jesus and John had some idea of what each wanted to do and John beginning his ministry could have been the trigger for Jesus to start His. When John said, "After me comes he who was mightier than I" (Mark 1:7). John recognized that Jesus' understanding of the relationship with God that was available to the Jews was more complete than his. That John began his ministry before Jesus did, I think was by design.

They both thought that time was short because of their age and because they believed the end of the world was near. Their messages were similarly centered on redemption and forgiveness of the sin of failing to live in the likeness of God. John wanted to change how people lived. Jesus wanted to change how people thought and felt. It is evident that John and Jesus had high regard for each other.

Jesus and John were concerned that the Jews were not living in accordance with the Covenant. Both saw that the Jew's failure to live in the Covenant did not come from the teachings of Judaism, rather the Jew's failure came from how the religious leaders were using Judaism for their own personal gain.

The description in Luke 3:2-3 of John coming out of the wilderness could put him around the Essene community, and he may have lived with the Essenes for a time.

In any case, John busted onto the scene out of the wilderness baptizing and proclaiming that the kingdom of heaven is at hand and calling for people to come forth be baptized and repent. He was in a hurry for the Jews to change how they lived before it was too late.

John felt it was his responsibility to warn the people that a new age was coming and to tell them to repent to be ready for the Messiah. The coming Messiah would separate the righteous from the sinners. John said that there was a "Day of Wrath" coming when the sinners would burn in an inextinguishable flame. Soon after John began his ministry, he was accepted as being a trusted prophet of God.

Jesus' approach was different than John's. Rather than being in a hurry, Jesus went where people were and made good use of what they knew and used. That is, He related to the people He met, for who they were. While He was frustrated that they could not make the leap from their lives to His life, He never gave up on them.

Neither John nor Jesus was about changing the Jew's world, rather they wanted the Jews to change how they lived in their world. Having their relationship with God at the center of all they did would put their lives into a whole new perspective.

FIRST THIRTY YEARS

This was an opportune time for Jesus and John to be born. The Jews, who believed in one God as described by Abraham and Moses, were looking for a major change to happen to straighten out the mess that their world had become. As described in chapter 4, the expectation was of a Messiah who would come down from the clouds and gather the believers or the righteous ones into a new existence.

The simple truth is that Jesus was a product of His time and upbringing. Unfortunately, we know next to nothing about His first thirty years. We can, I think, infer some things from what is known about the Jewish people in Jesus' time. For example, archeological excavations indicate that villages usually had one synagogue, which would have been a source of manuscripts for Jesus to read and study. Jesus' parents were religious, and the family would have gone to the synagogues on the sabbath.

There was not much, if anything, that would lead anyone to think that, while growing up, Jesus would someday proclaim the radical idea that the Jews could have their own, individual relationship with God. Jesus came from Nazareth, a town of poor, hardworking people. And He carried the added burden of beginning His life as being conceived out of wedlock. Other than His talks with the religious leaders when He was twelve, there is little, if any, record of His friends and neighbors seeing anything that would lead them to think that Jesus was destined to teach and demonstrate a new relationship with God that was available to each Jew.

The Jews were barely a majority in Galilee. There were many Gentile families who had settled in Galilee before and after the Jews moved in, all of whom had their own gods and religion. Regardless of their religious preference, the people of Galilee were similar in that they were poor predominately tradesmen and shepherds, who were working to feed their families and abide by their religious laws and the Roman laws and taxes.

We have little information on the beneficial effect Joseph had on his son Jesus. Jesus frequently used the term *father* in his reference to God, which indicates that in addition to teaching Jesus carpentry, Joseph taught and demonstrated to Jesus living in harmony with people and what it means to respect and keep God central in all that he did.

Surely, at some time Jesus would know of the circumstances of His birth. The stigma of being conceived out of wedlock was so strong that even a trip to Egypt could not hide the truth. Jesus saw and understood the strength of character and compassion Joseph had shown in marrying His mother and the steps he took to protect Mary and Jesus. Joseph's temperament that allowed him to accept the burden of marrying Mary, knowing the consequences of doing so in the judgmental atmosphere of the Jewish religion, along with the patience and strength he showed in keeping the family together, would have had a profound effect on Jesus, which Jesus incorporated into his understanding of God's relationship with the Jews. Joseph surely was the strong model of strength, compassion, dedication, and devotion that Jesus used for his own life.

As part of the Nazareth community. Jesus would have been able to observe the similarities and differences between the Jewish and Gentile families as He worked and played with His friends and neighbors. He was part of the working, poor citizenry, of mixed religious beliefs and duties. Regardless of what the people in Nazareth thought of Jesus, He was one of them. They were all in the same struggle to make ends meet. While this, by its-self, did not prepare Him for His ministry, this experience certainly could have become part of His approach to His ministry.

Jesus lived during a time of chaos and despair for the Jews. Jesus' family lived under three competing governments. The Jewish civil governmental structure centered on the tribe, clan, and family. This structure was in place before Abraham become the leader of the Hebrew tribe, and to a certain extent remains in place today. The second and controlling civilian government was the Romans.

Before the Romans there had been the Greeks who had been troubling, but they were friendly and responsive. The change to Roman rule brought with it a more controlling and oppressive government that imposed hardships and additional taxes on the Jewish population. The situation had become most intolerable. This just added to the long-standing problems for the Jews, of contenting with their inability to control their lives in their promised land.

The third government was the religious government, Judaism. Religion is not often thought of as a government; however, Judaism's authority over the Jewish people through its leadership interpretation and administration of Judaism certainly qualifies it as a government. While the Judaism leadership did not use Judaism to support the Jew's relationship with God, their leadership did allow the Jews to maintain some independence from Roman control. In the time of Jesus, the central Jewish civilian government was basically non-existent and completely subservient to the requirements of Judaism.

Another major part of Jesus' life was the divide that existed between Judaism and Samarian cultures and religions. After the death of King Solomon, the Kingdom of David was divided into two kingdoms, the northern kingdom of Israel, and the southern kingdom of Judea. Galilee and Samaria were remnants of the northern kingdom; however, starting back with the sons of Jacob, plus additional issues when Samaria was conquered by the Assyrians, the seeds were planted for a disagreement between Samaria and the rest of King David's Kingdom. At the time of Jesus' birth, Galilee and Judea were combined under one governor of the Romans and Samaria was under a different Roman governor. No love existed between Galilee and Judea on one hand and Samaria on the other.

If all that was not bad enough, the Jews bickered among themselves. The Pharisees, Sadducees, Herodians, Zealots, and various other parties were all vying for control; however, none of them were giving the Jewish people a reasonable solution for how to deal with all the chaos without despair. Additionally, there were bandits that roamed the countryside and the hill country that made traveling dangerous.

The Pharisees were a powerful party that strongly supported the leadership of the Jewish religion, Judaism. The Sadducees' party was composed of the wealthy, worldly people who took an intellectual view of Judaism and Jewish history. The Herodians were the people that supported the house of Herod, which ruled the Jews with a heavy hand. The Zealots were organized as a rebel force to fight the Romans, and in fact succeed in attacking and destroying Sepphoris, a Roman town four miles from Nazareth; however, the Romans brutally suppressed the revolt although they did not eliminate all the Zealot supporters. There are differing ideas about how strong the Zealots were and what were their actual accomplishments.

The fact that Herod of the House or tribe of Herod was the Roman's choice to be king simply meant that Herod's main concern was to keep the other tribal leaders from revolting or otherwise causing trouble. Similarly, the High Priest could maintain his independence from Roman control by keeping the Jews from revolting. His strongest tool for doing this was to make observance of the religious laws a requirement for access to the temple and as protection from being arrested for failing to show deference to the religious requirements. This requirement included a temple tax that made the religious leaders rich. With the additional Roman tax, most of the Jews had little left for living.

Some Jews formed a group called the *Essenes*. The Essenes were primarily made up of local Jews and Jews of neighboring countries who lived in communities in areas outside of Israel. One Essenes community lived in the desert. They were people who followed the basic Jewish beliefs with more purity and more rigor than the Pharisees.

Little was known of the Essenes before the discovery in 1947 of the Dead Sea Scrolls in caves next to an Essene community. Even with the information gained from the Dead Sea Scrolls, there are still many gaps in our knowledge of who these Essenes were and how they lived. The Essenes, seemly were content to quietly wait on the Messiah to come. As more is learned about them, the more intriguing the Essenes communities may become.

It is very difficult to appreciate the severity of the burden that was placed on the Gentile and Jews by the Romans, regardless of their religion, and the added burden placed on the Jews by the Jewish religious leadership. The Romans levied oppressive taxes on the people and Jewish leadership did the same. This led to four classes of Jews; the rich, the very rich, the working poor, and the poor who had been stripped of their livelihood and property and were reduced to begging because they could not pay their taxes. There was no middle class. This is the injustice and dire circumstance Jesus observed and lived with while growing up.

Although Mary and Joseph were poor people, Luke tells us that they made the trip to Jerusalem for the Feast of the Passover every year (Luke 2:41-52). As stated earlier, Jesus' parents were religious Jews who followed the requirements of Judaism.

We do not know how much of the Old Testament was available to Jesus as He was growing up. The official version of the Old Testament was not available before AD 100. However, copies of various Old Testament scriptures and other manuscripts were in existence and in use long before then. It seems that the manuscripts that were available to Jesus included the Law, which is the Pentateuch (the first five books of the Bible) and at least some of the Prophets. We know this because Jesus includes references from the Law and Prophets in His conversations. Hopefully, such books as Psalm, Job, Micah, Ruth, and Esther were also available. The importance of the available manuscripts on Jesus' understanding of the Jew's covenant with God cannot be overstated.

Without the information in the Old Testament, there would not have been a basis for Jesus' ministry. It was from His reading of the Old Testament that led Him to tell the Jews that the Pharisees, scribes, and priests; and therefore, the Jews, were not living in accordance with their covenant with God, and that the Jews were not being told that they could have a better life through a personal relationship with God.

Noss tells us that, "Somehow he came to know enough of the prophetic traditions to develop a distrust of whatever arid scholarship and
legalism the scribes and Pharisees were given to" (Noss pg. 594).

The Jews were highly literate. Being a carpenter's son in the small village of Nazareth would not have kept Jesus from having access to much
of the literature of the Jew's history and their relationship with God.
From his reading of the available literature and observing how the Jews
were living, Jesus began his ministry strongly convinced that living in
the Covenant with God would be living in the likeness of God.

Luke 2;41-52 tells us that when Jesus was twelve years old, He went
to Jerusalem with His family for Passover and went to the temple to
talk with the priests. Jesus' conversations with the priests indicated the
depth of His understanding of the core message of the ancient manuscripts and the relationship with God that was available to the Jews.

When the Feast of the Passover was over, He did not leave with His
parents. When they discovered that He was missing they returned to
look for Him. After three days, they found Him in the temple sitting
with the teachers amazing them with His "understanding and answers."
Jesus' depth of knowledge of Judaism far exceeded what a twelve-year
old boy was expected to know, which should have been a strong indication that He was special. However, the Jewish leaders failed to recognize Jesus' ability to develop a deeper understanding of the potential
relationship between God and the Jews than the leaders were giving
the Jews. That He was from Nazareth in Galilee, may have kept them
from recognizing His future potential.

Evidently, Jesus knew enough about the Jewish religion and had
thought enough about it to become so engrossed in His discussions
with the priests in the temple that He lost track of time and He did not
think about His parents not knowing where He was (Luke 2:41-52).
Not thinking to tell His parents certainly is not an unusual occurrence
for a twelve-year-old; however, the reason for Jesus' forgetfulness is
unusual for a twelve-year-old.

This story is our first indication of Jesus' struggle with the Jewish religion, a struggle that continued even after He established His own relationship with God. Certainly, He had studied enough of the available manuscripts of Jews history and their relationship with God, to have sorted out for Himself the writings that described the relationship with God based on the Jews Covenant with God.

Based on the events in the story being accurately retold and written over time, it gives us the first idea of Jesus' clear understanding of the Covenant between God and the Israelites, and the total misuse of Judaism by the Pharisees, scribes, and priests for their own financial gain and control. The ease with which Jesus turned aside the Pharisee's and scribe's trick questions during his ministry certainly came in part from the thoroughness of his knowledge of Jewish literature.

This story has a significant time, in this case, three days that Jesus' parents looked for Him before finding Him. It may or may not mean that Mary and Joseph spent three days looking for Him. In any case, they were very worried about their son and looked hard to find Him. When they did find Jesus, they were relieved, even though Mary scolded Him for worrying them half to death. This story has told us more than the amount of time that Jesus was missing and the worry, he caused his family.

The Concerns Jesus Faced

Once Jesus made His decision, there was no turning back. The peace of mind that came with His new life must have shown in the way He carried himself and the look on His face, for there is no record of Him having any trouble on His travels from His home to John the Baptist to be baptized or any of His travels after that.

Jesus spent much of His time during His ministry in Galilee, where the Jews were a bare majority. There were five main concerns confronting Jesus in Galilee. First was the Jewish religion, second was the Romans, third was the extreme poverty of the people, fourth was the presence of other non-Jewish religions, and fifth was the reluctance of the Jews to change the way they lived.

While all five concerns needed to be overcome, the Jewish religion was critical. It governed how He related to the Jewish people. He did not want to be enough of a problem to the Jewish leaders that they would have Him arrested. Being arrested would have quickly ended His ministry and His life.

The Jewish leaders had a sweet deal going. The Jewish people paid a variety of religious taxes which supported a rich lifestyle for the religious leaders. Having a carpenter from Galilee walking from town to town telling the people to change their ways, and that He was the new Law could be construed as preaching against the Jewish leadership. He surely was also aware of the concern both the Jewish leadership and the Romans had of another rebellion by the Jewish people.

That He lasted three years, which, based on how strongly He took the religious leaders to task, was probably as much time as could be expected. What the Judaism leaders did not count on; however, was that killing Jesus did not stop His ministry from continuing and growing after His death.

Escaping being arrested was more difficult than it sounds. His purpose was, after all, to convince the Jews that the religious leaders were wrong about how to live as God intended. He had to walk the fine line of describing a new and different lifestyle without appearing to preach blasphemy against the Jewish religious leaders.

Another critical concern was to not upset the Romans, who had civilian and military control over all the Jewish land. While the Romans were not interested in His ministry and how it affected the Jew's leadership, there were plenty of other areas where Jesus could cause the Romans to arrest Him. Complaining about the Roman taxes or objecting to the Roman rules are two areas where Jesus could be arrested. If Jesus was arrested, He would be turned over to the Romans for torture and death.

These two concerns were closely related. The Roman and Jewish leaders had an uneasy working arrangement. Each would not interfere with the other providing the Jews remained peaceful. Pontius Pilate, the Roman governor, was under orders from Rome to leave the Jewish religious rituals and laws alone if they did not interfere with Roman rules.

The Jewish religious leaders were hanging on to as much freedom from Roman interference as they could. Paradoxically, this meant that they had to require the Jews to strictly follow the religious laws. Jesus understood the dangers involved in His ministry. By simply disputing the religious leaders, He could be charged with blasphemy and put to death.

Regardless of what prompted Jesus to begin His ministry, He would have been aware of the serious problem of how the Jewish leaders and the Romans treated people who did not conform to Jewish laws and the requirement of the Roman rulers.

Both the Jewish and Roman leaders were afraid of another Jewish revolt. Viewed from Jerusalem, the crowds that followed Jesus looked suspicious. Could He and His small band of disciples be wandering around Galilee, and later Judea, raise troops for a rebellion? The Pharisees and scribes were sent out to follow Him and try to give the Jewish leadership cause to arrest Him.

The third concern, the poverty of the Jewish people, was what He saw and knew while growing up. It was an ever-present overbearing problem that certainly contributed to keeping the Jewish people from being able to grasp and take to heart the meaning of Jesus' message.

The fourth concern was that the religions of the non-Jewish friends and neighbors were often less demanding than the Jewish religion. As they and their neighbors struggled to survive each day it did not seem to the Jews that God was treating the non-Jews any different than they were being treated. So being blessed by God did not seem to be all that important.

Jesus carried two issues throughout His ministry. They were that He was thirty-plus years old and that He was not married. Marriage was an important part of the Jewish culture and men who were not married did not receive as much respect as men who were married. And the second issue was the issue of His birth coming so soon after Joseph and Mary were married? While the Bible does not identify either one as affecting His ministry, both had to be in the background any place He went in areas under Jewish control.

The fifth concern was the reluctance of the Jews to change. Jesus did not want to change the world, rather he wanted to change how the Jews *lived* in their world. He was not about improving the Jewish religion or the Roman's rule, but rather He talked about, and demonstrated, changing how the Jews coped with Jewish religion and the Romans. Jesus wanted to have a spiritual connection with God to be more important to the Jews than their worrisome and fearful thoughts. Having a spiritual connection with God would not, and could not, change the situation with the Jewish religion and the Romans, but it would change how the Jews lived in that situation.

These concerns were ever-present and affected how He lived and taught in His ministry. He wanted to explain and demonstrate His new approach to the Jew's relationship with God well enough for the Jews to change their lifestyle and for it to survive His death. He recognized that the purpose of His ministry, would in all probability, lead to His death at some point in the future.

Being God-centered was not going to change the requirements for growing and harvesting crops or herding and protecting livestock or paying taxes and fees to the Jewish religious leaders and the Romans. It would, however, change how they thought about doing these things, and how they lived each day. Getting them to realize the benefit of living in the blessing of God was Jesus' main purpose, and his inability to convince many Jews to change their thinking about living in the blessing of God must have been a great disappointment to him.

Jesus lived His faith in God. He lived as one whose spiritual connection with God was His primary guide in all that He did. Being guided by God freed Him from responding to the compelling issues of the day. While both Jews and Gentiles were suffering, Jesus' ministry was about bringing the lost sheep of Israel into the embrace of God's love and blessing.

The failure of the Jews to change their lives was the issue that Jesus continued to face throughout His ministry. Even with the miracles, which He did not like because they became the main attraction rather than a supplement to the message of His teaching, the Jew could not get beyond trying to have what Jesus did and said improve their current lifestyle, rather than looking at it as an opening to a new lifestyle to fully be what God made and saw was good.

What could one or two men do to make a difference? Neither John the Baptist nor Jesus would have been chosen to make a difference. The Jews were crying for a Messiah to come and save them from their world of Zealots, Pharisees, and Priests, the burden of Roman rule, and the chaos throughout the Jewish land. The poor that have been dispossessed were wandering through the county begging, the Zealots were just one of several groups that wanted to revolt, and bands of bandits were roaming the countryside stealing from the rich with little fear of being caught because the Romans did not care, and the Jewish government had little interest in hunting them down. All of this is most likely the reason the Essenes settled in the desert.

This was the chaotic world in which Jesus began His ministry about having enough faith in God to live in a relationship with God.

JESUS PREPARING FOR HIS MINISTRY

So, who was Jesus, and what do we know of Jesus as He starts His ministry? He was a Jew who was an accomplished carpenter. As He grew up in the small rural community of Nazareth, which was in a "backwater" part of Israel, he developed an understanding of the Jew's Covenant with God that had escaped others and established his commitment to keeping God central to all that He did.

Jesus' ministry was not about starting a new organized religion, after all, that was the type of offer the devil made in the third temptation. Jesus' core belief in a personal and friendly, but demanding God would have come from His observation of how Joseph interacted with the people, incorporating living his relationship with God in his relationship with His family and the people in and around Nazareth.

Jesus' personal relationship with God gave Him an understanding of God's goodness and God's love. As His relationship with God grew, He became at one, or atoned, with God. He was so aligned with being at one with God that He was willing to risk His life to spread His good news to the Jews.

Jesus recognized that the Jews could also have a God-centered personal relationship with God and wanted the Jews to believe they were what God made and saw was good. Jesus wanted the Jews to see that when they had a relationship with God they would live in God's unconditional love and be a blessing to others. That living in God's love would give them peace of mind while dealing with the Judaism leaders and the Romans.

Jesus' reading most assuredly included stories about Abraham's and Moses's relationship with God. Both Abraham and Moses strongly believed they were following God's intentions for the Hebrew-Israelite people. It was through Abraham's Covenant with God that Abraham's descendants would bring God's blessing to all mankind. The stories of Abraham and Moses may have guided Jesus' decision to live in the image of God. To date, Jesus' demonstration of living in the likeness of God is the most complete example we have.

Jesus lived in God's Covenant with the Jews. Jesus spoke of God the Father rather than God the Almighty. Jesus' ministry was guided by his strong and friendly relationship with God based on their mutual respect and love for each other. Without his relationship with God, Jesus would have remained a carpenter in Nazareth.

It was Jesus' decision to be spiritually committed with God, who, as His spiritual father, gave Him his strength of purpose for His ministry. So, what was Jesus' approach to the Jew's relationship with God? Jesus surely knew the first creation story and believed that the Jews were made in the image of God and could live in His likeness; however, they were not living up to that standard. The change Jesus wanted them to make was to live fully in the faith that God will be with them no matter the circumstances.

Jesus' message was simple. To become at one with God would require the Jews to change their lifestyle. In other words, to get different results they would need to think and act differently.

The underlying message of Jesus's life and ministry was that God's love was for all people regardless of how mean and unpromising a person's birth and life was. God would welcome him or her into living with His blessing.

Jesus' teaching had to be clear enough and direct enough for shepherds, carpenters, farm laborers, and other labors to take it in, believe it, and relate it to their lives. Jesus expressed His ideas by making good use of the things and issues that His followers knew and used. That is, He accepted the people that came to Him for who they were. This same approach, of using current things can be used today.

Jesus was an amazing man. From His reading of the manuscripts of the Jew's history that were available to Him, and from His observations of the world around Him, and from the lessons He received from His parents, Jesus developed His relationship with God and decided He would live His relationship with God. He surely knew the stories in Genesis and the message contained in them. Jesus determined that the God portrayed by the Jewish religion was not the God of Abraham and that the God of Abraham was still available to the Jews.

Jesus lived a strong message for the Jews. As He grew into manhood, Jesus had developed His unique understanding of what it meant to be spiritually connected to God. Jesus believed that with a strong faith in God's unbroken bond with the Jews and caring for the Jews, the Jews could be the "light of the world" (Matt 5:14). This Jesus is someone we all can emulate. Obtaining a personal relationship with God while working in a trade learned as an apprentice outside the main center of business is an accomplishment that all could and can emulate.

Jesus was convinced that living a God-centered life with a God-centered faith would give the Jews the spiritual strength and peace of mind needed to remove the stress, uncertainty, and hopelessness of their current existence. Being God-centered would not cause the Romans or the Jewish religious leaders to change their ways or go away, but rather would have the Jew's relationship with God be in control of their lives instead of the Romans and Jewish religious leaders. And as an additional benefit, they would be ready for the coming of the Messiah.

The life Jesus chose was not preordained, although many people think it was. The approach Jesus chose resulted in His message about having a spiritual relationship with God spreading to the people who would benefit the most from it.

So, what was the catalyst for Jesus to give up His carpentry business and leave His home and family to begin His ministry when He was thirty years old? The story of His birth could have caused His reluctance to begin His ministry. Being conceived out of wedlock would have been a concern and prevented Him from entering the temple; however, He was allowed on the porch of the temple.

There are several possible reasons for His decision to leave home and begin His ministry. One could have been the death of His father, Joseph. Joseph disappeared from the gospels after the birth of Jesus, but his presence was certainly an integral part of Jesus' growing up. As suggested earlier, the relationship between a father and the oldest son, who learned the carpentry business from His father, could have been very close, and the death of His father could have been devastating to Jesus and caused Him to leave home and begin His ministry.

Another reason for His leaving could have been as simple as the living conditions throughout Galilee had deteriorated to the point that He felt compelled to describe and demonstrate to the Jewish people that living in concert with God would improve how they lived in the existing conditions.

Still, another reason could have been that He believed He had a valuable message for the Jews, and He felt time was running short. Jesus believed that the end of the world as He knew it was close at hand as did His cousin John, the Essenes, and the Jewish people in general. This belief really took hold with the coming of the Romans and the accompanying misery the Jews were suffering. Deep down, the Jews were feeling that if God cared about His chosen people, He would send someone, the Anointed One, a Messiah, to remove the afflictions that had befallen them. And while Jesus did not see Himself as the "Anointed One," He did believe that He understood what was needed for the Jews to live in God's promise and for them to be ready for the Messiah.

As part of the age issue, it could have very well taken Jesus thirty years to get comfortable enough with His radical belief about the relationship the Jews could have with God to begin His ministry. The simplicity of His belief conflicted with the long-standing Jewish religious rules and requirements that were the basis for the Jewish government. To take on the established Jewish religion and staying clear of the Romans at the same time was a daunting undertaking.

Regardless of what Jesus envisioned His future to be, His decision to leave his family for an uncharted future, filled with unknowns and uncertainly would have been reached with trepidation. He was not leaving to visit a friend in the next village, with the expectation that He would be home that evening or in the next couple of days. He was leaving home knowing that He may never return. Additionally, traveling in Galilee was dangerous and many of the people He would see on the road were the people who made it dangerous. And He would be in their company on nights when He was outside a village.

Jesus, the son of a carpenter in Nazareth of Galilee, saw the shortcomings of the way Judaism was being administrated by the Jewish priests. He did not agree with the relationship with God that the Jewish leaders were telling the Jews to have. Instead of the priests' approach to God, Jesus determined that the central Judaism message was that a personal spiritual relationship with God was available to each Jew.

Jesus believed that getting each Jew to have a personal spiritual relationship with God was more important than anything else. He believed that, with God's support and God's blessings of forgiveness and grace, each Jew would have the strength to live free of the worry and stress they were enduring.

Jesus' Skills, Knowledge, And Understanding That Was The Basis Of His Ministry

In His quiet way, He was in command of His life and His surroundings. His calm assurance of God's love for the Jewish people in simple terms gave hope to the Jewish people. People felt better for having been in His presence. Jesus did not allow failures and disappointments to sway Him from His course.

Jesus had the ability to gain quick acceptance from people He met. His countenance was friendly, accepting, comforting, and non-threatening. He accepted the people He met as being what God made and saw was good. He gave each person His full, friendly attention. His compassion for the people was readily evident to all. There was a feeling of wellbeing that came over the people in His presence, a presence that gave pause to the scribes and Pharisees as much as His answers to their questions did.

It was the message of His ministry and His loving and caring interaction with the people that caused the crowds to gather wherever He went. In Jesus' presence, a person's belief in God enabled his or her healing. Jesus' gentle and firm belief in a person's ability to heal when they accepted God's love was often successful.

Being God-centered gave Jesus the peace of mind that led Him to give comfort and support to the people that gathered around Him. Jesus demonstrated that living with God's blessing was available to anyone who chose to have a God-centered relationship.

His belief that a relationship with God was available to everyone was so strong that people sensed it, believed it, and responded well to it, but unfortunately, their belief was not strong enough for them to change how they lived.

Jesus' freedom of spirit was reflected in His calm and commanding composure and His loving approach to all who confronted Him. His encouragement and the healing that happened in His presence of people who were hurting and distraught were what drew people to Him. There were many times when He could have easily shown anger, but instead, He showed patience and love. The few times He expressed anger or frustration was directed at Jesus' followers and the Jewish leaders for their failure to live as God intended. He was showing the Jews that they could free their spirit by having a strong, clear relationship with God.

His features and the way He approached and talked with people would have led people to accept and respect Him. Jesus was a strong, but gentle man, who was soft-spoken and friendly. He was a compassionate man of high character and strong sense of purpose and commitment to living in the likeness of God. Jesus had spent thirty-some years developing His ideas on what the relationship between the Jews and God could be and what the Jews could do to make it one of mutual support, trust, love, and understanding. He believed that His dream for the Jews could become reality through the Jew's faith in God and His promise of continuing to be their God throughout their future.

Jesus obtained His clear and uncluttered spiritual relationship with God by stripping away all the impediments made by man to gain control of the Jews, rather than to live in God's blessing.

Jesus had grown up living with the daily grind of getting enough to eat, paying religious taxes, following the Jewish laws, paying the Roman taxes, and not upsetting the Jewish leaders or the Romans. Jesus believed that living with God as their God and making their relationship with God their continuing top priority, would not make their daily hardships go away, but it would ease their worry and stress of dealing with their daily hardships.

The issues surrounding Jesus' birth underlies the discussion about when, and if, Jesus became divine. Was He born connected to God in a special way, different from the connection that everyone else had, or could have, or did He make his special connection later? Or was Jesus living in the likeness of God, so the connection Jesus had with God was available to all people? The scriptures give material to support each position and one can, and many have spent a long time arguing this issue.

Jesus certainly had an idea of what living with God's blessing meant. It meant living a God-centered life and putting trust in God first above all else. It meant going all in with a clear and open spiritual connection to God uncluttered with doubts, hesitation, and indecisiveness. Doing so would put the daily hardships in a much better perspective, by giving them strength and purpose from God's support. They could start life as a new day and each day thereafter would become a new day.

It is a mark of Jesus' relationship with God that, even with the stress of having the hostile Pharisees and scribes scrutinizing everything He did and said, He was able to demonstrate to the Jews the empowering quality of a spiritual relationship with God. Jesus' understanding of God's Covenant with the Jews was so different from how the Jewish religious leaders described living in the Covenant with God, that it was difficult for Jesus to live His relationship with God without giving the Pharisees and scribes cause to arrest Him.

Chapter 6

JESUS' MINISTRY

INTRODUCTION

The Jews had no reason to think of Jesus as being more than a carpenter before He started His ministry. The first indication the Jews had that Jesus was special came when He was thirty and had been baptized by John the Baptist, spent forty days in the wilderness, and depending on which gospel is used, Jesus either changed water to wine or taught and healed a man in the synagogue in Capernaum. See John 2:1-12 and Mark 1:21-26. Shortly after these events, it was reported that Jesus was a healer who drove out bad spirits, enabled blind men to see, and crippled men to walk.

His ministry was about the Jews having a personal relationship with God and living in harmony with a personal relationship with God. They would still have to work, that is, continue to be a carpenter, a farmer, or a shepherd, but living with God's blessing would replace their daily worry and stress from trying to meet all the rules and laws of the Jewish priests and the Romans.

It was Paul who recognized that Jesus' message of being right with God from the heart rather than by following laws set Jesus apart from the priests, scribes, and Pharisees. Without the burden of following the religious laws, Jesus was free to be guided by His relationship with God. Paul called it *casting aside the laws for freedom of spirit*. That His freedom of spirit set Jesus' ministry apart from all else was not well understood during His three-year ministry, nor is it well understood today.

Jesus was not interested in starting a new religion. Rather He was demonstrating living a God-centered life. Jesus was a Jew who believed in the message of the historical Jewish writings that told of their connection to God. Judaism was not the problem. Jesus knew and quoted the Old Testament writings that were the basis of Judaism. The Judaism priests' use of Judaism to feather their nests rather than using Judaism to lead the Jews to have a God-centered life was the problem.

It is difficult today to recognize how totally different Jesus' relationship with God was compared to the Jewish religious relationship to God. Jesus saw His ministry as being one of changing how the Jews approached life. This most significate change was for each Jew to have the freedom of spirit which would allow them to have love as the primary ingredient in his or her relationship with God and each other. God's act of creating man in His image and God's continual support, caring, and forgiveness of the Jews was His act of love. Jesus recognized God's love and simply wanted each Jew to accept God's love and live in the likeness of God with acceptance and love for themselves and each other.

Jesus was not just about changing how the Law was applied, but rather He was about a totally new way of living, without the Law, starting within each person's self. The old references were of no use. They were replaced with what Paul called *a freedom of the spirit*.

Jesus wanted to improve the lives of the Jews, not to start a religion. He was a Jew through and through, who believed that there was a God, who through His Covenant with Abraham blessed the Jews with the ability to be the light of the world, to demonstrate living in a spiritual God-centered relationship with God.

Jesus was convinced that the world as He knew it was going to end soon, and without a God-centered relationship the Jews would not be prepared to survive the end of the world and live in the new world.

Jesus believed in the relationship possibilities that were available from the interaction the historical Hebrew-Israel people had with God as described in the literature and history of the Old Testament; that is, the manuscripts that became the Old Testament.

Jesus believed that the failure of the Jewish leaders to lead the Jews into a God-centered relationship had put the Jews in the position of missing out on living within God's Covenant.

Jesus believed in the Jews. The historical literature was the foundation upon which He built His relationship with God. Jesus picked up the message of God's love for the Jews that threads through the Old Testament. For Jesus, God's message was found the core message in the Old Testament and was central to all that He said and did.

Jesus took the mystery and religion out of His relationship with God. His relationship with God was clear, direct, and uncluttered. Jesus chose to follow through with His ministry knowing full well what to expect from the Jewish religious leaders and the Roman leaders. He continued to preach and live in the blessing of God to the end, to show that living with God's blessing is greater than anything else, regardless of how it ends.

Even with the heavy burden of oppression by the Romans and the Judaism leaders, Jesus was most concerned about the people who heard His message and observed His lifestyle, but were unable to change their inward disposition, and make living with faith in God their priority.

THE GOSPELS STORIES OF JESUS' MINISTRY

Jesus' story is told in the four gospels. How important is it that the four gospels tell the story of Jesus' life and ministry differently? Is Jesus' story less valuable because the four gospels do not tell the same story on the events during Jesus' ministry? Or that only John describes Jesus raising Lazarus, or that only Luke tells the Parable of the Prodigal Son, or that each Gospel tells the story of the events after His death differently? Each gospel had a point to make or stress.

As we go through Jesus' three-year ministry, I will use Mark as the guide for the sequence of events described in the three synoptic Gospels of Matthew, Mark, and Luke. Mark is generally considered to first gospel to be written and was one of the sources for Matthew and Luke. The sequence of events in Mark is thought to closely follow the sequence described by Peter in his telling Mark the stories of Jesus' ministry. The authorship of the Gospel of Mark has been questioned; however, early Christians believed that it was written by Mark.

Mark recorded the events as Peter told them to him sometime after the death of Jesus. Although it is generally thought that Mark accurately wrote what Peter said, Peter's recall of the events may not have been complete or totally accurate, nor did he necessarily recall them in the order of their occurrence. Even with these issues, Mark's Gospel is probably the most accurate description of the events of Jesus' ministry.

It is strange that the Gospel of John has such a different beginning to Jesus' ministry. Turning water into wine was a major happening that you would think would not go unnoticed. One reasonable thought is that after Jesus started preaching and collected his first four disciples He and His disciples went to the wedding before going to the synagogue on the Sabbath, and either the water being turned into wine was not recognized until after Jesus and the disciples left, or that Jesus did not bring attention to what He did. An alternative explanation is that the description of turning water into wine was added later. There are other plausible explanations for the disagreement in how Jesus began his ministry, and this is not the only time that the Gospels have disagreements. Unfortunately, these disagreements cannot currently be resolved. It is my thinking that events happened or there was the need to make a point that over time became lost, which leaves us with what we have today.

Jesus' Baptism And The Three Temptations

Jesus and John the Baptist both recognized that having the well-established and respected prophet John baptize Him was an excellent way for Jesus to be introduced to the Jewish people. It would give credence and a spiritual start for Jesus' ministry.

All four gospels tell us of Jesus being baptized by John the Baptist and the Holy Spirit blessing Jesus; however, the circumstances surrounding His baptism differ somewhat in each gospel. All four describe God's blessing as being the spirit descending upon Jesus as a dove. All but John state ..." a voice came from the heavens, 'Thou art my beloved Son, with thee I am well pleased.'" All four Gospels have John the Baptist saying before he baptizes Jesus that he, John, baptize with water but the one who follows him will baptize with the Holy Spirit.

Matthew and Luke describe Pharisees and Scribes asking John to baptize them and being turned away. The book of Mark is the least descriptive and the book of John is the most descriptive of the baptism of Jesus and the surrounding events. See Matthew 3:11-17, Mark 1:7-11, Luke 3:15-17, 21-22 ND, and John 1:19-27, 31-34.

The story in the Gospel of John is substantially different from stories in the Gospels of Matthew, Mark, and Luke regarding the activities around the baptism of Jesus, the temptations, and the start of his ministry. These differences may highlight the different purposes of the synoptic gospels and the Gospel of John.

Matthew, Mark, and Luke have Jesus going straight from His baptism into the wilderness to experience his temptations. John does not mention the temptations and has Jesus selecting Andrew and Peter as His first disciples and then the next day selecting Philip and Nathanael as disciples.

Matthew and Luke describe three of his temptations during His forty days in the wilderness. Mark briefly states that he was tempted in the wilderness for forty days. Some of the details given by Matthew and

Luke may have come from other sources. See Mark1:12-13, Matthew 4:1-11, and Luke 4:1-13.

This brings up a problem that exists throughout the gospels. How did the writers find out about what transpired when Jesus was alone? If Jesus told one of the disciples did that disciple tell the others, or was someone other than the disciples who was special to Jesus and was someone He confided in? This is but one of the unanswered questions the Bible gives us to ponder.

The three temptations Jesus refused to follow defined His ministry. They drove home that Jesus would not allow any daily concerns to detract Him from living in His close personal spiritual relationship with God. They clarified and provided focus to His understanding of the underlying message of the Jews Covenant with God. Jesus articulated the Jews Covenant with God in a way that gave new meaning to the Jew's commitment to God.

He answered the first temptation, "If you are the Son of God command these stones to become loaves of bread," by saying, "Man shall not live by bread alone" (Matt. 4: 3-4). This defined Jesus' relationship with God as being spiritual, not physical. This temptation is the most encompassing temptation of the three. Jesus believed that being spiritually connected to God was the only way one could live in the blessing of God. It frees the mind from distractions like worry and stress. Being connected to God opens a clear channel with God to receive His blessing and steady and unwavering guidance and forgiveness.

I struggle with this the most.

This temptation is the same problem for the people who live in multi-million-dollar homes as it is for the homeless who survive, as best they can. It is not about having enough to eat, rather it is about having a personal relationship with God be a Jew's top priority.

As we will see, eating was an integral part of Jesus' ministry. So, the temptation was not about obtaining food, but rather, it was about the worry about obtaining food being a person's top priority. When obtaining food, and by inference, other material things, takes precedence over having a spiritual relationship with God, God is taken out of the picture. .

Jesus understood the problem this temptation speaks to. He grew up with people whose daily routine of feeding one's family, which was not always accomplished, was a consuming daily worry that blocked a clear channel for a spiritual relationship with God. It was very difficult for these people to have a spiritual relationship with God be more important than feeding their families.

Jesus believed that if the Jews were spiritually connected to God, they would be living in God's blessing and would have the freedom and vision to soar to new heights. Being with God would not eliminate the physical needs but these needs would be included in their overall relationship with God. This temptation highlights the constant problem confronting Jesus, that while the Jews like what they heard and saw, they were unable to adopt Jesus' message to their own lives.

In like manner the second temptation, "...throw yourself down ..." of throwing himself off the top of the Temple so God could save him was not what His relationship with God was about. It did not fit the spiritual relationship described in the first temptation. Jesus' response was, "You shall not tempt the Lord your God." Briefly and clearly, He states that setting conditions or bargaining with God was not part of having a clear, uncluttered spiritual relationship with God (Matt. 4: 6-7). If the Jews truly believed and trusted God, there would be no need to test God.

Jesus' understanding of the spiritual relationship with God was that God's part of the Covenant with the Jews was never in question, but rather, the Jew's part of the Covenant was continuously in question. God's commitment could not be made stronger by the Jews testing His commitment to them. That the Jews' commitment wavered from time to time did not change God's commitment to the Jews; however, the

Jews living with less than full commitment to their Covenant with God kept them from receiving any benefits from the Covenant.

The Jews needed to be fully committed to God. A part-time commitment did not work. It is all in or nothing. God cannot help those whose attention is elsewhere. Jesus' concern was about their spiritual well-being not about what their friends and neighbors think of them. Jesus' faith in his spiritual connection to God would not die with the death of His physical body.

This temptation and His response could have very well come from the example of His parents living in a spiritual relationship with God while providing a safe close family life, even with the circumstances of their marriage. Joseph having his faith in God be central to all that he did, including his family being part of the Nazareth community certainly had a strong impact on Jesus.

And finally, in the third temptation, the devil showed Jesus all the kingdoms and said to him, "All these I will give you, if you will fall down and worship me." Jesus' response was, "Be gone, Satan! For it is written, 'You shall worship the Lord your God and him only shall you serve.'" (Matt. 4:9-10).

Jesus' answer to the third temptation was central to Jesus' life and ministry. Jesus believed that a spiritual relationship with God took precedence over everything else. His relationship with God governed all that He said and did. This was the message He wanted the Jews to hear and embrace. He believed that having each Jew make his or her relationship with God be his or her number one priority would give them strength to live through the hardships they encountered.

Earthly power was not part of His relationship with God, for the connection with God was spiritual, not about earthly gains or needs and happenings. Jesus' relationship with God did not include physical power. He was not going to challenge Caesar to a battle for territory or political gain. He had seen enough of how political power corrupts and pulls people away from God. Gaining earthly control and power was not part of His decision to live His faith in his spiritual relationship with God.

God gave us dominion over the His gift of the world and everything on it without restrictions or instructions. He gave us the freedom to use His gift to the fullest, even beyond our wildest dreams. Jesus wanted the Jews to understand the freedom God gave each one of them, that they could live in the likeness of God. Rather than using their gifts as God intended, the Jews were stuck with keeping as much control over their lives as they could through what little political power they could muster.

The constant struggle between the Jews and the Jewish religious leaders and the Romans was what controlled the Jews lives. Without having a good spiritual relationship with God to guide their lives, they were allowing the Romans and the Jewish religious leaders to dictate how they lived.

Throughout Jesus' ministry, He stayed on point. Anything that diverted attention from a person's spiritual connection to God isolates that person from God. Jesus continually demonstrated living in His relationship with God by placing His faith in God above obtaining food and possessions, by not testing God, and by not working to have worldly power.

What would the change to the Jews be with a God-centered relationship? Accepting a relationship with God would give them God's constant guidance, forgiveness, and grace, regardless of who they were or what they did. God would be with them always.

God's commitment included the freedom to know that when one strayed away from his or her relationship with God, that each one would be freely and joyously accepted back by God. Regardless of the trouble Abraham got into when strayed from God, God willingly accepted him back without conditions or condemnation.

Jesus strongly believed that God fully intended for the Jews to set the example to the world for living in a spiritual relationship with Him. If the Jews could live in harmony with God's creation in their chaotic world that was controlled by people who did not have a God-centered life, they would show the way to fully accept and enjoy the life that God wanted them to enjoy, independent of what other people were doing.

The people with whom Jesus was most familiar and with whom He could best relate were the people who were having great difficulty understanding and accepting His message. It was difficult, if not impossible, for them to accept that what they had always done, e.g., find enough food each day, impress their friends and neighbors, and obtain as much power as they could to control their lives, wasn't part of what God was looking for in His relationship with them. As Jesus traveled through the country, the people who came to hear Him were in awe of what they saw and heard, but by and large, they could not make the leap of dropping all that they had struggled so hard to obtain to begin living as He lived.

His refusal to accept the devil's offers brought clarity to Jesus' thinking about how He could live in God's blessing. The temptations did not have anything to do with God being the Jews' God. The temptations were about the Jews accepting God's guidance.

Jesus realized that how well connected to God a person was depended entirely on the decision made by that person. God is fully available and ready to give each one of us His full blessing. The difficulty comes from how ready each person is to live in God's blessing. Could their belief and trust in God stay above the need to eat, or the need to impress others, or the need to be in control? Each one of these temptations offers easy excuses for not placing Jesus' answers to the temptations first.

Jesus' answers to the three temptations did not increase God's willingness to partner with Jesus, but rather they described Jesus' willingness to partner with God. By commenting to place His relationship with God first regardless of the hardships, distress, and negative experiences he would experience, Jesus found the peace of mind that comes with a close spiritual relationship with God. Using God's gifts as God intended removed the stress and worry that comes with the Jews doing things on their own. Jesus' demonstration of living in God's blessing is as true to us today as it was to the Jews in Jesus' time.

His partnership with God meant He would forego looking for food, testing God, or becoming a worldly leader. Everything He did and said from this time forward fit in with His response to one or more of these three temptations.

THE BASIS FOR JESUS' MINISTRY

For the better part of thirty years, Jesus had watched the Jews struggle with the adverse conditions that made their lives difficult and burdensome. They continued living the same way, with the unrealistic hope that something or someone would come along, and things would get better. They had failed to take advantage of the one thing that would make their lives better. Jesus saw that their faith was misguided. They did not recognize that a direct relationship with God was available to them to replace adhering to the Jewish religion, with its many rules and requirements.

It was not good enough that Jesus understood the Jew's role in God's Covenant. He had to demonstrate living in God's blessing, in the hope that the Jews would grasp it and take it to heart. He needed to do this in an environment of Jewish leadership control and Roman control.

I suspect that when Jesus started His ministry, He had at least some inkling that He would eventually be arrested. The gospels describe several instances when Jesus took the Jewish leadership to task and could have been accused of blasphemy, which was a crime punishable with death.

It is amazing that, for about three years, He lived and taught about having a direct spiritual relationship with God without being arrested. Jesus' core message was the Jew's way of living was wrong and He was giving them a new and very different way of living in God's blessing without the rituals and rules of Judaism. While His message set Him apart, it took the miracles that took place in His presence to draw the people to Him to hear His message. Unfortunately, the Jews interest in what they heard and what they saw was not strong enough to convince them to change their ways.

Jesus was putting His trust in His relationship with God when He decided to leave His carpentry trade and His family to walk from town to town to spread the message that the Jews could have a spiritual relationship with God while they worked in their trades and raised their families, without receiving permission from the Judaism priests. He believed that each Jew could establish his or her own communication with God and continue his or her daily life with the peace of mind of living in God's blessing.

Jesus wanted them to understand that if they centered their lives on God, He would support them and be with them in all that they did. The need for the Jews to change their ways, along with Jesus' belief that time was short underlies Jesus' three-year ministry. It was only after His death, that His followers began a struggling process of living Jesus' ministry, as disjointed, sporadic, and uncoordinated as their efforts were.

Jesus wanted the Jews to live in harmony with God as Abraham had. Jesus believed that the Jews were what God made and saw that it was good. He believed that God would bless and support them if they would live with Him as their one and only God, not as a nation but as individuals. This was the difference He brought to the Jews. The Covenant was not about rules, rituals, laws, and nations. It was about individuals living in God's creation with respect and loving care for each other and for God's creation. Jesus' dissatisfaction with the way Judaism was being practiced, as a source of power and money for the leaders through fear and domination, with little regard for the Jews, was the basis for His proclaiming the new way of living in the spirit of God.

God fulfilled his part of His Covenant by agreeing to be central in the Jew's lives.

To fulfill their part of the Covenant, the Jews must accept God as being central in their lives. God could only be with those who invited Him to be with them. This is as true today with both Jews and Christians as it was for the Jews in Jesus' time.

The story of Moses taking the Israelites out of Egypt is a case in point. God responded to the Israelites cry for help by calling on Moses to be His human representative to the Egyptians for the Jews. Ultimately, the results of Moses' relationship with God convinced the Israelites to have the faith in God that allowed them to make the monumental decision to leave all that they knew to follow Moses into a hostile unknown. The Israelites commitment to their relationship with God wavered from time to time, and that created hardships for them, not for Moses or God, but for the Israelites. The overall result of the Israelites finally adhering to their commitment to God, by taking actions based on their faith in God resulted in the Israel people returning to their promised land.

So, what is to be made of God and how He related to the Jews and, later, the Christians? What is God like, really? Only God knows why He created the world as a small part of the universe and what His expectations were for the world. From Jesus' ministry, we can get a sense of Jesus' understanding of God. Jesus spoke with deep-felt confidence of God's righteousness who never varied from His faultless justice as He went through the historical course of mankind.

Jesus believed God's love was unending. There was nothing mankind could do to cause God to withdraw His love for them. His relationship with mankind centered around God being available to all and allowed each person to make his or her decisions. God was not willing to control each person's life. God accepted each person and gave guidance when requested and God accepted them back, regardless of how many times they strayed, with forgiveness, redemption, and joy. Jesus believed each person should trust God without hesitation or worry and seek guidance and give thanks through prayer.

Jesus was not a Christian, He was a Jew, and His ministry was to the Jews, although He did minister to Gentiles. He did not support any of the parties such as the Zealots, Sadducees, or Pharisees, although His difference with the Pharisees was chiefly in emphasis. He was upset that the Pharisees did not practice what they preached. Matthew 23:1-39 is a long condemnation of their actions.

The Pharisees were a major problem for Jesus. The Pharisees were an elite class of Jews who were well educated in Judaism with all its structure and requirements, as well as what the Judaism leaders required of the Jews for God to be their God. Rather than living spiritually connected to God, and with their knowledge of God's Covenant with the Jews they instead chose to live in the splendor of accumulated riches and power, without concern for the wellbeing of the Jewish people or for living a God-centered life.

One of Jesus' big hurdles was that the Jews believed that by following the requirements of Judaism they were included in God's promise to Abraham. They had been told, and came to believe, that only through the Judaism priests could they have a relationship with God. Central to Jesus' was his recognition of the fallacy of their belief. Jesus knew that a personal spiritual relationship with God was available to them, and that God wanted each one of them to have such a relationship with Him. Without a spiritual relationship with God, the Jews were not living to their fullest. Jesus wanted the Jews to know that a relationship of trust and respect like Abraham had with God was available to them.

The Pharisees claimed to be living with God. As the Jews listened to Jesus and watched miracles, they could not help but see the drastic difference between what Jesus said and did, and what the Pharisees said and did. The Pharisees were following Jesus from village to village to see if Jesus would disrupt the relationship they claimed to have with God. Regardless of what Jesus said, it looked to the Jews like the Pharisees were living well and did not have to change anything, so why was Jesus telling them they had to change?

Having the Pharisees in the crowds citing religious laws and questioning Jesus was not as effective as the Pharisees had hoped. Even though Jesus was able to turn their questions against them the Pharisees, questions certainly caused the Jews to have concerns that Jesus was never able to totally remove. The Pharisees' presence certainly made the miracles more important to Jesus' ministry.

In the end, Jesus was never able to break the hold the Pharisees and priests had on the Jews. He could not get them to ignore the finery and splendor of the Pharisees and priests. He did not want them to think that God would give them what the Pharisees and priests had, but rather he wanted them to recognize that living with God's blessing will improve their own wellbeing. Today's Christianity with its magnificent churches, fine tapestry, and grand uniforms and robes, along with the wealth it consumes more closely relates to the Pharisees and priests than Jesus.

Jesus, as well as John the Baptist, the Essenes, and many Jews, believed that the end of the world as they knew it would soon be upon them, and that there would be a Messiah who would save the righteous followers of the Covenant. Although Jesus, and the Essenes all believed the end, The Wrath of God, was near, Jesus was not going to sit quietly and meditate while waiting for it to come like the Essenes.

Jesus was comfortable with the poor Jews and had compassion for their suffering. Jesus had grown up as a village carpenter and, as such, He understood the problems these Jewish people faced daily. The expectation of the religious establishment and John the Baptist was that the Jewish people would come to them. Jesus resolved to go to the people.

There was no magic in Jesus' relationship with God or in His expectation of what God would do. God was not going to make the Romans go away or the Jewish religious leaders change their ways. Jesus did not predict that the hardships facing the Jews would go away, but rather He was telling them that if they would change their lives and become spiritually connected to God and keep their lives God-centered, God would be with them giving them the mental and spiritual strength and direction needed for them to live with the hardships they faced without the worry and stress that weighed them down.

I think that it is no coincidence that the Old Testament Prophet, Micah, and Jesus, both being from small villages of common Jewish families, were able to see through the pomp and glitter of the Jewish religion, with its corruption and privilege, to get at the heart of the Covenant the Jews have with God. Jesus' message to the Jews is simple enough for shepherds, carpenters, and tax collectors to grasp and they could live the message if they were willing to make the changes necessary for them to do so. The message of Micah 6:6-8 is also simple and direct.

> 6. With what should I come before the Lord, and bow myself before God on high? Shall I come before him with burnt offerings, with calves a year old? 7. Will the Lord be pleased with thousands of rams, with ten thousands of rivers of oil? Shall I give my first-born for my transgression, the fruit of my body for the sin of my soul?" 8. He has showed you, O man what is good; and what does the Lord require of you but to do justice, and to love kindness, and walk humbly with your God?

Verse 8 is a clear, concise definition of what God expected of the Jews and later the Christians. God did not look for all the glitter, the material offerings, majestic buildings, or the pomp and grandeur that was, and is, part of religion. I am a great admirer of the grand cathedrals, and the religious jewelry, and art that are dedicated to God. And while God may appreciate them all, He really is only glorified when He is first to each person as each person is to him. How can He help people who do not believe in Him or trust His promise, or who think that wondrous works are necessary to get His attention?

Jesus' message can be seen in Micah's verses 6:6-8.

The New Testament, even with its many translations and copying errors, and its later additions, it continues to clearly describe Jesus' ministry.

JESUS' EARLY MINISTRY

The beginning of Jesus' ministry in Mark 1:14-39 is comparable to Matthew 4:12-25 and Luke 4:14-15. Mark tells us that as Jesus walked along the Sea of Galilee, He asked four fishermen Andrew and his brother Simon (Peter) and James and his brother John, sons of Zebedee, to join him, which they did. John seems to indicate that Simon and Andrew were disciples of John the Baptist before becoming disciples of Jesus. This is when John has Andrew telling Simon that "We have found the Messiah." John records this as happening a few days after Jesus was baptized.

John has Jesus beginning his ministry at a wedding feast. Jesus enjoyed wedding feasts and banquets, so much that the scandalized Pharisees, afraid of all form of ceremonial defilement, went about complaining that Jesus ate with tax-collectors and irreligious people, did not observe dietary rules, and never fasted.

So, what better way for John to tell the story of how Jesus started His ministry than to have Jesus go with His disciples to a wedding feast in the town of Cana (John 2:1-12.). Weddings and the celebrations that followed were a way for the Jewish people to have fun and relieve their daily routine. This wedding may have been with family friends because Jesus's mother, Mary, was present. A person who could join such an activity would be someone the people enjoyed. This is where Jesus was comfortable. Apparently, Jesus was there to relax and enjoy the party with friends. Things were going well when the wine ran out. He was not happy when Mary asked Him to solve the problem.

There is an interesting exchange between Mary and Jesus. Jesus did not want to get involved and tells Mary His time to start His ministry had not come yet. Mary ignores Jesus' complaint and tells the servants to do what He says. Jesus, the Son, does what Mary, the mother, wants. And the exchange indicates that Mary knew the ministry Jesus had chosen and wanted Him to get started on it.

Jesus surely would have talked with Mary about His ministry as He was developing it. In any case, it appears that Mary had accepted the angel's message that Jesus was special. Jesus, who developed His understanding of His ministry while He was at home, appeared to be hesitant about starting His ministry and his mother was telling Him it was time to get started, with her blessing.

Returning to the three synoptic gospels, Matthew, Mark, and Luke describe a different beginning to His ministry. They have Jesus began His ministry in Galilee. After His forty days of temptations and upon hearing that John the Baptist had been arrested, Jesus began by preaching the word of God. In Mark 1:14-15, Jesus said, "The time is fulfilled, and the kingdom of God is at hand, repent, and believe in the gospel." The footnote for Mark 1:15 states, "The whole of Mark is an expression of this verse." The term "gospel" probably is a later addition since the Old Testament was not assembled until AD 100 and the New Testament was not written until after Jesus' death.

So, what does *repent* mean. It means to change direction of your life. It means having a relationship with God and trusting His guidance and accepting His forgiveness and grace instead of following the dictates of the Jews and Romans laws and directions. It means to follow God's guidance in how to use God's gift of having dominion over all living things and the world itself. In short, it meant to live in the likeness of God.

In simple terms, repent means that if you want different results, you must change the way you live. Jesus' call for the Jews to repent was not a command but a statement of reality. To participate in the kingdom of God, the Jew's relationship with God had to change and take precedence over all else.

The synoptic gospels beginning to His ministry clearly and simply states Jesus' mission. Jesus strongly believed that to better their lives the Jews must redirect their primary purpose to living in a close relationship with God. Unfortunately, they simply were not able to dismiss their continual worry about what the Romans and Judaism leaders would do if they changed by making God central to how they lived.

Once Jesus began His ministry, the positive impact of His message and lifestyle served as an example of living with God's blessing. It did not take long for the word to spread of Jesus' dynamic message about the personal relationship each Jew could have with God. Unfortunately, the message of His ministry was not strong enough to serve as the change agent that He had hoped it would be.

Jesus was not telling them to be ready to die and go to heaven, but rather to fully live their gift of life with God's blessing. The idea that the Messiah would save them from their world required them to first save themselves by living fully in their God-given gift of life to be ready for the Messiah when he came. Jesus believed that God knew that they could do it. After all, God made them in His image to live in His likeness.

Continuing the story in Mark, the four disciples left their boat and went to Capernaum with Jesus. On the Sabbath, He was accepted to teach at the synagogue in Capernaum. The synagogues had someone, most probably the Rabbi, who looked after the synagogues and organized the service on the Sabbath. Jesus would have received permission from that person to speak in the synagogues.

Mark's dry recital of Jesus' teaching in the synagogue does not do justice to the drama that must have come from His teaching and healing. While people would come to Capernaum from time to time to preach in a synagogue, they would be people of note, such as religious leaders, but not some unknown carpenter from a small out-of-the-way village called Nazareth who would talk to them about a new life centered on belief and faith in God.

What Jesus said and how He said it was critical to His acceptance by the congregation. Mark 1:22 tells us that the audience, "was astonished at his teachings, for he taught them as one who had authority, and not as the scribes." And immediately, a man stood up who believed he had an unclean spirit (a demon) that was causing him his illness and called out for healing. After Jesus rebuked the demon, the man went into convulsions and then the man was well. The audience was amazed and questioned among themselves at the event and the power Jesus had. (See Mark 1:14-27. Also see Matthew 4:17-22, 7:28-29, and Luke 4:31-37.)

While we will never know what He said, Jesus surely would have talked about having a new God-centered life, which awakened their hopes and dreams of a better life. He was giving them hope by telling them that they could receive God's blessing by making God first in their lives, above all else. It was a message given in simple everyday language that clearly spelled out God's love for them and His commitment to be with them on good days and bad. His message was given in a way that allowed the congregation to believe that what He was describing was possible. The point is, Jesus had the congregation excited about His message, and His message opened the opportunity of the man with unclean spirits to be healed.

The separation of the two events, what Jesus said and what Jesus did, is important. Unfortunately, this separation was not clearly made in this story, just as it was not clearly made in the stories of other events.

The two separate events are repeated in the three synoptic gospels. First, Jesus teaches the Jews of the bright new future that awaits them when they become disciples of God, accepting God's support and guidance above all else. This message, in and of itself, was joyously received.

As things are quieting down, up jumps the man with the demon. There is no indication that the man knew Jesus, so his asking Jesus for help must have come from the man being amazed by Jesus' teaching. Jesus rebuked the demons, and the man was healed. For the second time in a few minutes, the people were again astonished and amazed again.

Jesus' reason for being in the synagogue was that he wanted to tell the Jews the good news about the relationship they could have with God. A relationship that God gave them in their Covenant with Him. They could have God's blessing if they would make having a personal relationship with God their top priority.

Jesus did not go out looking for people to heal. The people came to Him. Jesus was traveling from town to town spreading the good news that each Jew could have a personal spiritual relationship with God which would improve their lives. Living with faith in God would improve their outlook of their world and be the critical ingredient in a person's healing. When someone was healed, Jesus said, "your faith has made you well." When Jesus ran into someone who did not have faith there was no healing. Jesus' role was to be the catalyst for the healing. Without the person's faith nothing could be accomplished.

The causes of illnesses were often a mystery in the time of Jesus. The causes could be mental and/or physical. Changing the mindset from continual worry to having hope can do wonders. Recent studies have confirmed that the mental state of a person is very important in the healing process.

There just was not much that could be done in Jesus' day to improve one's health except to improve one's mental state. The standard explanation for illness or bad things happening was that a person had fallen out of favor with God or that there was a demon involved. Anyone who could improve a person's health or the circumstance of the lives of people were thought to have had a special relationship with God that allowed him or her to bring wondrous things into being. They did not realize that the special person could be any one of them.

Giving the man in the synagogue new hope that he could live with a spiritual connection to God could have been enough to give him a new outlook on his life. This would have seemed to be a miracle to the man and the people in the synagogue. That the man was healed in the presence of Jesus indicates that they were hearing his message. In Jesus' presence, people could be cured was attributed to Jesus rather than to their connection with God at the time of their healing. Even with Jesus' disclaimer that the person's faith made him well, the people declared that Jesus healed the person who had asked for healing to occur. This misunderstanding by the Jew occurs throughout Jesus' ministry and continues today.

The miracle did two things. It showed that much can be accomplished with faith in God and it separated Jesus from the many itinerant ministers in Galilee and Judea claiming to have a special relationship with God. Jesus was mindful of other ministers and recognized that some may have enjoyed God's blessing. He was not threatened by their success, as Jesus demonstrated when He rebuked John for telling a man to stop casting out demons because he was not with Jesus (Mark 9:38-41 and Luke 9:49-50). Anyone could promise to have insight into a better life through the blessing of God, but it apparently took preforming miracles to add credence to the claim.

Mark 1:29-39 tells us that Jesus immediately left the synagogue and went to the house of Simon and Andrew where Simon's mother-in-law lay sick with a fever. When Jesus took her hand and lifted her up her fever left her, and she served them. Further, it seems the synagogue audience told everyone they saw because a crowd gathered at Simon's house to be healed by Jesus. The Bible tells us, that many were healed, and demons were cast out.

I think that Jesus started His ministry believing that He had a clear understanding of the covenant between the Jews and God. As Mark tells the story, within the first week or so, Jesus had confirmed His belief. On the first few days of His ministry, He asked four men to join Him in His ministry and they agreed. Then He delivered a message of hope and caring and awakened some of the Jews of Galilee to God's love and explained God's wish that the people would turn their lives around and live in God's grace. And He had facilitated the healing of people. In addition to the above biblical references, portions of these stories are also found in Matthew 8:14-17 and Luke 4:38-41.

The events of the day may have been as surprising to Jesus as it was to the synagogue audience, and as it was to the crowd at Simon's house. While it seems reasonable to think that Jesus believed that his spiritual connection to God gave him a new message of God's blessing for the Jews and the ability to facilitate healing, the extent of the healing power the Jews had in Jesus' presence may have surprised him, for Mark 1:35-38 tells us that Jesus got up before dawn of the next morning and went to a lonely place to pray, where the four disciples and others later found Him.

Jesus going off by Himself to pray was, I think, Jesus checking in with God on His thoughts on the previous day's happenings. His reaction to the crowds defines the issues Jesus was having with His new position. It seems He was still working out how best to use that power while staying in touch with His purpose and the people. He wanted nothing to do with what He has seen power do to others and His last temptation was about this very issue. And to make matters worse, while He was sorting out these things the crowds kept crowding in on Him.

As Jesus continued His ministry, He was surprised and perplexed by the crowds that followed Him and the reaction of the crowds to His teaching and His ability to cause healing. He spent time alone in prayer searching for guidance and asking if He understood God's intended relationship with the Jews. As we will see later in His ministry, He will become more comfortable with the reaction to His ministry and be more confident in His ministry.

The story of activities of the first days of Jesus' ministry is one of the many times the Bible indicates the poor condition of life for the Jews at the time of Jesus. Everywhere Jesus went, there were people wanting to be healed, or to be given hope, and people gathering to hear Him speak. The Jews cry for help was apparent throughout Jesus' ministry. Unfortunately, it is also apparent that the Jews could not take the help they so desperately wanted even though it only required them to put their trust and faith in God instead of accepting their situation without trusting God.

So, what can we make of the first days of Jesus's ministry? He came quietly on the scene with a powerful but simple message that resonated with the Jews who heard Him in the synagogue and who lived in the area served by the synagogue. This same message was powerful enough for Simon and Simon's brother, Andrew, and the sons of Zebedee, James, and John. They left their daily work that put food on their tables, to follow Jesus, who offered nothing more than a new relationship with God. That was it, no pay, no food, no shelter, and no idea of where they were going or when they would come back.

We know nothing of the families of these first four disciples except that Simon was married, and his mother-in-law was living with him and Andrew. We do not know if the other disciples were married or if any of them had children. All we know is that Jesus spoke, and they stopped what they were doing to follow Him. If Andrew and Simon were disciples of John the Baptist, they may have already met Jesus and heard some of what Jesus had been saying, but we will never know if that was the case. Even if they had already met and heard Jesus it was still a large leap of faith to drop everything they knew, regardless of how miserable it was, and walk into an unknown future.

Undoubtedly, fishing was not an easy or highly desirable job. For that matter, all jobs open to the poor Jews entailed hard work, long hours, and little job satisfaction. In the time of Jesus, there was no middle class to speak of. You were either poor or rich, or very poor, or very rich. The lack of money caused the economy to be based on barter as well as money. Jesus grew up in this economy and understood the language of the poor Jews and understood their hardships and failed hopes and dreams in a way that the scribes, priests, and Pharisees could not.

The Jews had developed the idea of the coming "Day of Wrath" that John the Baptist had talked about. The religious leadership surely knew about the "Day of Wrath" idea, but Jesus was the first person to put in the language of the common people a strong voice to the belief that the time was near for God to render His judgment on the world and the believers that God favored would be saved. He framed His message in the language of the poor Jews. They did relate to Jesus' message. This is evidenced by the outpouring of joy and respect He received, which continued to varying degrees throughout His three-year ministry. It is also evident that even through the Jews related to Jesus' message they could not embrace it, as being central to their lives.

Some of the healings and other miracles that the gospels described Jesus performing are not easy to explain. There is difficulty in trying to sort out the descriptions of the actual activities of Jesus from later additions. There were other individuals and their followers wandering throughout Galilee and Judea during the time of Jesus, all proclaiming in some fashion that they were prophets of a god. That Jesus facilitated the healing of people set Him apart from most others and gave Him an added level of credibility. After the death of Jesus, the need to have Jesus achieve miracles during His ministry became greater as the church relied more heavily on Jesus being divine.

Over the years, since the time of Abraham and Moses, the Jewish religious leaders, in their attempts to fulfill the Covenant, had made Judaism into a regiment of rules and legal requirements, rather than worship of God's wonders and thankfulness for His grace. The history of the Jews was of Jews repeatedly falling out of favor with God, to their detriment, and God's acceptance and grace when they finally wake up and renew their reliance on God for guidance.

Jesus's ministry was about fixing the problem, by cutting through all the requirements that the leaders said had to be met to be acceptable to God, living his message of receiving God's blessing, Micah 6:6-8 clearly states how God wanted the Jews to live.

Even if all he was doing was giving the Jews hope, I think that Jesus was improving the lives of the Jews He met to a much greater degree than He thought He was.

Jesus did not take credit for the healing but rather said such things as, "your faith has made you well" or "take up your pallet and walk." Said another way, He was saying that He had awakened their faith in God which allowed their bodies and minds to heal. I think that this is a critical point to understanding His approach to His ministry and His relationship with God. He could not help a person unless He could awaken that person's belief that he or she could be healed through his or her faith in God. Jesus was the catalysis that enabled a person's faith to be the healing force he or she needed.

Mark 2:1-12 gives an example of His approach to healing. This is the story of Jesus returning home in Capernaum and having a crowd gathered at His home. When four men arrived, carrying a paralytic, but the crowd was so thick that they could not get through to Jesus, they went up on the roof, which was a flat roof of sticks, straw, and packed earth, and breaking a hole in the roof, lowered the paralytic down into the room next to Jesus. When Jesus saw their faith, He told the paralytic, "My son your sins are forgiven." This got the scribes in the crowd wondering," Why does this man speak thus? It is blasphemy! Who can forgive sins but God alone?" Jesus responded, "Which is easier, to say to the paralytic, 'Your sins are forgiven, or to say, 'Rise and walk'?" He went on to say, "the Son of man has authority on earth to forgive sins and then tells the paralytic, "I say to you, rise, take up your bed and go home," which the paralytic did (Matt. 9:2-8 and Luke 5:17-26).

As is the case with many of the stories in the gospels, there is much to this story in addition to the healing of the paralytic. Since His first Sabbath, He had been going through towns preaching and enabling healing wherever He went. Even though this apparently was early in His ministry, His local fame has grown to almost unmanageable proportions. The healing in this story comes from the faith of the paralytic and the four men who brought him in to Jesus.

Two things were required for the paralytic to be healed. First, the four men had to have enough faith in what they had heard about healings associated with Jesus that they took the difficult journey of carrying their friend to Jesus. And second, without the paralytic's faith in God, he would not have healed. That was it, no magic poultices. The paralytic had it within him to be well. Jesus did not claim to heal him. For whatever reason, the paralytic and his friends believed he could not walk. Simply by awakening his faith in God, Jesus released the paralytic from his belief that he could not walk, and the paralytic was free to be well.

As Jesus went from the healing of the paralytic and was walking in the area, He saw Levi (Matthew), a tax collector, and asked Levi to follow him, which Levi did. Why would a man with the job of collecting taxes, which would lead to a life of riches and plenty, leave that life for a life of unknown future? Collecting taxes was not the way for Matthew to make friends or to have people want to be with him. Matthew was drawn to Jesus because he saw a man who attracted people and was at peace with His life, in other words, Jesus had what Matthew had been looking for. Matthew may not have known for sure what Jesus had, but he knew for sure he wanted to be included (Mark 2:14, Matt. 9:9 and Luke 5:9- 27-28).

Jesus was also drawing a crowd of scribes and Pharisees who pretty much question everything Jesus did and said. When asked why His disciples did not fast as did the Pharisees and the disciples of John did, he asks, "Can the wedding guest fast while the bridegroom is with them?" He goes on to say that one day the bridegroom will be gone and then they will fast (Mark 2:19 -20, Luke 17:22).

This refers to the fact that He knew that He could not defy the Jewish leadership forever. Jesus was aware of how narrow the path was that He was walking, that if He strayed off the path His life would be over. He knew that the Pharisees and scribes were following Him to find a reason to arrest Him. Any time He gave the Pharisees or scribes cause to arrest Him, they would and that would be the end of His ministry. The little latitude He had was strengthen by the crowds that followed Him, but he still had to be careful what He said and how He said it.

After Matthew joins the disciples (Mark 2:14) Jesus goes on to describe the changes needed to live in God's blessing by using examples that the people listening to Him could well relate (Mark 2:21-22 and Matt. 9:16-17). He explained that no one sews a piece of new cloth on an old garment or puts new wine into an old wineskin. The garment will tear ruining the garment and the wineskin will burst, losing the wine. He was saying that He was bringing the Jews a new message of God's love for them, and they could accept God's love, which was the new wine and new cloth, by replacing the Judaism and Roman laws by making living in their relationship with God their top priority.

Making a new life with God had to start with throwing out the old life, that is the old garment and old wineskin of daily worries and fears. The cloth of the new life will serve well as the new garment of God's blessing. The new wineskin of new life would hold the new wine of God's love and forgiveness. Jesus was the embodiment of such a new relationship with God.

This was the strong message to the Jews, that they could not incorporate new life into their existing lives. They must change to a new life centered on their relationship with God. This was a most difficult leap for the Jews to make and was a major barrier to the Jews enjoying the benefit of being spiritually God-centered.

The Jews had spent their total lives earning enough to live, whether it was by farming, shepherding, laboring, or begging while staying out of harm's way from the Jewish and Roman authorities. That was all they knew. Now Jesus was telling them that their daily activities would not change; however, they would replace their worries about the Judaism leaders and the Romans with living in their new relationship with God and receiving God's blessing and grace. Jesus wanted them to replace their fears with unconditional love and spiritual support from God. This required the leap of faith that many could not make.

Then on a Sabbath, Jesus and his disciples were walking through a grain field picking grain to eat. The Pharisees complained that it was unlawful to pick grain and eat on the Sabbath. Jesus' response was simple and direct. "The Sabbath was made for man, not man for the Sabbath; so, the Son of man is Lord even of the Sabbath."

Jesus went from the grain field into a synagogue where a man with a withered hand was. The Pharisees watched to see if Jesus would break the law by healing the man on the sabbath. Jesus knew what they were thinking and just asked a simple question, "Is it lawful on the Sabbath to do good or to do harm, to save life or to kill?" Pharisees were silent and Jesus healed the hand. They were not happy with Jesus and began plotting His destruction (Mark 2:23-3:6). There are similar stories in Matthew 9:14-17, 12:1-21, and Luke 5:33-39, 6:1-11.

You do not have to be divine to know why the Pharisees were so interested in what Jesus would do. Jesus was openly flaunting the Pharisees by ignoring the rules of Judaism.

And the question remains, did Jesus heal the hand or did Jesus, by standing up to the Pharisees and supporting the man give the man the strength and commitment needed to heal the hand? Throughout Jesus' ministry people reported what they saw without realizing the role the person being healed played in the healing. The idea that, "all things are possible with God" did not fit into the Jews experiences.

Throughout His ministry, Jesus continued to ask the Pharisees questions that identify the untenable positions the Jewish laws created. The above stories are examples of Him identifying what was called for and what change looked like.

His answers to Pharisees clearly defined His approach to living with God in the chaos of His time; however, the Pharisees heard it as violating Judaism. The priests and Pharisees of Jesus' time had boiled Judaism down to following the religious manmade rules and rituals, instead of having a relationship with God. Judaism was a closed society available only to those who had the time to study the Law and the money to pay the Judaism leaders. To be on the inside of the Jewish society was to be rich and to be held in high regard by the Jewish people while being outside the society was to be poor, isolated, and live at the mercy of the Judaism leaders.

Jesus had read the manuscripts that described the relationship the Jewish ancestors had with God and the support, caring, and forgiveness God gave the Jews ancestors when they strayed from Him, and the happy welcome they received when they returned. Jesus recognized that the rituals and rules that controlled Judaism were later additions that did not change God's relationship with the Jews even though it changed the Jew's relationship with God. God's relationship with the Jews ancestors was still available to all Jews, as it is to all people today.

Jesus had eliminated any doubt the Pharisees may have had about His thinking about Judaism. He was a danger to their interruption of Judaism that supported their way of life. He needed to be stopped. The Bible tells us that after healing the hand on the Sabbath, the Pharisees immediately held counsel against Jesus with the Herodians. The battle lines were drawn. Jesus would continue His ministry of caring and giving hope to the poor and oppressed, and the Jewish leaders would continue to look for a way to shut Him down without inciting his followers. I marvel at the masterful way Jesus continued to confront the Jewish leaders without being arrested.

Much of Jesus' message was delivered through parables. The Jews related to the parables Jesus used to explain His messages. There are three parables in Mark 4:1-33, the parables of the Sower, the lamp, and the mustard seed, that describe how Jesus sees His world. Starting with the parable of the Sower, Jesus, the Sower of seeds, recognized that not everyone would take His message to heart and fully appreciate the fullness of God's promise. Going further, He identified the problem the Jews who took His message to heart were having living in God's blessing because of interference of other influences, such as the Jews leaders but, He knew great things could happen from the mustard seed effect of the few who heard him and took His message to heart.

The parable of the lamp simply says that one does not light a lamp and put it under a basket or hide from view by others. Jesus is saying that some will like what they hear but will hide Jesus' message about a new relationship with God from their friends and neighbors.

And the parable of the mustard seed is that from a small seed a large tree will grow. This was Jesus' message that each one of them, no matter how insignificant they think they were, with a God-centered relationship they would be a positive influence on the Jews.

Matthew and Luke also have a fourth parable about leavened bread. When the cook puts into bread dough some leavening (yeast) the dough will expand (Mark 4:1-34). Also, see Matthew 13:1-52 and Luke 8:22-25 for these and more parables. The message of these parables tells of the improvement in the Jew's lives that will come when they add the leavening of a relationship to God.

All four gospels describe Jesus' effort to have the Jews see the benefit of centering their lives on God. Living with a spiritual connection with God would make what appears to be insurmountable into something manageable. Jesus did not promise their daily grind would disappear if the Jews would repent and allow God in their lives, but they would have the strength and peace of mind to better live with the daily grind. The Jewish religious leaders and the Romans would not suddenly be nicer to the Jews but with God's blessed, responding to either Romans or the Jewish leaders, or both would be less wearing and consuming for the Jews.

He made his decision to live spiritually connected to and be guided by God. His ministry was so different from what the Jews were getting for the Judaism priests that the Jews liked hearing what Jesus said and seeing how Jesus lived; however, to change their lives to emulate how Jesus lived was more than they could do.

Sermon On The Mount

To continue the story of Jesus' ministry, we turn to Matthew and the Sermon on the Mount (Matt. 5:1-7:29). The footnote pertaining to the Sermon on the Mount states that the writers of Matthew inserted into the Sermon on the Mount portions of Jesus' teaching on other occasions.

The writers of Matthew did a great service by assembling Jesus' teaching into the Sermon on the Mount. While Jesus' message is told throughout the New Testament, the Sermon on the Mount gives Jesus' input on a broad range of subjects in the language of the Jewish people, using examples and terms familiar to the Jewish people.

The Sermon on the Mount clearly states Jesus' belief that the Jews could live in harmony with each other and in harmony with God without the rituals and rules that had become Judaism.

The Sermon on the Mount starts with the Beatitudes. The Jews that Jesus knew were poor people who could personally relate to the Beatitudes. In a few minutes, He told them that He understood what was bothering them and gave them a future they could embrace, by telling them that God believed in them. Jesus was telling them that God recognized the good in them.

The message in the Beatitudes was about more than just the point of each Beatitude. The total message of the Beatitudes describes an attitude toward life that God wanted for people who were willing to live in harmony with Him. Although the Beatitudes may have suffered much through the years of translations, copying errors, political corrections, and lost manuscripts, I believe that they remain true to Jesus' primary message.

For example, the current definition of the word "meek" may not accurately represent the meaning of the original word. My sense is that meek in the Beatitude describes having strong convictions that are firmly held, while being gentle, soft-spoken, and forgiving of others. Mahatma Gandhi, Dalai Lama, Nelson Mandala and Jesus come to mind as people who exemplify being meek in the context of the Sermon on the Mount.

Next, after the Beatitudes came Jesus' strong statement of God's recognition of the importance of the Jewish people, a message that they had seldom if ever, heard. Normally they were told how insignificant they were. Jesus told them that they were a valuable and important part of God's creation. Regardless of what the Jewish leadership or the Romans did or said, the future of the Jewish people and the future of all people rested with them.

As the salt of the earth, the Jews were the one ingredient needed to complete the spiritual connection with God. Jesus was telling them that it was not the Jewish leaders and Roman Emperors that will make a lasting difference in the world. Rather they, the people who were considered unimportant and of little or no value, were who would make the lasting difference. Even though they were thought to be of little worth, they were the foundation of the Jewish nation.

As the light of the world, when they were in darkness no one could see and know them, but through their connection with God they would shine with the love and blessings from God for all to see. Jesus was telling the Jews that it was through them that God could reach all people.

When Jesus said *I have not come to abolish the law, but to fulfill the law*, He was not saying that He would replace Judaism with a new Judaism, with new rules and rituals. Rather, He was saying that He was showing them a new simpler God-centered relationship available to them, with no temple tax, no religious sacrifices, and no multitude of manmade rules. The new law was love. Love themselves and all they meet as God loves them.

No matter what the Jews did to other Jews, they could not force God to stop loving them. Admittedly the gold calf incident caused God to rethink His Covenant commitment to the Israelites; however, He continued His commitment. Jews were not born bad. God did not make bad Jews. God gave the Jews what they need to live in His likeness. It was up to the Jews to choose to live in God's likeness. Jesus wanted the Jews to live in God's likeness to receive God's blessing. God's continued commitment to the Jews was the guiding message Jesus gave the Jews and through them the world.

Jesus talked about the old law vs the new law. The difference between the old and the new is covered in Matthew 5: 21- 48. He described issues regarding how to treat each other, to eliminate relationships based on hate and to not repay mistreatment with mistreatment but with love and forgiveness. In each instance He gives examples of how to deal with adversity. He told them that anyone who kills another would be subject to judgment, that they should reconcile their differences when upset or angry. He set higher standards to be met for adultery and divorce, He told them not to swear for any reason, and explained that instead of an eye for an eye one should love one's enemy.

One example, which surely caused some aggravation was His admonishment that, "if anyone forces you to go one mile go with him two miles" (Matt. 5:41). This would have been particularly burdensome when applied to the Roman troops. As the troops moved from one place to another, they could order Jews to carry their things. Jesus is telling the Jews to do more than they are told to do, instead of being angry and resistant. Carrying the soldier's heavy load was hard enough without carrying hate and misery as well. Jesus was saying not to get worked up about having to help the Romans, instead, do more than was required or expected, like carrying the Roman's load farther than required.

Jesus lived in the same world as the Jews and certainly understood the hardships and misery they endured. He continued to stress that having a spiritual relationship with God as the number one priority would give the Jews a better perspective of their life. Regardless of the adverse situation, the positive or negative effect the situation could have on each Jew depended on the reaction of each Jew. It was up to each Jew whether he or she would become anxious and hateful or would accept the situation and make the best of it. Calmly making the best of a situation would be better for the Jews than the effect on them from the anxiety and anger they were living with.

Jesus demonstrated that living spiritually connected to God gave Him the strength of purpose and the freedom to stay on message and starting anew each day, even though the disciples and His followers were not making living connected with God their top priority. He could have easily allowed these failures to become central to His life, just as the Jews allowed the hard times, worry, and misery to be central in their lives. Even though He was not getting the changes He wanted in the Jew's lives, He stayed true to His ministry to them and His spiritual relationship with God. He continued His effort to have the Jews realize that they were God's people regardless of what they were told by the Jewish religious leaders. God wanted each one of them to have their own uncluttered relationship with Him.

Jesus restated His thinking that we are made in God's image in Matthew 5:48, "You, therefore, must be perfect, as your heavenly Father is perfect." This statement summarizes Jesus' understanding of God's expectations of the Jews. To continue in the image of God is to live as someone blessed by God. If the people who were created in the image of God, would choose to live in likeness of God, they could incorporate God's forgiveness of their transgressions and his steadfast love into their daily lives.

God never required them to earn their right to have a relationship with Him. It has always been freely given. No one had to study manuscripts or pass a test. All each Jew had to do was initiate a relationship with God based solely on each Jew's trust and belief in God.

A better translation of this passage may have been to use "complete" rather than "perfect." Someone who is complete will be spiritually connected to God and will live at one with God. A person must create a spiritual connection with God to receive His guidance and support and His freely given grace and love.

There is an old saying that goes like this,
Be who you is.
For if you is who you ain't,
You ain't who you is.

Aside from the bad grammar, because you are made in God's image, you are yourself when you live in the likeness of God.

Jesus continued by talking about not making a public display of piety. Public prayer does not win any points with God. Prayer should be sincere, not full of meaningless impressive phrases. This led to the Lord's Prayer (Matt. 6:9-13). I do not believe anyone has ever improved on this example of how to pray to God.

161

It is glorious in its direct simplicity. It applies equally well today as it did in Jesus' time. The prayer opens with reverence for God and the acceptance of God bring in charge. This is followed by a request concerning our needs, and for His forgiveness based on our willingness to grant forgiveness. It closes with a request to be free of situations that could cause us to violate His trust to protect us from evil.

Jesus continued in Matthew 7:1-5 with a very powerful message.

> 1. Judge not, that you be not judged, 2. For with the judgment you pronounce you will be judged, and the measure you give will be the measure you get. 3. Why do you see the speck that is in your brother's eye, but not notice the log that is in your own eye? 4. Or how can you say to your brother, 'Let me take the speck out of your eye,' when there is the log in your own eye? 5. You hypocrite, first take the log out of your own eye, and then you will see clearly to take the speck out of your brother's eye.

This passage struck me as being very important during a church youth group study several years ago. It has remained with me since that meeting and, on more than one occasion, it has kept me from being critical of others.

I believe that failing to adhere to the above message in Matthew 7: 1-5 is a major cause of pain and suffering throughout the world. There seems to be an inherent need to correct the short comings of friends and acquaintances.

Years ago, when I was in the Air Force, I attended a staff meeting during which a list was handed out composed of many words and actions that people did not like. Everyone was to mark the items on the list that he or she did not like in other people. Without exception, the traits each one of us do not like in others were the same traits we did not like in ourselves. While the exercise was enlightening, it also was very difficult to accept what it said about each one of us. What Jesus stated clearly and simply, required a concentrated effort for the meeting attendees to recognized and accept as being true in each of us.

Matthew 7:6 is another troubling verse. "Do not give dogs what is holy; and do not throw your pearls before swine, least they trample them under foot and turn to attack you." My first thought is that the word "pearls" is a translation of the original word, to which many Jews could not relate. My understanding is that God did not require the Jews to give away things that were dear to them unless they were interfering with the Jew's relationship with God. Rather, Jesus wanted the Jews to change their priority of following the Judaism leaders and worrying about the Romans, to having a relationship with God. If their relationship with God was not their top priority, they were allowing their lives, their pearls, to be trampled under the Judaism and Roman rules and taxes.

God loved the Jews regardless of how rich or poor they were. The problem comes when being rich or poor being more important than having a God-centered relationship with God.

There is much more in the Sermon on the Mount than what I have highlighted. I can think of no better way to understand the teaching of Jesus than to spend time reading the Sermon on the Mount. Some of what is in the Sermon is in different places in Mark and Luke, but the writers of Matthew did a great service putting such a large part of Jesus' teaching in the Sermon on the Mount.

JESUS' CONTINUING MINISTRY

Continuing to follow Matthew, a centurion, an officer of the Roman Army, approached Jesus to heal his sick servant. The discussion between the centurion and Jesus results in the servant being healed because of the centurion's faith that through Jesus his servant could be healed. Jesus marveled at the centurion's faith and told him that He (Jesus) had not found the centurion's faith in Israel. (Matt. 8:5-13. The story is also found in Luke 7:1-10 and John 4:46-53).

This is one of several instances when a person was healed because of the faith of the person looking for healing. In this case, the person was a Roman solider. Being thrown into outer darkness is to be without God and the weeping and gnashing of teeth describe the misery and distress that engulfs someone who has forsaken God. Being thrown into darkness could also refer to when the end of time comes, when God will gather up his own, those who believe in Him, and the rest will be left out in the cold.

Jesus is helping a person who is a member of the oppressing Romans, so His message is for everyone, not just the Jews. Jesus, the Jew, is teaching the Jews about their relationship with God, and that with such faith as the Centurion had, Gentiles can also be in God's favor. With this example, Jesus demonstrated to the Jews how they, as God's chosen people, can interact with Gentiles as God intended, regardless of who they are.

Continuing with Matthew, chapter 8, verses 18-44 tell us that when a scribe asked to join Jesus' group. Jesus tells him, "Foxes have holes and birds of the air have nests; but the Son of man has nowhere to lay his head." Jesus then tells the disciple who wanted to bury his father before he joins Jesus' group to, "Follow me and leave the dead bury their own dead." Both comments make his point that having a true spiritual relation with God is more important than any of the other relationships or concerns for physical comforts.

Being descendants of Abraham and carrying the blessing God gave Abraham gave the Jews a special relationship with God that carried the special responsibility of setting the example of living in harmony with God. As followers of Jesus, Christians, carry the same blessing and carry the same responsibility of having their relationship with God set the example of being more important than all else.

Throughout his ministry, Jesus did not seem comfortable with the miracles. The excitement over the miracles kept the people from recognizing the importance of Jesus' simple response to the miracles by saying the person's faith has made that person well or a similar message.

He repeatedly tried to impress upon the people that through their faith in God each one had the power to heal themselves. Jesus was troubled that the people could only equate the healings to the presence of Jesus rather than the healing that came from the person's faith in God in the presence of Jesus.

Jesus' presence, it seems promoted healing by strengthening the faith of the healed person. Even with His reluctance to do so, Jesus evidentially felt the need to improve the life of the Jews by showing them the healing power of God. He worried that the excitement over the miracles would detract from His message of life through the covenant with God.

His call for the people to repent, to turn their life around was extremely important to Jesus. In His mind, it overshadowed His miracles. It does seem that His concern about the miracles was well-founded.

The writers of the gospels also failed to recognize how important the faith of the person being healed was to that person's healing. Several sites in the Bible describe a person proclaiming that he had been healed by Jesus without recognizing his or her part in the healing.

Jesus certainly knew the Old Testament stories of men who, with God's help, accomplished great things. Jesus also knew of the Jewish belief that a Messiah would come to rescue them; however, Jesus did not see Himself as the Messiah, but rather as God's messenger who was preparing the people for the coming Messiah at the end of the world as they know it. The truth is that Jesus knew that He did not meet the requirements of being the Messiah, nor did He believe that He needed to be the Messiah to get the Jews ready for the Messiah. It is also evident that the people did not see Him as the Messiah, for even with His message and healings He did not fit their image of the Messiah.

The term "Son of man" comes up in Matthew 8:20 and in Mark 2.10. This is a good time to look at this term. The footnote for Mark 2.10 is worth repeating.

Son of Man, a title which Jesus used of himself, probably seemed to his listeners to carry either of two meanings: (a) that Jesus called himself a typical human being in accordance with the common meaning of son of (see Matt. 5:45n), or (b) that Jesus (contrary to the humble conditions of his daily life) linked himself to the prophesied figure of Daniel 7:13-14 who was popularly regarded as the coming Messiah (see Acts 7:56 n). Jesus nowhere fully discloses his own understanding of the term (but see 8:32n). However, each meaning by itself, as well as both together (see Matt. 25:29n), could have appealed to him. It also was characteristic of him to speak in such a way as to oblige his hearers to determine their own personal attitudes toward him as part of the process of understanding his words. (See Matt. 13:3n)

Jesus' understanding of His relationship with God is never fully answered in the scriptures that describe His teaching and healing. God simply did not give Jesus a book of instructions and Jesus did not give the Jews, or us, a book of instructions. As the footnote says, He wanted the Jews to make up their own mind about His healing and teaching. God gives us the ability to figure it out on our own and Jesus expected the Jews to do just that.

Mark tells us that after healing many, Jesus left Capernaum and preached in the surrounding towns. He then returned to Capernaum where He continued to preach and heal people. Jesus continued to draw large crowds from Galilee, and now Judea, beyond the Jordan and around Tyre and Sidon. He continued to deal with the crowds that gathered wherever He went. And adding to that issue, shortly after beginning His ministry the scribes and Pharisees began following Him and tried unsuccessfully to trip Him up with their theological questions.

Jesus was initially surprised at how quickly the Jewish people seem to accept His belief that the central piece of God's Covenant was His love for the Jewish people. By simply accepting God's love, and returning it in kind, the Jewish people would complete the Covenant. God's love is an ultimate love that gives gifts and the freedom to use the gifts without restrictions.

Jesus' optimism in the Jew's response to His ministry was quickly dispelled with His realization that He was only getting superficial acceptance that needed continual reinforcement rather than the internal change He hoped would happen. I think His terrible realization of this fact came when He watched his followers being more impressed by His miracles than by His example of living in God's love.

Jesus went up into the hills with His chosen few, apparently recognizing that He needed help managing the reaction He was receiving from His ministry. Jesus selected twelve to be His disciples (later after his death, called apostles), from the few that went into the hills with Him, to be sent out to preach and have authority to cast out demons. These were twelve men who agreed to live with Him as He lived, in accordance with His ministry. These were very different men who brought their differentness with them, which showed up from time to time, but who stayed with Jesus until His death. They were Simon whom He surnamed Peter; James the son of Zebedee and John the brother of James, whom He surnamed Bo-aner'ges, that is sons of thunder; Andrew, and Philip, and Bartholomew, and Matthew, and Thomas, and James the son of Alphaeus, and Thaddaeus, and Simon the Cananaean, and Judas Iscariot who betrayed Him (Mark 3:7-28, Matt. 10:1-4, Luke 6:12-16).

As the gospels often do, the description of Jesus choosing His twelve disciples does not include any accompanying information. In this case, any information about why He chose these twelve men. How well did He know these men before He chose them? Mark tells us that Andrew and Simon were casting their net and James and John were mending nets when Jesus met them and ask them to go with Him. Were these the first four fishermen Jesus saw, and if so, why stop at four? Surely, there were more than the four fishermen in the area.

It seems reasonable to think that He knew or knew of the four fishermen, Andrew, Simon, James, and John. The Gospel of John tells us that Andrew and Simon were disciples of John the Baptist. This being the case, Jesus could very well have known of them, and it would have been an easy connection to make with James and John.

The remaining eight disciples were chosen from the group of people that had been following Jesus. It would not have taken long for various members of the group to stand out in one way or another. I do not think that Jesus' choices were random, but rather were based on Jesus' observation of the men. It is a much stronger statement of Jesus' faith in God for Jesus to have made His choices based on His own observations rather than on God's intervention.

Just as important as why Jesus made His selections, is what prompted the ones He chose to agree to travel with Him. There was a big difference between following Jesus and becoming a committed member of Jesus' group that stayed with Him through all that could come up. The men and Jesus took a leap of faith in each other and, except for Judas, stuck with their decision through good times and bad for the rest of their lives.

Judas' act of turning on Jesus was more an act of frustration than of betrayal although the distinction may be hard to see. Aside from his questionable activities as the disciples' treasurer, Judas believed that Jesus would eventually see the futility in His approach to changing the lives of the Jews and become the sword-bearing leader that Judas hoped he would be.

After selecting the disciples, Jesus went home with the crowd following Him and bothering Him so much that Mark tells us that He and the disciples could not eat. Jesus has brought a message of hope and a bright future to the crowd which excited them and had them wanting more. As their excitement grew and more people joined the crowd it apparently overwhelmed Jesus and the disciples. His friends, possibly His family, went to rescue Him from the intense emotions of the crowd. They feared for His safety and his sanity. Mark says that He was, "beside himself." Because He was so upset the scribes that were in the crowd claimed that He was possessed by Be-el 'zebul or the demons or Satan. He responded, "How can Satan cast out Satan? If a kingdom is divided against itself, that kingdom cannot stand" (Mark 3:20-25). Both Matthew12:22-37 and Luke 11:14-23 start this event with Jesus curing a man who is blind and dumb which leads to the scribes' comment that he was Satan and Jesus' response.

Mark chapter 3 continues in verses 31-35 with Jesus' mother and His brothers came; and standing outside they sent to Him and called to Him. A crowd was sitting about Him; and they said; "Your mother and brothers are outside, asking for you." And He replied, "Who are my mother and brothers?" And looking around on those who sat about Him, He said, "Here are my mother and my brothers! Whoever does the will of God is my brother, and sister, and mother."

This story confirms Jesus' priorities. His commitment to God was greater than His commitment to His family, which surely would have been a difficult reality for His family to accept. This comes in a time when family was central to all the Jews did. While family was important to Jesus, He knew that to fully enjoy the benefits of being in a family one must first be at one with God.

The question of Jesus' power comes up more than once and while the people did not seem to be concerned, the Pharisees and scribes were obsessed with this question. After all, if His power came from God, they were not needed anymore. Proving that Jesus was a fake would give them job security. The healings and parable stories, and Jesus' response to the scribes and Pharisees are described in Mark 1:38 to 4:34 and are also found in Matthew and Luke (Matt. 8:2-4; 9:1-8, 14-17; 10:1-4; 12:1-4, 22-27 and ch.13; Luke 5:12-26, 33-39; 6: 1-16, 43-45; 8:4-18; 11:14-23; 12:10; 13:18-21).

When Jesus selected His twelve disciples from the group of people following Him, it seems that He had resolved whatever doubts He may have had about His message and its reception by the Jews. However, He continued to be disturbed by the crowds and the constant demands by the Jewish people. He was raised in a small village that provided little reason for the people to get together as a crowd. Crowds and the requests for healing were continuous and troubling companions to Jesus throughout His ministry. They were a mixed blessing. On one hand the crowds gave Him a larger audience and the healings gave Him creditability, as well as helping to keep Him from being arrested. On the other hand, it was hard for Him to get any time for Himself, and He felt that the healings interfered with His message being fully understood and accepted.

Jesus' message of *repent and believe in God* was central to His ministry. He developed His message from His study of, and conversations about, the historical writings of the Jewish people and their religion. Nothing in His first thirty years prepared Him for, or ever gave Him an inkling that He would be dealing with the large crowds, or that the healing of people in His presence would be such an overpowering part of His ministry.

Jesus demonstrated and described His vision of what life will be like for the Jews who live in the Covenant and the promise of God. The disciples and crowds, and even the scribes and Pharisees were amazed and confounded by what they saw and heard, for it was unheard of for a person of Jesus' stature and background to be doing the things He was doing and saying the things He was saying. For the Jews who came to hear Him, He was a breath of fresh air. Here was one of their own telling them that their God was available to them without paying taxes to the priests or following the religious rituals and rules. For the scribes and Pharisees and the Jewish leadership, He was scary dangerous.

Toward the evening of a day telling parables and preaching to the crowd, Jesus decided to get into a boat with His apostles to escape the crowd. While Jesus was getting some sleep in the boat a storm came up that scared the disciples. This was not an average, run-of-the-mill storm. It was strong enough to scare four fishermen, who had experienced the chancy weather of the lake. So, they woke Jesus asking Him to do something. With a hint of anger, He calmed the wind and rebuked the disciples for their lack of faith. And they continued to the east side of the lake.

Once again, His power was demonstrated, only this time it involved natural forces rather than human and physical issues. It also shows how limited the faith of the disciples was. Even with the disciples seeing the healings, and now His power to calm the storm, they could not make the leap of faith connection to Jesus' faith and His wondrous work. Nor could they conceive that they too could have a Jesus like spiritual connection with God.

Jesus' power came from His commitment to God. It did not come from some man-made equipment or material, but rather it came from His trust and faith in God and God's commitment to the Jews. Jesus' commitment was not something that could be seen directly. The disciples did not recognize that Jesus' calm presence and the ability of Jews to trust God enough for them to improve their lives when they were with Jesus' came from Jesus' relationship with God, a relationship each one could have with God.

Upon landing on the eastern shore, they encountered a demoniac (mentally troubled) man who asked Jesus for help. Jesus cast the demons out of the man and into a herd of swine that were nearby. The herd ran downhill into the lake and perished. The herdsman ran into town telling the people what had happened. The town's people came out and asked Jesus to leave (Mark 4:35-5:17). Matthew 8:28-34 and Luke 8:22-37 tell the same story except that Matthew states that there are two demoniac men.

The town's peoples' request certainly was reasonable considering what He did to their swine. That loss of the swine was a concern of the town's people indicated that the town's people may not have been Jewish, although recent archaeological findings seem to indicate that the Jewish prohibition about eating pork was not as strong as it was thought to be. In any case, Jesus may have once again healed a non-Jew or Gentile.

So, as Jesus got back on the boat to head back across the lake, He had much to ponder. In the last few days, He had seen the amazement and excitement of the crowds the followed Him, the limitations of the disciples' faith in their new life, and the success that He, a Jew, had helping Gentiles in need. His success to date confirmed that, based on His belief that a new day was coming soon, He still had much to do and so little time to do it.

A great crowd was waiting for Jesus as He reached the shore. Jairus, a ruler of the synagogue, was waiting to ask Jesus to heal his sick daughter. As Jesus went with Jairus, "a woman who had had a flow of blood for twelve years, and who had suffered much under many physicians ... and was no better but rather grew worse touched Jesus' garment." When she touched Jesus garment her bleeding stopped, and she was well. Jesus felt her touch and looked for the person who had touched his garment. The woman fearfully fell at his feet. Jesus said, "Daughter, your faith has made you well; go in peace and be healed of your disease." At this time, a servant came saying that Jairus' daughter was dead, but Jesus told Jairus, "Do not fear, only believe." He then proceeded to Jairus' house and went into the room where the daughter was and took her hand and told her to raise, which she did (Mk. 5:21-43, Mt.9:18-26 and Lk.8:40-56).

From there, He and His disciple went to Nazareth in Galilee, and, on the sabbath, He went into the synagogue and began to teach. Many began to question His teaching. How did He get so smart? After all, wasn't He the son of Mary and Joseph the carpenter? Wasn't He Jesus, the carpenter, who used to build plows, cabinets, and other things for the people of Nazareth? They had watched Him grow up and take over the carpentry business when Joseph died until one day He just took off.

They took offense to Him trying to teach them about their relationship with God. The people in Nazareth wanted to know, what made Him so special? And where did He get all this information about God's covenant with the Jewish people? They simply were not ready for one of their own to come back to Nazareth with such profound and unsettling ideas.

It apparently did not enter their minds that, if a man with his background could have a special relationship with God, then they could also have a special relationship with God. So, as Jesus says, in Mark 6:4, "A prophet is not without honor, except in his own county, and among his own kin, and in his own house." It sounds like it just was not only the people in the synagogue that did not accept Him, but His own family and Gentile neighbors were also giving Him a hard time. He could do little but marvel at the unbelief of the Jews He had known as He grew up into manhood (Mark 6:1-6). Matthew has his experience in Nazareth later, Matthew 13:53-58 and Luke has his experience in Nazareth early in His ministry, before He selected his twelve disciples (Luke 4:16-30).

Mark and Matthew say that because of the lack of faith Jesus could only heal a few sick people. This supports Jesus telling the people that they must have faith in God, and believe all things are possible with God, to be healed. Without their faith in, and acceptance of, being made in God's image, Jesus could not help them.

This experience had to be a profound disappointment for Jesus. These were the people with whom He had grown up. These were the people He thought about as He developed His approach to His ministry. What was enthusiastically received in other parts of Galilee fell on deaf ears of the very people He thought He knew best. His message could not get past Jesus' being a local boy but acting better than them.

He left this bad experience and collected His disciples and sent them out two by two, and gave them authority over unclean spirits, with the instruction that they were to take nothing for their journey except their staff and sandals.

> 10. ... He went on to say, "Where you enter a house, stay there until you leave the place. 11. And if any place will not receive you and they refuse to hear you, when you leave, shake off the dust that is on your feet for a testimony against them." The disciples were successful. They preached that men should repent, and they cast out demons and anointed with oil many who were sick and healed them. Mark 6:7-13

Luke 9:1-6 closely follows Mark; however, Matthew 10:1-42 expands the instructions quite a bit. The version in Matthew is more poetic in its expanded instructions. It includes such statements as, "Behold, I send you out as sheep in the midst of wolves; so be wise as serpent and innocent as doves" (Matt. 10:16). And do not fear those who kill the body but cannot kill the soul; rather fear him who can destroy both soul and body in hell (from Greek "Gehenna") (Matt.10:28). And finally, "And whoever gives to one of these little ones even a cup of cold water because he is a disciple, truly I say to you, he shall not lose his reward" (Matt. 10:42). This last passage refers to a child, which Jesus sometimes calls His disciples. It may better fit with Matthew 18:6, although referring to the disciples as children does fit well here. Luke10:1-16 also describes Jesus appointing another seventy disciples to go out and teach and heal calls His disciples the twelve. In Luke 10:17-20, the seventy returned with success stories to tell.

Christianity has assigned several qualities and purposes to Jesus' ministry; however, His instruction to His disciples clearly limits the scope of His ministry to changing the Jews' lives by convincing them to follow in Abraham's footsteps by centering their lives on their relationship with God. His purpose did not include changing the lives of Gentiles or the Samaritans. However, when they asked, He included them in His ministry without allowing their inclusion to dissuade Him from His primary mission, convincing the Jews to live a God-centered life. Jesus was open to receiving all who came to hear Him; however, He reserved some of His harshest criticisms for the disciples who committed to be with and follow Him. Even in the rarefied air of Jesus living His God-centered life the disciples could not embrace Jesus' trust and faith in God.

With the acceptance that He and His message were receiving from the people, and His failure to adhere to the dictates of the priests, scribes, and Pharisees, it is little wonder that the religious establishment was worried. Here was an unknown person, with no education or ties with any religious organization. He did what many other itinerant ministers wandering around the countryside, had not been able to do, that is, to have large crowds collect in each village He entered, with a smaller group traveling with Him from village to village.

Jesus was viewed as having the potential of upsetting the religious and governmental order of things. The history of the Jews was that there were periodic revolts and uprisings. The Maccabean uprising was only 200 years past and the Zealots revolted in AD 6. They captured the town of Sepphoris, which they burned and destroyed. While the Romans bloodily suppressed the revolt, they were unsuccessful in eliminating the Zealots, at least one of whom was a disciple of Jesus.

The Zealots originated in the northern area of Galilee, so the Jewish leadership had some reason for concern. I wonder if any of the priests remember the boy who, eighteen years earlier, stayed in Jerusalem after Passover asking questions and was holding His own in discussions? In a nutshell, Jesus looked like trouble that they did not need. He got crowds excited with His unconventional message of conforming to Gods' will, not to the Jewish religion will, through personal prayer and changing how they lived. That was dangerous.

The Jewish leadership might not have been so worried if they had known of His trouble in his hometown of Nazareth (Mark 6:1-6). Mark tells us that when Jesus spoke in the synagogue in Nazareth all the people were upset, and they questioned how a local boy could be so smart.

Mark next tells us that John the Baptist was beheaded by King Herod, sometime after Jesus' commission for the twelve disciples to go out on their own (Mark 6:14-29, Matt. 14:1-12, Luke 9:7-9). In any case, the Bible does not give us more information than what is in the above-referenced sections. It seems reasonable to think that the death of His cousin was an unexpected blow to Jesus. John, his friend, and confidant, the one with whom He could try out ideas and share His thinking was gone. This was a void Jesus was never able to fill.

It is true that John and Jesus may not have been close cousins who supported each other as they develop their ministry, but the circumstantial evidence of their mothers being close and that they had similar messages, although their approaches were different, and John, knowing that Jesus would follow him, and that Jesus came to John to be baptized is compelling. That does not mean that they were necessarily in agreement or had decided what to do beforehand, but rather that they were aware of each other's thinking and ideas, and that John's death was a major loss for Jesus.

When the disciples returned and told Jesus all that they had done, He told them to find a lonely place to rest and eat. This seems to be a surprising lack of reaction by Jesus to the news of the disciples' success. Once again, the Bible does not fill in any details. Was Jesus' lack of reaction to the disciples' success due to Jesus expecting more, or was it due to how fast the disciples reverted to their former attitude? Jesus' lack of enthusiasm may have come from the problem He seemed to be having with the miracles and healings, as part of His ministry. If the sequence of events in Mark is correct, Jesus may also have been dealing with John's death. Obviously, Mark believed that nothing more needed to be said, but it would be helpful to have information about what was going on between Jesus and the disciples.

It was a strong message about Jesus' ministry that, after being with Jesus for a short time, the disciples could preach the word of God and heal through the peoples' newfound faith. What more evidence of the validity of Jesus' message did the disciples need to live as Jesus lived? That they missed the importance of their own success of living in the likeness of God had to be a great disappointment to Jesus.

Jesus has taken twelve very different Jewish men who were of mean occupations and converted them into men of faith who, through what they said and did, gave the people the faith in God that was needed for healing to happen. Their joy and excitement they experienced from their successful mission were not enough for them to incorporate their experience into who they were.

Apparently, the spiritual connection with God the disciples had, and their successful ministry to the Jews in the surrounding area were quickly lost when they reverted to their old ways upon their return.

They did not realize they could retain their personal connection to God in the presence of Jesus. Their sense of servitude to Jesus may have gotten in the way of their connection to God.

We can only speculate on how different the world would be if the disciples had retained their soul connection with God and continued their ministry throughout Judea. That could have been the revolution the Jewish leadership was so afraid would happen. It would not have been for prestige, money, and conquering land. It would have been about changing how people thought and lived and recognizing that each person was important. It would have created a new way of living that totally changed what was guiding people in their daily livings and changed what they believed were the important things in their lives. There would have been a place for everyone in such a peaceful revolution.

Mark goes from the return of the disciples in Mark 6:30-31 to Jesus telling them to go to a lonely place to rest. They ended up taking a boat to a different location; however, the people ran ahead of them to the local where they landed. The people come from villages and the surrounding area to this place until a large crowd gathered, Mark reports there were 5,000 people in the crowd. The number 5,000 probability only referred to the men in the crowd. Often, women and children were not counted.

Mark tells us that Jesus "... had compassion on them because they were like sheep without a shepherd; and he began to teach them many things." It grew late as He continued to teach, and the disciples asked Jesus if they should go into town to buy bread to feed the crowd. Instead, Jesus told them to gather the available food and distribute it to the crowd. After Jesus blessed the food and the crowd was fed with five loaves and two fish, to everyone's amazement, they ended up with twelve baskets of bread and fish. (See Mark 6:32-44. Also, Matthew. 14:13-21, Luke 9:10-17, and John 6:1-15. See 2 Kings. 4:42-44 for similar message.)

The increased amount of food after everyone had eaten can be explained in a couple of ways. One is that it is a miracle caused by Jesus' prayer.

The other explanation is that everyone brought some food with them. There were no fast-food restaurants scattered around the neighborhood. If someone was going to be away from home for a few hours, it was common for them to bring food with them. They would not willingly share what they had until they saw that Jesus wanted to share equally all the available food. Jesus' ability to convince the crowd to share what they had was, in and of itself, a miracle for having enough food was a constant problem. So, either way, Jesus' giving nature changed the minds of the people, for a short time, to be what God made, and saw was good.

This story points out that the disciples had enough money on hand to go into town and buy enough food to feed 5,000 plus the wives and children. Apparently, the disciples received enough donations that they had a treasurer and having money on hand was not a concern. The Gospel of John 12:6 states that Judas was the treasurer for the disciples.

I am curious to know what town would have been able to supply enough food for 5,000+ people on such short notice. This is another case of the Bible not giving any more information than is necessary to make the point of the story.

After the food had been distributed and the excess collected, Jesus immediately had the disciples get into the boats and leave for the other side of the lake and He dismissed the crowd and went into the hills to pray. Later that night He saw that the disciples in the boat were in distress, and He walked across the lake on the water and got into the boat with the terrified disciple to calm their fears. As Mark says, they "were utterly astounded" as well they should have been. They did not understand the loaves and now on top of that they had to digest Jesus walking on water. Who wouldn't be overwhelmed? Mark finishes this scene be stating "...that their hearts were hardened" (Mark 6:45-52. Also see Matt 14:22-33, John 6:15-21).

The hardened hearts comment was about the disciples' lack of faith. With their return from their successful mission of teaching and healing, followed by Jesus' teaching and feeding the crowd, topped by His praying, and then walking on water, they simply could not compre-hend all that was happening, and the opportunities that were avail-able to them. Having to digest in such a short time Jesus' rejection in Nazareth, which surely was disheartening to them, and then the high of the joy and excitement from their successful mission trips, followed by Jesus feeding the 5,000, all of which had just been topped by him walking across the water to their boat, causing a serious overload of their ability to make sense of it all. It sounds like Jesus expected them to understand what they had seen as coming from having faith in God, but they could not make that leap. They simply could not see them-selves doing on a steady basis what they were seeing Jesus do.

As is true with other events, the timing and sequence of Jesus' rejec-tion in Nazareth, commissioning the disciples and then return, feeding the five thousand, and Jesus walking on water is different in the three gospels.

The disciples' struggles with making sense of all that was, in part, due to their inability to release themselves from the religious culture they have followed all their lives. The permission Jesus was giving them to freely live outside the rules and structure of the Jewish religion was not strong enough for them to give themselves the freedom that would come from living in the blessing of God.

The return of the disciples is also reported in Luke 9:10, but not in Matthew. John does not report the commissioning of the disciples. All four gospels report feeding the 5,000, and Mark reports another similar occurrence of Jesus teaching and feeding to a crowd of 4,000 with two fish and seven loaves of bread, which probably is an alternate descrip-tion of the same event. (See Mark 8:1-10 and Matthew.15:32-39.) In both stories of feeding the gathered crowd, the numbers 5,000 and 4,000 count the men in the crowds. Aside from that, the descriptions of feeding the 5,000 are very similar in the four gospels, all though the events before and after it differ in each gospel. Luke does not mention Jesus walking on water, while Matthew and John repeated Mark's story (Matt. 14:22-33 and John 6:15-21). So, what is one to make of all that?

Mark has things moving at a fast pace. Without knowing what the time span is for all the activities of Jesus' ministry through feeding the 5,000, it is hard to tell where we are in his three-year ministry. It seems that we are well past the early part of His ministry, and He is more comfortable with his ministry. He understands and accepts His relationship with God. It also seems that things are moving faster than the disciples can comprehend. The basis of their faith has been shaken and they are being left behind. Feeding the 5,000 and walking on water were well beyond the disciples thinking. The disciples were common people who were used to solving practical problems for daily living, and Jesus is telling them to have faith in God beyond what they needed for daily living. They were having a hard time making the transition from material living to faith in God living. One wonders what our reaction would have been to all that was going on if we had been there.

The Pharisees and scribes continued to follow Him and question Him in the hopes of getting Him to say something they could use to arrest Him. In Mark 7:1-23 they questioned, "Why do your disciples not live according to the traditions of the elders but eat with hands defiled?" Jesus answered them with the admonishment, "You leave the commandments of God and hold fast the traditions of men." He goes on to say that the traditions followed by the Pharisees kept a man from honoring his father and mother as required by Moses. He explained to the crowd and disciples that nothing for the outside can defile a person, but rather what comes out of a person, such as," evil thoughts, fornication, theft, murder, adultery, coveting, wickedness, deceit, licentiousness, envy, slander, pride, foolishness," can defile a person. Neither the crowd nor the disciples could grasp His meaning or apply it to themselves. Interestingly, the Bible notes that He has declared all foods are clean. The footnote in the Bible for Mark 7:1-23 summarizes Jesus' response best as, "Whereas the common people were moved by elemental needs, and Jesus was aroused to compassion for human suffering while the religious leaders were concerned with details of ritual."

After this encounter, He quietly went to Tyre and Sidon. There is a woman, which Mark says was Greek, Syrophoenician by birth, came and fell at His feet begging Him to cast out the demons from her daughter. The exchange is interesting. Jesus said, "Let the children first be fed, for it is not right to take the children's bread and throw it to the dogs." She answered," Yes, Lord; yet even the dogs under the table eat the children's crumbs." Jesus says, "For this saying you may go your way; the demon has left your daughter." She went home and found that to be true (See Mark. 7:24-30.)

Matthew also recorded this event in Matthew 15:21-23, except He called the woman a Canaanite and He added that the disciples wanted Him to send her away, for it seems she had been pestering them. Matthew also included Jesus saying, "I was sent only to the lost sheep of the house of Israel." After the exchange between Jesus and the woman, He was impressed with her faith and the daughter was healed. Although Jesus' primary purpose was to convince the Jews to change their lives, Jesus repeatedly healed Gentiles because of their faith. It would have been a tough realization for the Jews to accept that the Gentiles could receive healing through their faith in God just as the Jews could.

Jesus returned to Galilee from Tyre and Sidon and continued to teach, creating a healing atmosphere, and sparring with the Pharisees.

In Mark 8:31-33, Jesus explains that His time is short, that He could not keep on disputing the Judaism leadership without being arrested and killed. He added that three days after being killed, He will rise. In Matthew, Jesus led into His comments by saying that He had to go to Jerusalem, apparently to celebrate Passover.

The Bible does not say how often Jesus went to Jerusalem to celebrate Passover. Mark has this discussion toward the end of his ministry, which could mean that Jesus knew that going to Jerusalem, the strong center of Judaism, would be an ideal time for His arrest by the Judaism leaders.

In Mark 8:29, Peter called Jesus Christ and in Mark 8:31 Jesus said that He will rise three days after He is killed. I think that both statements are late additions. While Christ was one term used to identify the Messiah, Jesus was not thought as the Messiah until after His death, not before

His death. There were instances when people thought He could be the Messiah they were desperately hoping for, but not a savor. Jesus and the Jews were expecting the Messiah to come with the end of the world. Jesus did not fit their description of the Messiah.

If Jesus did say that He would rise after He was killed it should have been in the forefront of the disciples' minds when He was crucified. The surprised and astonished reaction of the disciples to Jesus being raised indicates that there was little. if any forewarning that He would rise.

Jesus' Continuing Frustration With The Disciples And Jews

After Jesus' comments in Mark 8:31-34, Jesus continues teaching in Mark 8:34-38 by telling what one must do to be immersed in a relationship with God such as He was.

> If any man would come after me, let him deny himself and take up his cross and follow me. For whoever would save his life will lose it; and whoever loses his life for my sake and the gospel's will save it. For what does it profit a man, to gain the whole world and forfeit his life? For what can a man give in return for his life? For whoever is ashamed of me and my words in this adulterous and sinful generation, of him will the Son of man also be ashamed, when he comes in the glory of his Father with the holy angel. (Also see Matthew 16:24-28 and Jn 12: 25-26)

The term *gospel* is most certainly another later addition. Neither the disciples nor the people who were following Jesus wrote about Jesus' ministry until after His death. So, there would not have been a gospel or book for Jesus to reference. Removing *gospel* doesn't detract from the meaning of Jesus' message. Losing one's existing life, for a God-centered life, as described and lived by Jesus, was what Jesus wanted for the Jews.

Mark 8:34-38 is one of times when Jesus explained what it meant to live in the likeness of God. It summarizes the values that are the basis for all that Jesus has said and done up to this point. It also is an acknowledgment and acceptance that He is delivering God's message. To have the same type of relationship with God that Jesus had requires the relationship with God to take precedence over all else, it could not be incorporated into the disciples and Jewish people's existing daily life. This was the heart and soul of Jesus' message. This new relationship did not fit in the old wine skin of their daily lives but must be put into a new wine skin that could stretch and bend as needed to have their relationship with God take precedence over everything else.

The second point that He makes, by speaking of an individual rather than a group, is that the relationship each person has with God is that person's alone. It is separate from the relationship all other people have with God. Being a member of a group that believes in God does not cut it. Such a group may help an individual develop a personal relationship with God, but that group could not be a part of a person's personal relationship with God. A person's relationship with God does not depend on the consensus of the members of a group or a person's neighbors or friends. Only God's acceptance is what counts.

It really goes back to the creation story. If each one of us is to live in the likeness of God, we would respect each other and all of God's creation. The Ten Commandments (Exod. 20:1-17) describe in some detail how we should respect God and treat each other as a part of caring for God's creation. The fact that this requirement is simple does not mean that abiding by it is easy or simple. The relationship between God and mankind, and mankind to mankind is certainly a large part of the Old Testament. In His ministry, Jesus further describes these relationships.

The use and protection of the land and nonhuman living things are not clearly described in either the Ten Commandments or the teachings of Jesus. I think that is because they were not the source of the Jew's misery. It is the inhumanity of man to man that was the main violation of God's creation that concerned Jesus, although there certainly was mistreatment of animals and the land.

There was a tremendous difference between what Jesus was saying and doing and what the Jewish people had been told by the Judaism leaders they had to do, as well as the hardships imposed upon them by the Romans. The Jewish people liked what Jesus did and said but were not able to bring themselves to live as Jesus' lived. Doing as Jesus was doing would have been very difficult because it would have been a total change in their daily activities. And they were apprehensive about what would happen.

Look at the disciples, who went so far as to leave their families and the only life they know to follow Him, who could not get their minds around the simple idea of Jesus' message. No matter how exciting Jesus' ministry and lifestyle were the total change the Jews would have to make was beyond their ability to make. The gulf between what the Jews were excited about and how they would live as Jesus lived was too great.

He continues in Mark 9:1, "Truly, I say to you, there are some standing here who will not taste death before they see the kingdom of God come with power." Again, Jesus expresses His concern that the time was short, and the people needed to immediately change their ways. He was convicted that the kingdom of God was at hand. He was raised in a time of great distress among the Jews and their strong belief that God would send down a Messiah to save them. The problem, as Jesus and John the Baptist saw it, was that following the dictates and requirements of the Jewish religion was not the same as living in accordance with God's covenant with Abraham.

Jesus did not want the Jewish people to miss out on being with God because they had been misled. His major concern during His ministry was that, regardless of how well His message and actions were received, the Jews were not taking to heart His message and changing their lifestyle. It had to be particularly frustrating that the disciples, who were with him day and night were also failing to make the change to living in God's blessing.

The next activity that Mark describes, is the *Transfiguration of Jesus.* Mark 9:2-11 states that Jesus took Peter, James, and John up a high mountain, and Jesus was transfigured before them with His garment glistening white, and Elijah and Moses appeared and talked with Jesus. In verse 7, it states, "And a cloud overshadowed them, and a voice came out of the cloud saying, 'This is my beloved Son; listen to him.'" As quickly as Elijah and Moses came, they disappeared. As Jesus and the three disciples walked down the mountain, Jesus told them not to tell anyone about what they had seen until after the Son of man has risen from the dead. They kept the matter to themselves while questioning what rising from the dead meant (Matt. 17:1-8 and Luke 9:28-36).

Even with this experience, they could not make the connection with what they marveled and what they admired about Jesus could also be theirs if they changed their thinking to a new approach centered on God. God's comments after Jesus was baptized, came before Jesus had started His ministry. This transfiguration experience is the first confirmation in the gospels that God approves of what Jesus is doing. Jesus' teaching and His healings and miracles amazed the people in Galilee and gave them new hope; however, that did not validate that what He was telling them was God's message for them. The validity of Jesus' teaching could only be given by God and this transfiguration experience was God validating Jesus' teachings.

Throughout His ministry, Jesus told the disciples not to tell people about what they had seen and heard. Jesus knew that He was stepping on toes. In both the Jewish and Roman law, a person could be arrested, tortured, and killed for as little as questioning an action of a leader. When the Pharisees and scribes were questioning Jesus, it was not to find out what He thought, but rather it was to have a reason to arrest Him and thereby get rid of a troublemaker. Jesus never gave them what they wanted until the very end. His ability to avoid the traps that the Pharisees and scribes continued to set for Him is evidence of His knowledge and understanding of the law and Jewish history as well as a demonstration of His sharp mind and His understanding of the people around Him.

The issue of what can be accomplished if one has faith in God comes up frequently throughout Jesus' ministry. One of the very clear demonstrations of this is the story of the healing of the epileptic child as told in Mark 9:14-29 the father of the epileptic son had asked the disciples to heal his son, but they were not able to do so.

These were the same disciples who had been recently sent out on their own and had successfully healed people; however, they had apparently lost their faith to do so when they were in the presence of Jesus. Jesus responded to their lack of success by saying, "O faithless generation, how long am I to be with you? How long am I to bear with you? Bring him to me." The father brought the son to Jesus and tells Jesus, "... if you can do anything, have pity on us and help us." The way the father framed his request is the way he would have framed a request to a priest, scribe, or anyone of standing. Jesus responded with some irritation, "If you can! All things are possible to him who believes." The father cried out (other ancient authorities add "with tears") "I believe; help my unbelief!" After Jesus rebuked the unclean spirit, the boy was healed. It sounds like the father came to Jesus with hope rather than faith that Jesus could cure his son. Without faith you have nothing. Once the father gained his faith his son was healed. This story is also told in Matthew 17:14-21 and Luke 9:37-42.

If you will remember when Jesus sent out the twelve disciples to the surrounding communities to teach and perform miracles, the disciples came back proclaiming the success they experienced. So, even with their experience, the disciples did not understand that the success they had was a sample of what life would be if they kept their faith in God first in their lives.

Jesus was frustrated with the disciples' continuing inability to stay connected to God. The disciples, who had witnessed this combination of Jesus' faith and the faith of the healed person working time and time again, and with their own experience of the combination of their own faith and the faith of the healed person working when they were on their own, still did not have strong enough faith in God and themselves for them to promote healing in the presence of Jesus.

Jesus' faith in God was not enough. He was helpless to heal a person without that person's faith in God, or as shown in the above story, through the father's faith in God. This key message of Jesus' ministry is repeated throughout the synoptic Gospels and remains the most unappreciated message of his ministry. Remember back to his lack of success in Nazareth, when what Jesus was telling the Jews did not renew their faith in God as it had for the man with demons in the synagogue in Capernaum. Once again, Jesus' faith in God alone could not help the Jews.

As Jesus continued His ministry, His disciples continued to have trouble understanding what He was telling them. The disciples continued to try to fit what they were hearing into their existing way of living. As an example, Mark tells us in Mark 9:33-37, that when Jesus heard that the disciples had been discussing who was the greatest, he told them that, "If anyone would be first, he must be last of all and a servant of all." He then took a child and said, "Whoever receives one such child in my name receives me; and whoever, receives me, receives not me but him who sent me." (Also see Matt. 18:1-5 and Luke 9:43-45). That the first must be last is a new and strange concept that was not practiced in the Jewish religion or the Roman Legions, or any other organizations of that day, or for that matter, not by many, if any, organizations today.

Since the disciples had decided to stay with Jesus as He traveled from place to place, it seems that the idea of the first being last and the last being first would have been an idea that they could accept; however, it was so different from what they had known all their lives, they simply could not see how such an idea would work. So, once again no matter how hard they tried, the disciples could not fit Jesus' ministry into the Jewish society that the disciples knew and accepted.

Mark 9:38-40 provides further insight into Jesus' thoughts on living in the Covenant with God. John apparently saw another person causing healing as competition and tells Jesus, "... we saw a man casting out demons in your name, and we forbade him, because he was not following us." But Jesus said, "Do not forbid him; for no one who does mighty work in my name will not be able soon after to speak evil of me. For he that is not against us is for us". (Lk.9:49-50)

It would have been reasonable for Jesus to accept someone else who had been awaking to God's promise as He had been. After all, that is what Jesus wanted all Jews to be able to do. It was evident on more than one occasion during His ministry that He welcomed all who had faith in a God-centered, spiritual relationship with God.

Jesus was giving a strong statement that, with faith in God, anyone can facilitate healing. The sad truth from John's comment is that even with their own experience of healing people, they could not see the better life that comes with living with faith in God.

It is unfortunate that we do not know what happened to the man that was casting out demons. Was he also attested and killed in a similar manner as Jesus was, or did he manage to stay outside the Jewish and Roman leadership control and, after a long time of faithfully serving the Jews, die a peaceful death? That would be the happy ending; however, history has shown that a happy ending is not often the case.

Jesus goes further explaining the penalty for working against God. In Mark 9:42-48, He states. "Whoever causes one of these little ones (his followers) who believe in me to sin, it would be better for him if a great millstone were hung round his neck, and he were thrown in the sea." He goes on to say that if your hand or foot causes you to sin cut them off for losing one of them is better than going to hell. The notes in the Bible state that the word hell comes from the Greek word "Gehenna" and the word sin comes from the word "stumble." (See Matthew 18:7-9 and Luke 17:1-2.)

Several other times during His ministry Jesus talks of being out of God's grace as being in a hellish existence (Mark 5:25-34, 10:23-27, 11:22-26, and Luke 10:17-20, 12:4-7 and 16:23). The Jews did not have to die and go to some far-off place to be miserable. They could be miserable wherever they found themselves. Many of the poverty-stricken people were living a hellish existence and went to Jesus to change their lives.

So, what did Jesus give the Jews that would show them what living in God's grace looks like? When God created mankind in his image, He did His part. To fully enjoy His gift, mankind needs to live in the likeness of God, or live as God would live. It did not take much imitation for the Jews to understand that a better life was available through believing and trusting in God.

Jesus' life was their primary example of living in God's grace. His handling of the Pharisees, scribes, and priests was one example. That in Jesus' presence, Jews develop the trust in God that promotes healings was another example. Jesus' telling the Jews of the relationship with God that was available to them, in clear language, they could understand was Jesus's third example of what living in God's grace looks like.

The importance of what happened in the stories of healing is not given enough coverage. Jesus called forth healing for a variety of physical and mental disabilities. Regardless of the illness brought to Jesus the critical and necessary ingredient was faith in God. Jesus' faith in God was a given, but by itself, it was not enough. It was always the faith in God of the ill person, or a person or persons associated with the ill person, that completed the healing connection that made the person well. Jesus said that a person's faith made that person well time after time, but they could not apply the message of someone being healed to themselves.

Jesus' continued teaching, such as is described in the Sermon on the Mount. He told them that they were made in the image of God, and that God believed in them. Living in God's grace plainly meant changing their priority from daily survival to living a God-centered life based on their unwavering belief and trust in God.

Going back to chapter 3, the ancient Hebrews' belief in demons was of minor importance. It was in the third century BC that it was decided that the demons were organized and had a leader named Satan (Shaitin). This idea seems to have been taken from the Zoroastrianism religion. At about the same time, the concept of there being a last judgment came from Persian sources with little change. The ancient Hebrews believed that the dead descended into the pit of She'ol, which was like the Greek Hades and Babylonian Aralu (Noss pg.556-557).

It is important to recognize that the concepts of hell and Satan did not originate with Judaism and were not included in the writings of Judaism until some 1500 years after God made His covenant with Abraham. I think it is also important to recognize that the perception of the known world, from before the Hebrews journeyed into Canaan, through the time of Jesus, and well into the Middle Ages, was much different than our perception of that same world today. There was little thought that the earth was a ball rather than a flat surface, or that it was located on a small, out of the way section of the Milky Way galaxy rather than in the center of God's universe, or that it rotated around the sun. With what the Hebrews, and later, the Jews could see and knew about their world it would be logical to think there was a place off in the far reaches of God's kingdom, as Satan's domain, to send evil people.

There is no question that the concepts surrounding Abraham's relationship with God had been revised and added to be the time of Jesus. I think that Jesus recognized this; however, He lived and taught a relationship with God that returned to the simple and direct relationship Abraham had with God.

Mark starts Chapter 10 by having Jesus leave Galilee and go to Judea and the area beyond the Jordan River. As crowds gathered, He would teach them as he traveled. Mark 10:2-12 tells us what Jesus' response is to the question asked by a Pharisee. Is it lawful for a man to divorce his wife. Starting at verse 6 Jesus responded with "But from the beginning of creation, God made them male and female. For this reason, a man shall leave his father and mother and be joined to his wife, and the two shall become one. So, they are no longer two but one. What therefore God has joined together, let not man put asunder."

When the disciples were alone with Jesus, they asked about what He had just said. He was more direct in His response to them saying, "Whoever divorces his wife and marries another, commits adultery against her, and if she divorces her husband and marries another, she commits adultery" (Matt. 5:31-32, 19:1-12). These are powerful statements for two reasons.

First, they describe a major change to Jewish law of the time, which allowed a man to write a certificate of divorce, "to put her away." He is telling the Pharisee and the disciples that God's intent for the marriage commitment to be forever, rather than a temporary convenience. This is the expectation God had for the Jewish people. It is the expectation He also has for Christians. It indicates that Jesus is at one with God. The expectations of God are simple and direct; however, they can be difficult or inconvenient to follow. Jesus continued to describe what God wanted for the Jewish people as situations arose.

The second reason the marriage statements are so powerful is that they put man and woman on an equal basis. At that time women were second-class citizens. They were not counted by the government in the census. The number 5,000 in Mark 6:30-44 probably did not include the women in the crowd. As indicated by the marriage law that came from Moses, the man had a free hand in the society and women were dependent upon the decisions of men. While Jesus' comment on marriage did not solve the lack of equality for women, it certainly put a spotlight on the issue.

Mark 10:13-16 tells us that Jesus was blessing children when the disciples stopped them from coming to Him. When Jesus saw what was happening, He was indignant, or justifiably angry, and said, "Let the children come to me, do not hinder them; for to such belongs the kingdom of God. Truly, I say to you, whoever doesn't receive the Kingdom of God like a child shall not enter it" (Luke 18:15-17). A similar comment by Jesus is found in Mark 9:36-37.

This is a strong statement against the requirements and rituals of the Jewish religion and certainly can equally be applied to Christian today. Jesus again emphasizes the idea that a child did not have to read the laws or followed the religious rituals to be acceptable to God. A child was acceptable to God just as he or she was, no input from mankind was needed.

This idea surely gave the religious leaders heartburn. The idea that a child's simple faith in the world as they saw it, was good enough for God went against all the Jewish people had been told all their lives. It goes against what Jesus had been told growing up, but He saw through it just as He saw through the Jewish Religion of His day.

There is much to take from this. All the religious robes and trappings, and the temples and magnificent buildings, laws and rules, rituals and theology are of no value in our relationship with God, and surely are detrimental to someone having the simple faith that God asks of the Jews and us. None of these things or the religious studies and observation of holy days provides anyone an entrance into the kingdom of God. We spend a considerable amount of time, money, and energy to be able to enter the kingdom of God, all for naught. The simplicity of a child's trust and faith in God is all that is needed. The footnote to Mark 10:15 (pg. 1227) states, "To receive the kingdom as a child is to depend, in trustful simplicity, on what God offers."

For the Jewish religious leaders, the downside to this idea was, it is next to impossible to tax a child's trust and faith or to require them to go to worship services to obtain what they already have.

Christianity would look much different today if all the rituals, doctrine, denominations, and procedures were eliminated and accepting people as you find them while trusting in God was all that was required to be a Christian.

There is a constant theme throughout Jesus' ministry. Receiving the blessing of God requires only that one has a simple trusting faith in God. How can anyone expect God to be with them through thick and thin if they are not willing to have their priority be their faith in God, to live in harmony with God, and to trust in God through good and bad. It does not require some grand event but rather, making the lives of other people better. The little thoughtful things are what matters to God, not the grand structures and gestures.

As Jesus was leaving the children, a rich man kneed before him and asked, "What must I do to inherit eternal life?" He told Jesus that he has observed the commandments since his youth, and Jesus tells him he must, "... sell what you have and give to the poor, and you will have treasures in heaven, and come follow me." Upon hearing this, he went away sad for he had great possessions (Mark 10:17-22, Luke 18:18-23).

The disciples were amazed by Jesus' words as He explains further, "It is easier for a camel to go through the eye of the needle than for a rich man to enter the kingdom of heaven" (Mark 10:17-31, also see Luke 18:18-30). It seems that in Jesus' time the entrance gates of a town wall had a small gate to the side of the main gate that was used at nighttime when the main gates were closed. This small gate was just big enough for a person to go through. Apparently these gates were called the "eye of the needle" and it would be nearly impossible for a camel to go through it.

The story of the rich young ruler has not received enough attention for it describes the key to a dilemma the Jews faced. They wanted to incorporate Jesus' message into their existing daily life and Jesus continued to say it could not be done. On one hand, the rich man's experience provides a clear picture of the tremendous difference there was between the man's life and the life Jesus had chosen. Because the man confronted with the choice was a rich man, the common Jews did not relate the message to themselves and what they needed to give up, to follow Jesus. They could not relate to a man having to give up what they never had to them giving up what they did have. Not being able to give up their existing life was keeping them from joining with Jesus.

It has always been my assumption that being rich was an insurmountable barrier for the man to enjoy eternal life, which made him sorrowful. An exception to my thinking came from a comment that was made during a *Faith at Work* conference several years ago. One of the leaders raised the possibility that the man was sorrowful knowing that he would give up his wealth and all that went with it, the prestige and respect he received, to follow Jesus. He knew giving up all that he had worked to obtain would be a great loss that would be necessary to go into a new unknown life.

It seems evident that existing life, with all its advantages, was not fulfilling enough to keep him from searching for a better life. The is the same problem the followers of Jesus were having. They were not able to free themselves of their existing life to clear their lives for the new life with God.

Having heard what Jesus told the rich man, Peter said to Jesus, "Lo, we have left everything and followed you." If Mark's sequent of events is right, this is the first time Peter raised the issue of what the disciples can expect since they left everything to follow Him. Jesus tells him that anyone who left everything to follow Him would receive a hundredfold what he or she left. Jesus also once again tells Him that the first will be last and the last first (Mark 10:28-31).

Another parable that illustrates the conflict between wealth and having God first is found in Luke 21:1-4. It tells of the rich putting their money in the temple offering box and a poor widow putting in two copper coins, which were of little value. While the donations from the rich were of much greater monetary value than the widow's paltry amount, the rich donations were a small token of their abundance and did not endanger their lifestyle, while the widow's donation came from the little that she had and meant that she would do without something. Being at one with God was more important to the widow than anything else. Maintaining their wealth status was more important to the wealthy than being at one with God.

Both Jesus' answer to the rich young man and His observation at the offering box describes the difficulty rich people have in balancing their lifestyle with the need to make their spiritual connection with God their top priority. With all that Jesus did and said, each person must make God his or her most important priority to have a relationship with God such as Abraham and Jesus had.

Having money is not the problem, for Jesus and his disciples had enough to warrant having Judas be the group's treasurer, and the disciples apparently had enough money to buy food to feed the 5,000. The problem is the place that money holds in the Jew's lives. For the rich having money and making money was the driving purpose of their lives. For the poor not having money and trying to get money was the driving purpose of their lives. Only by making a relationship with God their primary purpose, without regard to how much money they did or did not have, would both the rich and the poor be able to live with God's blessing.

Living with God's blessing does not necessarily require changing what a person does. A carpenter could still be a carpenter and a vineyard owner could still own a vineyard. The change must come from within oneself, how one lives his or her daily life. One does not need to change jobs, or change what one does, but rather change how one thinks about and approaches people and situations he or she meet each day.

A continuing problem between the disciples and Jesus is well demonstrated in the exchange between James, John, and Jesus, and the reaction of the other ten disciples afterward, as described in Mark 10:35-45. The story starts out with James and John telling Jesus, "'Teacher, we want you to do for us whatever we ask of you.' He asks, 'What do you want me to do for you?' And they said to Him, 'Grant us to sit, one at your right hand and one at your left, in your glory.' But Jesus said to them, 'You do not know what you are asking. Are you able to drink the cup that I drink, or to be baptized with the baptism with which I am baptized?'" Simply by asking the question, James and John showed that the answer to Jesus' question was *no*. It also showed how disconnected James and John were from Jesus' ministry.

They continued the discussion and when the other ten disciples heard what James and John had done, they were indignant, to say the least. Jesus ended the discussion by repeating His earlier statement "...but whoever would be great among you must be your servant, and whoever would be first among you must be slave of all." And then He continued," For the Son of man also came not to be served but to serve, and to give his life as a ransom for many." As is often the case there is much to learn from this exchange. (See Matt. 20:20-28 and Jude 22:24-27.) Jesus is still trying to get the disciples to understand the idea that the first must be last in the here and now, not in some future existence. Simply allowing God to be first in their daily lives rather than retaining their current life, eliminating the need to worry about the pecking order in their group or what might happen next.

The disciples primarily saw Jesus as their leader, so they kept missing the message Jesus gave them just like they did every time someone was healed because of that person's faith rather than Jesus' faith.

James and John so misunderstood what Jesus had been teaching and demonstrating with the healings in His presence that the audacity of their request escaped them. And then when the other ten disciples found out about it, things must have gotten tense, to say the least.

The twelve disciples were a mixture of men from different parts of the Jewish community. Each one chose to follow Jesus for his own reasons, and each was trying to figure out what it meant to be a disciple of Jesus and how to fit that into what they knew. Each of them had gone out in pairs and preached and healed, as instructed by Jesus, with great success; however, that one experience was not strong enough to overcome their lifetime experience of living under the Jewish religion and of seeing the strong being in control.

Their experience with the Jewish religion and in the villages was that someone was in charge and some other people had duties to fulfill. The only one of the twelve that had a duty was Judas as treasurer for the group, and it seems that Judas saw that as an advantage rather than a responsibility (John 12:6). Apparently, Jesus had not appointed a chief disciple and assigned other duties, which was in line with His teaching that the greatest must serve. Nothing they were doing; however, was strong enough to overcome their lifelong experiences. Even after almost three years with Jesus, the pecking order in the group was still important to the disciples. Based on the comments and explanations that Jesus made, He knew that the disciples were not taking His message to heart and using it as a blueprint for changing their lives to live in harmony with God. If they were, there would be a major change in how they thought about their world and their position in it. Their priorities would be totally different. How they lived and approached the issues that confronted them would have been different, but the issues would be the same.

Once again, the disciples were having trouble getting their minds around Jesus' message. While they liked Jesus' message, they seem unable to adjust their thinking to fit His message. If they were having trouble with Jesus' message it seems a given that the crowds were having the same problem.

Their life experiences formed the barrier that was keeping the disciples from recognizing that they were all made in God's image and therefore all had the same potential as Jesus to live in God's blessing.

This is another example of the disciples and the followers of Jesus being unable to change their thinking about their daily lives. The first thought of a fisherman who finds a productive fishing spot is to keep its location a secret, but Jesus wanted them to share all that they had. Jesus set the example with his willingness to share with the 5,000 the little they had, which led to the great amount that fed the 5,000. He was not holding back anything. He willingly shared all his knowledge and skills for living in God's favor with everyone He met, and He was not threatened by someone who was also living in God's favor.

So, why did disciples stick around, and why did the Jews keep following Him? While we may never know the answers to these questions, some reasonable conclusions can be made. Undeniably, the first reason that comes to mind is the healings and miracles. These were evidence that in Jesus' presence great things happened in support of His message. Jesus' fear was probability true. That the healings and miracles were interfering with His message for them to repent. It was a dilemma for Jesus, the miracles and healings brought the people to Him, but they also kept the people from taking the next step of living as Jesus lived.

While there may have been several other reasons for the disciples to remain with Jesus, one is that they thought of His miracles, healings, and teachings as a prelude to the main event. When was He going to take up the sword, descend upon the dastardly oppressors and relieve the Jewish people of their burdens so they could enjoy their lives? Judas certainly was one who thought like this. A related idea was, because the Jew believed that the end was near, and a Messiah would come down from heaven to save the righteous and Jesus was obviously doing God's work, they wanted to be with Him when the world came to an end, not realizing that it would take more than being with Jesus when the end came.

Whatever was prompting the Jewish people to stick with Jesus, it seems to center around the expectation that Jesus would make their lives better. Although He kept saying that only they could make their lives better, it did not register, and they kept looking elsewhere for something improve their lives.

His air of quiet authority certainly could have given them hope of there being more that what He was giving them. That His message of God's love and grace, which filled a hole in them that the Jewish religion did not and could not fill, certainly gave them hope of more to follow. God did not want them to be beaten down. Rather, God believed in them and wanted them to believe in themselves. Jesus waited them to see themselves as being what God saw was good. The part about repent, turn your life around, was the part of the message that the disciples and the Jews could not bring themselves to do.

Jesus was not telling the Jews and disciples that they would not have to keep working hard for long hours. But rather, He was telling them that believing in God would give them the strength to persevere through their struggles and hardships.

How many of you know of a person who has had one bad thing after another happen and can barely get by, but he or she continues to be cheerful and pleasant to be around, but still goes out of his or her way to help others? That is what Jesus was explaining and what the disciples and the crowds did not recognize as being an improvement to their existence.

The disciples who traveled with Him and the crowds that gathered when He came into towns were mainly from Galilee, with some addition of the people of the Judea area, which may have included the rich man. Jesus went to the people and talked with them rather than *to them*. This helped them feel that He cared for them and that He would fulfill the promise of helping them remove the daily burdens they were carrying. Even with all He had said, they still were having difficulty making the mental leap to a new life.

They did not believe that the change could be within them and be so simple. They had lived their lives under the complexities of the Jewish religion and the Roman occupation, and now Jesus is telling them of the simple life with God that he was living; however, He did not say that making their lifestyle changes would be easy. They kept looking for the key to opening the door to the new life. The simple answer given to the rich man passed by them. The inability to make necessary life changes was what they could not overcome.

This issue may be that one of the reasons Jesus was rejected in Nazareth. His statement of God's message was simple and direct without grand pronouncements or high drama. They had been told that the "Anointed One" would be a supernatural person who would descend from the clouds to the sound of trumpets and surrounded by angels. So, where did this carpenter's son, who they watched grow up from a baby to manhood get off telling them he was giving them God's message? There must be more to it than what this upstart was telling them.

Following Mark's sequence, we are now beginning the final week of Jesus' ministry with His entrance into Jerusalem on Palm Sunday for the feast of the Passover. From the beginning of His ministry, the Pharisees, priests, and scribes had been dogging Him trying to build a case against Him of blasphemy and being a fraud. And now during the upcoming week, He would be available to them, in their home ground, to complete their mission of His death.

During His ministry, Jesus, on more than one occasion, predicted His death. I believe that this comes from His understanding that He could take shots at the Jewish leadership only for so long before they would shut Him down. Jesus' predictions came solely from His understanding of what He was up against. That His ministry lasted about three years was due to the Jewish leadership's inability to get enough on Jesus that they could arrest Him without causing an uprising from Jesus' followers.

Being arrested meant being charged with a high crime, such as blasphemy, and being put to death, which in Jesus' time was a torturous, inhuman, drawn-out process. Jesus was not talking about the end of time that He believed was coming; but rather He was talking about the end of His ministry. He hoped that the disciples had picked up more of His ministry than they seemed to have.

Jesus had been delaying coming to Jerusalem. His predictions of His arrest and resulting death would be much easier to accomplish with him in Jerusalem for that is where the leaders of the Jewish religion and the Roman governor were. He had an alternative. He could go into the hill country and delay for some time or completely avoid a confrontation with the Jewish religious leaders and the Roman Governor. To do so, however, would go against His message of trust and belief in God, and His message not to fear what people can do to them. With God's love their spirit will endure. So, knowing full well what was in store for Him, He entered Jerusalem.

ADDITIONAL STORIES

At this point, I will stop and pick up some stories in Matthew and Luke that are not in Mark. I will cover the Gospel of John in a separate chapter.

The first of these stories is about forgiveness and is found in Matthew 18: 21-35. Peter came up to Jesus asking how often he should forgive his brother who sinned against him. Peter suggested seven times and

Jesus replies, "... seventy times seven." Jesus then tells a story concerning a king who wanted to settle accounts with his servants. The first servant brought to him owed him ten thousand talents, which the servant could not pay. A talent was worth about one thousand dollars. The king ordered him to be sold, with his wife and children and all that he owned to make the payment. The servant fell on his knees begging the king to give him more time to pay the debt. The king took pity on the servant and released him and forgave him his debt.

Then, when this servant left the king, he saw a fellow servant who owed him one hundred denarii. He seized the man by the throat, demanding payment. A denarius was worth about twenty cents. This servant also asked for patience and more time to pay the debt. The first servant denied the request and had him put in jail. When other servants told the king what had happened, the king summoned the first servant to him and rebuked him saying the since the king had forgiven him his debt shouldn't he have shown his fellow servant the same mercy that the king had shown him? In anger, the king had the first servant thrown into jail. Jesus concluded, "So also my heavenly Father will do to every one of you, if you do not forgive your brother from your heart." This clearly describes a basic message of Jesus' ministry. Regardless of your station in life, the treatment we show others is the treatment God will show us.

The second story in Matthew is in Matthew 20:1-16 about an owner of a vineyard who early one morning hired some men to work in his vineyard for a denarius. Three times throughout the day, he hired more men to work in his vineyard for the same payment of a denarius. At the end of the day the owner paid the last men one denarius, the same as the first men he hired. The first men hired were upset and grumbling about this being unfair. The point that the owner made to the first men he hired was that he, the owner, had lived up to his agreement with the first men he hired. Must he have their approval to do what he wishes with his money after he paid the first men? Jesus ended this story by again saying "... the last will be first and the first last."

Our thinking of today does not follow this story. We spend a lot of time, energy, and money trying to make sure that all people are treated to same for the same work, and hard be the judgment on a vineyard owner who did not treat the men he hires equally for the time and work they perform. The issues of freedom of choice and treating individuals as individuals can get lost in rhetoric on equality. Ronald Reagan, as he was so capable of doing, states the issue described in the vineyard story clearly and concisely.

> The American dream is not that every man must be level with every other man. The American dream is that every man must be free to become whatever God intends he should become. (Google Ronald Reagan Saying Quotes American Dreams)

So, while we are a long way from having accomplished this dream, and it certainly has its own set of issues, giving each person such a dream is a much better goal than trying the impossible task of making everyone equal.

Jesus did not expect or require that all the Jews should be treated the same, but rather that they be given the freedom to have their own relationship with God without the dictates and rules imposed by the religious leaders and the Roman leaders. It was not about the money per se, but rather it was about the requirement to support the Jewish leadership rather than each Jew having his or her own relationship with God.

When God made us and saw that it was good, it included the freedom of choice. That includes making bad choices. Whether the results of a person's choices are bad or good, the results are that person's responsibility. So, if the Jewish religious leaders were more like the vineyard owner the power to choose would have benefitted the Jewish people, granted not equally, rather than creating undue burdens for all of them to carry. One can only speculate on what the world would look like if all companies and governments followed the vineyard owner's thinking.

Now, turning to Luke and the stories of Mary Magdalene. Mary first appears in Luke 8:2-3. At some point after He had selected His twelve disciples, Jesus and his disciples were going from town to town and were joined by three women who had been healed. Of the women, Mary Magdalene had been cured of seven demons; Joanna was the wife of Herod's steward and Susanna were the women who joined Jesus. These three were of means and well respected, although some thought that Mary Magdalene was, "a woman of the city," as mentioned in Luke 7:37. Apparently, Mary Magdalene was an important part of Jesus' followers. She was at Jesus' crucifixion remaining true to Jesus through to the end. John describes her as being the first to Jesus' tomb on the third day and the first person that Jesus talk to after He had risen.

It is in Luke 10:25-37 that Jesus gives us the parable of the Good Samaritan. In response to the question ask by a lawyer of what he must do to inherit eternal life, Jesus asked the lawyer what the law said. (See Matthew. 22:23-40 and Mark 12:28-34 for the lawyer's questions throughout the Good Samaritan story.) The lawyer answered, "You shall love the Lord your God with all your heart, and with all you soul, and with all your strength, and with all your mind; and your neighbor as yourself." Jesus told the lawyer that he had answered right and to go do that and he will have eternal life.

The lawyer asked one more question; "And who is my neighbor?" And that is the lead-in for the story of the Good Samaritan. Luke 10:30-37 tells the story.

> A man was going down from Jerusalem to Jericho and he fell among robbers, who stripped him and beat him, and departed, leaving him half dead. Now by chance a priest was going down that road; and when he saw him, he passed by on the other side. So likewise, a Levite, when he came to the place and saw him, passed by on the other side. But a Samaritan, as he journeyed, came to where he was; and when he saw him, he had compassion, and went to him and bound up his wounds, pouring on oil and wine; then he set him on his beast and brought him to an inn, and took

care of him. And the next day he took out two denarii and gave them to the innkeeper, saying, 'Take care of him; and whatever more you spend, I will repay you when I come back.' Which of this three, do you think, proved neighbor to the man who fell among the robbers?" The lawyer said, "The one who showed mercy on him." And Jesus said to him, "Go and do likewise."

This is the most definite story Jesus tells to describe the senseless thinking that makes people enemies of each other because of where they live or what religion they follow. Jesus was a Jew who saw His primary purpose as telling and showing the Jewish people that, as God's chosen people, they could show the world how to be right with God and His creation. There are examples of Jesus helping Gentiles, but this is the only time that Jesus forced a Jew, the lawyer, to give an answer that went against the Jewish mindset.

Because of things that had happened in the distant past, the Samaritans and Jews had little use for each other. The Samaritans and Jews came from the same ancestors but could not overcome the past differences to be able to enjoy each other. Carry that thought back further. Regardless of which creation story you like, we all go back to the same starting point, regardless of where we live, the language we speak, our religious beliefs, or the color of our skin—we are all on this world together and God would like for us to get along a whole lot better than we are, and to be neighbors to each other.

Luke 10: 38-42 follows up the story of the good Samaritan with Jesus and his disciples stopping in the house of Mary, Martha, and Lazarus. Although Matthew and Mark do not mention this family it seems that these three were very important to Jesus as will become apparent in chapter 7 of the Gospel of John. The story explains that while Martha was busy preparing and serving food and drink Mary was at the feet of Jesus listening to Jesus's teaching. Martha complained to Jesus that Mary should be helping her serve their guests. Jesus answers Martha, telling her she is troubled about many things while she should allow Mary to continue what she is doing. This story goes directly back to the three temptations, that one's spiritual wellbeing is more important than providing for one's physical needs.

Luke also gives us the well know story of the Prodigal Son, (Luke 15:11-32). It tells of a man with two sons, the youngest of whom asks his father for his share of his inheritance and goes his own way. It did not take long for the son to spend his inheritance and end up working for a man feeding the man's pigs and going hunger. The son finally came to his senses and returned to his father asking to be hired as a servant. Instead, the father welcomed him back and rejoiced for his return. Now when the eldest son, who stayed at home and continued to work found out what was going on, he went to his father complaining about the injustice of rewarding his wayward brother. The father said that the eldest son will have all that is the father's and to be happy that his brother who was lost has be found.

The message is simple and clear. One can separate himself or herself from God and as the person's life becomes more difficult, God will not go looking for that person to bring him or her back but will rejoice when that person decides to return. God gave us the freedom and ability to make our own decisions and God would not interfere with us doing so; however, when we get lost and confused and decide to turn around and come back under God's blessing, God will welcome us with joy and gladness.

On the way to Jerusalem for Holy Week, Luke records Jesus telling the Parable of the Pounds in Luke 19:11-27. Summarizing the story, a nobleman went away to receive "kingly power" or a kingdom. Before leaving, he calls in ten servants and gave each one of them a pound. A pound was worth about twenty dollars. He tells the servants, "Trade with them until I return." The citizens hated him and did not want him to rule over them; however, he returned as the king. He called the servants in and asked them how they did. The first servant reported that he had made ten pounds with the pound he had received. The king was pleased and gave him ten cities to govern.

The second servant reported that he had made five pounds with the pound that he had received. The king was pleased and gave him five cities to govern. The third servant gave back to the king the one pound saying that he was afraid of the king because he was a severe man. The king was mad at the servant saying that if he knew that he was a severe man the least he could have done was to put it in a bank to earn interest. The king took away the one pound and gave it to the servant with ten pounds. Jesus does not tell us what happened to the remaining seven servants, but they may be the ones saying to the king, "Lord, he has ten pounds." He answers, "I tell you, that to everyone who has will more be given; but from him who has not, even what he has will be taken away ..."

If we think of the pound as God's blessing, then the two servants that expanded God's blessing to include others would continue to receive God's blessing to give to others. The servant that did nothing with God's blessing lost it and would suffer from losing it.

We will now go to chapter 7 in the Book of John.

Chapter 7

GOSPEL OF JOHN

INTRODUCTION

The fourth gospel explains the mystery of the person of Jesus. Like other men, He is yet unlike them, standing above them in unique, solitary grandeur. Whence this uniqueness? (Introduction to the Gospel of John, all biblical references in this chapter are RSV)

There may have been more contributors than the Apostle John to his gospel and some sections appear to have come from other writings. Some scholars think that a disciple of John's wrote much as Mark had written from his conversations with Peter.

There is a question of when the gospel was written. Since it does not reference the destruction of the Jewish temple in AD 70, some believe that it was written before then; however, many think it was written around AD 90. It appears that John was written late enough to be strongly influenced by the writings of Paul. Paul and John were alive at the same time and, since Paul knew the Jerusalem apostles and the early Gentile followers of Jesus, Paul and John surely knew of each other and, may have known each other and met and discussed Jesus' ministry.

While Paul wrote that Jesus was divine, but not the Messiah, it appears that early Christians quickly began describing Jesus as the Messiah, without knowing the Jewish interruption and understanding of the term. The writers of John, as well as the writers who added Jesus being the Messiah to other gospels, are part of the early Christians who tried to make sense of what they knew about Jesus. Since John was a Jew, it seems unlikely that he would have called Jesus *the Messiah* rather than *divine*; however, there is no doubt that the writers of John believed Jesus was more than a man with a special relationship with God.

Noss states,

> But it is in the fourth gospel that we find the divine character of Jesus most clearly presented. The writer sought to write a gospel that would find the living, subjectively experienced Lord of Paul in the historical objectively known Jesus of the Synoptic Gospels. Noss, page 629

The writers of the Gospel of John were interested in going beyond simply recording the events and associated activities during the ministry of Jesus. The three synoptic gospels had already done that. The Gospel of John, however, interprets the events and actions as Jesus was bringing God to the Jews and the Gentiles in simple terms. The Jewish belief that the Son of Man or the Messiah was going to come down from heaven accompanied by angels had to be overcome for the Jews to accept Jesus as being divine.

It is amazing that, with all the turmoil of the time and the powerful forces opposed to them, the early follows of Jesus were successful in retaining their identity and increasing their numbers.

In that light, the need for a strong statement of Jesus' divinity to open the Gospel of John becomes more apparent. The first three gospels did a good job of identifying and explaining events during Jesus' ministry and describing his message. What was lacking was a thorough explanation of "... the mystery of the person of Jesus."

The prologue of John (John 1:1-18) is a brilliant and compelling statement that Jesus came from God as a human witness to God's glory and returning to be with God. John described Jesus as coming directly from

God as His Son to get the Jews to change how they lived. The gospel opens with, "In the beginning was the Word, and the Word was with God, and the Word was God" (John 1:1). So, the point was that before Jesus was a man He was with God. This is the setting of the narration in the Gospel of John. The first eighteen verses of John set this tone of the book.

John and the three synoptic gospels show John the Baptist introducing Jesus to his followers and to the priests and Levites that would be questioning him. John the Baptist came out of the wilderness, "... preaching a baptism of repentance and forgiveness of sins" (Luke 3:3). His message was well received by the Jews, and He had gathered a large following as he traveled the land. While all four gospels have the message from heaven proclaiming that Jesus was the Son of God with whom God was well pleased, it was after Jesus was baptized by John the Baptist, that the Gospel of John goes farther in proclaiming Jesus the Messiah.

Stories Of Jesus' Ministry

From the baptism of Jesus, John has Jesus beginning His ministry by changing water into wine at a wedding party (see chapter 6). From the wedding feast at Cana in Galilee, John shows Jesus going to Jerusalem where He cleanses the temple of money changers, which is what the synoptic gospels describe Jesus doing during Holy week (John 2:13-25). Either John places the cleansing at that time to make his point of Jesus being the Messiah, or Jesus did this twice. Because cleansing the temple would be such an affront to the Jewish priests, it would have been highly unlikely that they would have allowed that to happen twice. The money changers were, after all, one of the Jewish priests' sources of money. It seems highly probable the Jesus cleansed the temple only once and that John put cleansing the temple at the beginning of Jesus' ministry to make the point that Jesus was the Messiah.

John followed up the temple cleansing with a meeting of Jesus and Nicodemus, a Pharisee and member of the Sanhedrin. The Sanhedrin was the court that made the final decision on claims and criminal charges. Some references say it was solely concerned with religious matters and other say it was concerned with religious and political matters.

In this meeting, which was held at night, undoubtedly because Nicodemus did not want to be seen talking to Jesus, Nicodemus was trying to make sense out of what Jesus was saying and doing. In John 3:1-21, Jesus made a very powerful statement of His message to the Jews. Jesus started out by saying that one must be born anew (or from above) to see the kingdom of God. Said another way, Jesus was saying that one's spirit must be united with God to be in the kingdom of God. Earthly control and power are not part of the union with God.

Nicodemus was having a hard time getting his mind around this idea. Jesus made the distinction, "That which is born of flesh is flesh and that which is born of the Spirit is spirit. The wind blows where it wills, and you hear the sound of it, but you do not know whence it came or whither it goes; so, it is with everyone who is born of the Spirit" (John 3:6-9). John went on with Jesus saying, "For God so loved the world that he gave his only Son, that whoever believes in him should not perish but have eternal life" (John 3:16). Jesus continues, "For God sent the Son into the world, not to condemn the world, but that the world might be saved through him" (John 3:17). The much-quoted John 3:16 was only half of that message. John 3:17 gives the reason for God sending Jesus into the world as being to save the world, not to condemn it. Combining 3:16 with 3:17 gives a much stronger message of Jesus' ministry.

Verses 3:1-21 are a clear and strong proclamation of Jesus' ministry. Jesus starts by telling Nicodemus that to have eternal life, or life in the likeness of God's, one must be renewed through the Spirit. Jesus likens the Spirit to the wind. The wind is something the Nicodemus could grasp just as it is for us today. It is a force of unknown source and destination that was continually with him. He could feel the wind but could not see it. He could only feel and see the results of its passing.

What other way can the Spirit be described? How can the Spirit be identified so that people will know when they are in His presence? Those who are in God's spirit will view themselves differently and the surrounding world will look and feel different. Those in the Spirit are living in God's blessing and know that they are living in the Spirit without having other people define or identify the Spirit. For all others, He is less definable than the wind, for there is nothing to define, only something to wish for, and know when you have Him.

John 3:13-15 is troubling. These verses start out with, "No one has ascended into heaven but he who descended from heaven, the Son of man." They continue with, "And as Moses lifted up the serpent in the wilderness, so must the Son of man be lifted up, that whoever believes in Him may have eternal life."

Using the definition of the words in John 3:13-15, we are faced with an inconsistency. The Bible tells that Moses, who was born of a woman, died, and was buried in the valley of Moab (Deut. 34:10-11). He ascended into heaven and came to Jesus during the transfiguration. Also, this implies that only through following Jesus can one participate in God's life, which leaves out all those who died before Jesus started is ministry. This passage greatly diminishes the meaning of Genesis 1:1-31, that we are all made in God's image. This may be a late addition by someone who was not familiar with the Old Testament nor was he or she with the thinking described in the footnote for Mark 2:10, which describes Jesus' willingness to allow the Jews to describe for themselves the meaning of Son of man. See the footnote for Mark 2:1-12 or chapter 6: JESUS' MINISTRY.

From His meeting with Nicodemus, Jesus and his disciples traveled in Judea and then went through Samaria, stopping at Jacob's well near the City of Samaria where He encountered a Samaritan woman. It was about noon and Jesus, wearied, had sat down at the well while His disciple went into the city to buy food. As the woman was drawing water, Jesus asked her to give Him a drink. The Jews and Samaritans did not get along so, the Samaritan women asked why a Jew was asking for a drink from a Samaritan. This began a conversation between the two.

The conversation began as a conversation between a Samaritan and a Jew; however, as the conversation goes from talking about drawing water to drink to talking about each other. As Jesus offered the woman a life with God, the woman was stuck on dealing with the practical issue of drawing water from the well. After Jesus identified that she was unmarried and had been with more than one man, as they continued to talk the woman became convinced that Jesus was a special person who was spiritually connected to God. When she said that she knew that a Messiah was coming and Jesus states He was the Messiah she ran to the city to proclaim that Jesus was something special (John 4:1-42).

Women would come to the well to draw water in groups early in the day rather than alone in the heat of the day. Because the woman was drawing water by herself at noon, Jesus surmised that she wasn't respected by the other women in the town, which meant that she had, at the very least, been sleeping around and probably was a prostitute.

The woman rushed into the city proclaiming that she had met a man who knew all that she had done, and she wondered if He was the Messiah. Even with her low standing in the city, what she said and the way she said it convinced the city people to go out to see and hear Jesus for themselves. They were so taken with Jesus that they asked Him to stay with them, which He did for two days. The Gospel of John tells us that this all came about because of the woman's testimony.

This entire meeting with the Samaritan woman and later the town's people, highlights Jesus' ability to be accepted by people and to quickly gain their respect and trust. It is interesting that the Bible does not record that Jesus healed anyone, just that He taught while in the town. Apparently, this is one of the few times when healing and miracles were not required. John also stated that after hearing Jesus speak the towns-people told the woman that their belief in Jesus no longer was because of her testimony. This seems to indicate that she would continue to make her trips to the well at noon by herself.

Jesus' interaction with the Samaritans seems to go against the purpose of Jesus' ministry of ministering to the "...lost sheep of the house of

Israel" (Matt. 10:6). I believe that rather than indicating a change in Jesus' ministry, it is an example of how the Jews should be friends to the Samaritans rather than continuing that animosity that stemmed from long past activities.

After the prologue in the first eighteen verses of the gospel proclaiming that Jesus came from God, John began describing the ministry of Jesus with the baptism of Jesus, as did the three synoptic gospels. The next three events in John are not in the synoptic gospels. The first event was turning water into wine at the wedding feast, the news of which surely was spread far and wide by word of mouth. See chapter 6 for the Cana wedding. His other two, his conversation with Nicodemus and the Samaritan woman were conversations held with these individuals apparently with no one else around.

John was either at the wedding feast or found out about turning water into wine from the disciples who were there or other people who were at the wedding feast. But how did John find out about Jesus' conversations with Nicodemus? Jesus could have told the disciples later, but that being so, why didn't the other disciples think this event was worthy of being included in the synoptic gospels? More compelling, why wasn't the conversation with the Samaritan woman included in the synoptic gospels? John and the other disciples were at the well and in the city with Jesus.

John reports these three events as major events that establish Jesus as the Messiah, but for some reason, these events were not worthy of even being mentioned in the synoptic gospels. Once again, we should assume there were events at the heart of these gospel stories, even if the stories were not included in all the gospels. If the other disciples knew about the events but deemed them to be much less important than John did, or they did not hear the events being described in the same way as John did, that could explain why John is the only one describing them.

After His conversation with the Samaritan woman, Jesus continued to Galilee and healed the son of an official in Capernaum (John 4:46-54).

From Capernaum Jesus next returns to Jerusalem. At the pool by the sheep gate where lame, sick, and paralyzed people waited for the water to ripple so the first person in the water would be healed, one man had been waiting for thirty-eight years to be healed but despaired because he had no one to put him in the water when it rippled.

Jesus told him to pick up his pallet and walk. And the man did just that. Jesus did this on the Sabbath which caused the Jewish leaders to want to arrest Him (John 5:1-18). This is one of the clear examples, if not the clearest example, that mankind can correct the frailties that possess it, and that Jesus had the ability to awaken this capability in the Jews. It also is another indication that Jesus was a strong commanding presence, not by His words alone, but also by His carriage. In the presence of Jesus, people wanted to believe in the caring God that Jesus talked about and demonstrated throughout His ministry.

At this point, John tells the stories of Jesus feeding the 5,000 and Jesus walking on water in similar fashion as the synoptic gospels (John 6:1-21). The next event recorded in John is the woman caught in adultery being brought to Jesus while He is teaching at the temple. According to the law the woman was to be stoned to death. The Pharisees and scribes asked Jesus what to do, hoping to catch Him breaking the law so they could arrest Him. Jesus's answer, which has often been repeated, was, "Let him who is without sin among you be the first to throw a stone at her." All leave, leaving Jesus alone with the woman and Jesus asks her, "Woman where are they? Has no one condemned you?" She said, "No one Lord." And he replied, "Neither do I condemn you: go and do not sin again." The footnote in the RSV, for this story (John 7:53-8:11) explains that this event is not in many ancient manuscripts; however, it appears to be an authentic incident in Jesus' ministry.

Although it was not originally part of the Gospel of John, it has been accepted as an integral part of the Gospel of John. It gives another example of Jesus' ability to defuse a tense situation with a simple statement or question back to the Pharisees and scribes for which they have no response. Jesus' understanding of the law and the frailties of the Jewish people gave him insights that apparently escaped everyone else.

John continued to stress that Jesus was the Messiah throughout his gospel. He has Jesus saying that he is the Son of God or the Messiah through his miracles and his teaching in between his miracles. Additional examples are in 2:16, "Destroy this temple (body) and in three days I will raise it up." In 5:24, "Truly, truly, I say to you, the hour is coming, and now is, when the dead will hear the voice of the Son of God, and those who hear will live." In 6:35, "I am the bread of life: he who comes to me shall not hunger, and he who believes in me shall not thirst." In 7:33, Jesus then said, "I shall be with you a little longer, and then I go to him who sent me; you will seek me and you will not find me; where I am you cannot come." And in 8:12, Jesus spoke to them, saying, "I am the light of the world; he who follows me will not walk in darkness, but will have the light of life."

The ultimate miracle was the raising of Lazarus from the dead (John.11:1-57). It stands as John's ultimate argument for Jesus being the Son of God who has come as the Messiah for the Jewish people.

Lazarus was the brother of Mary and Martha who lived in Bethany. All three were important to Jesus. John 11:5 tells us that, "Now Jesus loved Martha and her sister and Lazarus." I have heard several speculations over the years about how Mary and Martha fit into the life of Jesus during his ministry. The Bible tells us in John that Jesus knew and cared deeply for Mary, Martha, and Lazarus, and that they cared very much for Jesus, and believed in His ministry. It is intriguing that John described a loving relationship between Jesus and this family and Luke tells us that Jesus was familiar enough with the family that Jesus went directly to their house when He went to Bethany without further explanation. They evidently had been with Him enough to have faith in him and to accept his ministry on faith. Yet, Luke and John barely mention the three, and Mark and Matthew ignore them.

The threats from the Pharisees and priests against Jesus become so strong that Jesus had crossed the Jordan to be outside Judea and escape arrest when He received word that Lazarus was ill. John states that Jesus waited two days before crossing the Jordan back into Judea to go to Bethany.

When Jesus arrived in Bethany, He found that Lazarus had been dead for four days. This is significate because pious Jews believed that the souls stayed for three days and left on the fourth day. Martha and Mary were being consoled by neighbors and friends when Martha receives word of Jesus' arrival. Martha went to greet Jesus while Mary stayed with the friends and neighbors. After Martha greeted Jesus, she went back and told Mary, "The Teacher is here and is calling for you."

Mary came to Jesus, saying:

> "Lord, if you had been here my brother would not have died." When Jesus saw her weeping, and the Jews who came with her also weeping, he was deeply moved in spirit and troubled; and he said, "where have you laid him?" they said to him, "Lord come and see." Jesus wept." John 11:32-35.

The sadness of Mary and Martha, and their friends weighed on Jesus and caused the sadness to overcome Jesus. His feelings for this family ran deep. When they led Him to the tomb, Jesus asked that the stone blocking the entrance be moved. Martha told Jesus that Lazarus had been dead for four days and there would be an odor. Jesus proceeded to have the stone removed and after saying a prayer called for Lazarus to come out. Lazarus came out and Jesus commanded the people to, "unbind him and let him go" (John 11:45).

John describes the reaction to Lazarus being raised as being mixed with some believing in Jesus and others rushing off to the Pharisees to report on what had happened. When the Pharisees and priests got together the raising of Lazarus heighten their concern of allowing Jesus to continue His ministry. They expressed their concern that if everyone believed Jesus, the Romans would destroy the holy places. The high priest went further to say that the Jewish nation would be destroyed.

This presents a clear picture of what Jesus has been up against during His ministry. As Jesus' continued to be met with large crowds and He continued to deflect the Pharisees questions with His answers, they had become more determine to justify killing Jesus to save their wealth and status.

The synoptic gospels make no mention of Lazarus being raised from the dead. It is difficult to know how such an event as this could escape the noteworthy attention of the other disciples. What did the other disciples see and what really happened? Did the other disciples think that this was just another healing and saw no special significance to this one? The increased pressure to discredit and arrest Jesus and the continuing pressure on Jesus' followers after His death could have influenced the disciples to not report Lazarus' raising. There are other possibilities; however, there does not appear to be any good answer to this dilemma.

Jesus was staying out of sight. He with His disciples stayed in the small town of Ephraim near the wilderness. The Passover was coming up and the Pharisees and priests had told the people coming to Jerusalem to tell them if they saw Jesus. They want to find Him and arrest Him.

Six days before Passover, Jesus went to Bethany to visit the family of Mary, Martha, and Lazarus (John 12:1-8). This may be the same visit by Jesus to the family as is described in Luke 10:38-42. Luke does not indicate when Jesus visited their house. John's story is a little different from the story in Luke.

In the story in John, Mary brought out a pound of expensive ointment and anointed the feet of Jesus. Judas Iscariot said the ointment should be sold and the money given to the poor. Jesus said to let her alone and let her keep it for His burial. Jesus continued saying, "... the poor you will always have with you, but you do not always have me." This confirms that Jesus was aware of the plot against Him, which with all the questioning by the religious leaders and His flaunting the religious leaders should not have been surprising. Both Mark and Matthew describe a similar event happening during Holy Week in the house of Simon the leper. In this event, a woman pours ointment over Jesus' head, then Judas left this house to go to the chief priest to betray Jesus.

(Mark 14:1-11, Matthew 26:6-10, and Luke 7:37-39 has a woman washing Jesus' feet.)

The combination of the two stories in John, raising Lazarus and Jesus joining the family for a meal, confirms this family as having a special place in Jesus' heart. Again, the Bible leaves us with little information about the relationship Jesus had with this family. Sometime in his life, possibly during His ministry, Jesus met this family and formed a respectful and caring relationship that went well beyond other relationships described in the Bible. It was a loving relationship that exemplified living in the likeness of God.

Luke has many things happening between Jesus' visit in Bethany and Palm Sunday; however, John having Jesus' visit with Mary, Martha, and Lazarus, shortly before Palm Sunday, as the last major activity Jesus does before going into Jerusalem. So, the visits that Luke and John describe may not be the same; however, both give preference to Mary over Martha. They both in their own way identify Jesus as the Son of God. Because of the similarity of the message in these two stories I think the stories are two versions of the same event.

Now is the time for Holy Week.

Chapter 8

HOLY WEEK

PASSOVER

The Feast of the Passover was the reason Jesus was going to Jerusalem. The importance of Passover to the Jews cannot be overstated. The Passover is celebrated every year to commemorate the night when the Egyptian first-born were killed, and the Israelite first-born saved, as the last plague brought on the Egyptians by God to convince the Pharaoh to release the Jewish people from their servitude, so Moses could lead them out of Egypt.

Jesus was aware that the religious leaders were plotting against Him because His teaching conflicted with their use of Judaism. However, it would not be true to His own ministry if He did not celebrate Passover. He was committed to doing as much as He could in the short time remaining. Jesus knew that by entering Jerusalem it was highly likely that Jewish leadership would attest him. Jesus' need to celebrating Passover was of greater importance than the need to preserve His life.

PALM SUNDAY

The story of Jesus entering Jerusalem on Palm Sunday is told in Mark 11:1-11, Matthew 21:1-9, Luke 19:28-38, and John 12:12-19. Summarizing the versions, when Jesus drew near to Bethany, at the

Mount of Olives, He told two of His disciples to go to a small unnamed village to get a donkey colt for Jesus to ride into Jerusalem, which they did. They threw garments on the colt and Jesus sat on it. As Jesus entered Jerusalem, a crowd that had gathered laid garments and tree branches on the road in front of Him crying "Hosanna in the highest." Matthew has all the city asking who He is and the crowd saying, "This is the prophet Jesus from Nazareth of Galilee." John has the crowd declaring that Jesus is the King of Zion.

As a practical matter, the crowd that welcomed Jesus into Jerusalem was made up of the people, mainly from Galilee, who had followed Jesus into Jerusalem and the people in Jerusalem who had heard Jesus and been impressed with his teaching. Thousands of people were in Jerusalem for the Passover, from Judea, Israel, and many other areas of the known world, with the group following Jesus being a small part of this mass of humanity. As was the case throughout Jesus' three-year ministry, he was known by the small number of people from the regions He had passing through. His presence in Jerusalem was not known very much outside this small group of His followers and the Jewish leaders who were after Him. No matter how large the crowd was that welcomed Jesus into Jerusalem, it was just one part of the total crowd in Jerusalem for the Passover.

The events surrounding Jesus' entering Jerusalem are reported differently in each gospel. Matthew has Jesus going from entering Jerusalem to the temple and throwing out the money changers and healing the sick and teaching before going back the Bethany for the night (with Mary, Martha, and Lazarus?). When He came back to Jerusalem in the morning, he encountered the fig tree that bore no fruit (Matt. 21:12-19). Mark has Jesus entering Jerusalem and looking around and returning to Bethany for the night. The following morning, He sees the fig tree that has no fruit on the way into Jerusalem, and after cursing the fig tree, He goes to the area around the temple to chase out the money lenders and then began teaching (Mark 11:12-17). Luke simply has Him going to the temple and chasing out the money changers (Luke 19:45). John is silent on what happens after He enters on the donkey

(John 12:12-13). John had Jesus clearing out the moneychangers earlier in His ministry.

The significance of Jesus' entrance needs to be recognized more than it is. Some Jews were looking for the Messiah that was to come down from the heavens on a cloud with angels around Him to collect the righteous to live in Gods' blessing together. Other Jews were looking for a Savior to ride in on a white horse with a sword in hand to rescue them from their misery. Instead, Jesus came to them riding a donkey to symbolize His humanity and humility. Apparently, the joy of the Jews who welcomed Him was not diminished by Jesus' entrance.

The story of the fig tree in Mark 11:12-14 is simple and straightforward. Jesus was hungry, saw the fig tree, and went to get some figs, but there were none. Jesus said to the tree," May no one ever eat fruit from you again." Matthew repeats this story and both Mark and Matthew add that the fig tree withered, Matthew at once, Mark by the next morning. Both Mark and Matthew continue with Jesus saying then if you have faith and never doubt you can move mountains (Mark 11:20-25, Matt. 21:18-22). The footnote to Mark and Matthew both state that it was not the time for the tree to have figs.

Luke has a different story. In Luke 13:6-9, Luke has Jesus telling a story about the owner of a fig tree wanting to cut it down because it hadn't had any figs for three years, but his employee told the owner that he would dress the roots with manure and if it doesn't have figs next year, he will cut it down.

These stories are perplexing, to say the least. Obviously, what Peter told Mark was not good enough for Luke and John ignored the whole event. So, what does one make of this story? The Gospel of Mark, being the first gospel to be written and coming from Mark's conversations with Peter, has the best chance of being the most accurate.

Jesus' anger at a tree could have been a way of His expressing anger at His situation. He had little to show for his last three years teaching about the Covenant between Abraham and God and God's love for

Jewish people. The Jewish people of Galilee, who constituted his largest following and who had seen and heard His ministry, and benefited most from His ministry, were still waiting for Him to change their daily existence. What good is Jesus' ministry if it could not put more food on the table or relieve them of the Jewish religious and Roman tax burdens?

Jesus had described a new existence where one lives humbly with God. Jesus demonstrated this with His lifestyle and His teachings, and with the healings and miracles that happened in His presence, which He worried were distracting from His teachings. His life and ministry set the example of living in God's grace instead of living without God's grace in their world of oppression and poverty. He had also shown that living in God's grace was available to all people when He sent the twelve disciples out on their own to teach and heal, in which they were successful.

Jesus had not been able to convince the Jews that He was not talking about attaching His teachings to their existing lives, which would be akin to putting new wine in an old wine skin or sewing a new patch on old cloth. Even with these everyday examples the Jews could not make the changes necessary for them to experience new life. Instead, the Jews kept the old wine skin that they liked having even though it no longer served a useful purpose, and the old cloth with a hole in it rather than getting a new cloth that would better meet their needs. Jesus' frustration came from, no matter how He stated the failure of their lives, they could not bring themselves to change their lives to a much better life living in the blessing of God.

Even with the high regard the disciples and common people had for Jesus, He still could not convince them to take the next step from being on their own to living humbly with God.

EARLY HOLY WEEK

For three years, Jesus had thumbed His nose at the Jewish leaders. So far, He had avoided being arrested but He knew that time was against Him. The Pharisees and scribes that had been following Him continuously tried, unsuccessfully, to establish a reason to arrest Him. they continued to hope their quest would eventually be successful. He had predicted His arrest and death at least three times in the synoptic gospels and at least once in John. There was still time for Him to escape back to Galilee and continue His ministry in the hills and back county of Israel. If He went to the hill and back country, He would be harder to catch, and the Jewish leaders desire to catch Him would decrease; however, that would not demonstrate His trust in God.

His whole message had been that His spiritual bond with God was stronger than anything created by man. The only option left for Jesus to convince the disciples to take His message to heart was to show that His belief in God was so strong and complete that He would continue living in His spiritual connection with God, even after His death. The finality of His ending, while there were still many Jews who had heard Him, but would not commit to living in God's guidance, had to be a sad and troubling realization for Him.

The Pharisees and scribes continued to question His authority as they had throughout His three-year ministry; however, it seems that they were stepping up their questioning and felt like *this time* they must find a reason to arrest Him.

Mark 11:27-33 describes an exchange between Jesus and the chief priests, scribes, and elders. The Pharisees were not identified as being involved this time. Jesus was asked, "By what authority are you doing these things, or who gave you this authority to do them?" He said that He would ask them a question and if they answered it, He would answer their question. So, Jesus asked, "Was the baptism by John from heaven or from men?" This caused them to argue among themselves for if we say, 'From heaven,' He will say, 'Why did you not believe him?' But shall we say, 'From men,' we are afraid of the multitude; for all hold that John was a prophet.' The chief priest, scribes and elder said, "We do not know." And Jesus said, "Neither will I tell you by what authority I do these things" (Matt. 21:23-27, Luke 20:1-8).

Once again, Jesus escapes the trap set by the Jewish leaders. Of all the wandering ministers throughout Galilee and Judea, why did Jesus create such a problem for the Jewish leaders? First, Jesus treated them with disdain by claiming that He was the new law; and therefore, He was not following their rules. Second, Jesus was reported to have produced miracles, confirmed by the Pharisees and scribes that followed Him, and He had a large following wherever He went. Third, they could not have an uneducated carpenter freely running around telling the people that the current system, their system, did not meet what God intended for the Jews. And fourth, and maybe the most troubling reason was that they feared that Jesus was a rebel who was building an army as He wandered through Galilee and Judea. Having another rebellion was to be prevented at all costs.

For the last three years, their efforts to arrest Him and stop His foolishness had failed. They were desperate enough to confront Jesus in front of a large crowd that could turn on them, and most certainly would quickly spread the news about the results of the confrontation. His failure to give them a reason to arrest him meant that they were going to have to come up with another plan. So, while their attempts to stop Him continued to fail they simply could not allow Him to continue.

In the meantime, Jesus continued to teach with parables such as the parable of the vineyard. This is the story of a man who planted a vineyard and leased it out to some tenants. When he sent a servant to collect some of the fruit of the vineyard, the tenants beat the servant and send him back empty-handed. After sending several servants who were either beaten or killed, he sent his beloved son. The tenants reasoned that if they kill him, they will inherit the vineyard, so they killed him. The owner destroyed the tenants and gave the vineyard to others (Mark 12:1-12, Matt. 21:33-46, Luke 20:9-19).

For those who were tuned into what Jesus was saying, this parable would have been upsetting, particularly after the events of the next few days. This parable surely describes God's, the vineyard owner, reaction to the death of Jesus, the beloved Son. Jesus had foretold His death before with no apparent reaction from His disciples. He knew that He was not going to get away with upsetting the Jewish leaders much longer and He was aware of what happens to people who upset the Jewish leaders. After torture was death. I think that He was hoping that at least one of His disciples would continue His teaching after his death, but none were responding as He had hoped.

The Jewish leaders had not given up but sent some Pharisees and Herodians to test Him again. They started out by complimenting Him by saying that He "...truly teach the way of God." Then, thinking that they had set Him up they asked, "Is it lawful to pay taxes to Caesar, or not?" Jesus' answer, "Render to Caesar the things that are Caesar's and to God the things that are God's" was simple and profound. (See Mark 12:13-17 Also see Matthew 22:15-22 and Luke 20:20-26.) He defeated them once again with a simple, easily understood statement that gave them nothing to do be walk away again.

While Jesus' response silenced the Pharisees, it may have done more damage than the Pharisees recognized. Jesus' answer was troubling to his disciples and followers. Paying taxes to Caesar was a heavy burden that they simply could not get around. The taxes kept the Jewish people poverty-stricken. It was one of the burdens they were looking for Jesus to remove from their lives. Instead, Jesus seemed to support paying the taxes. What good was eternal life if they still had to pay taxes to Caesar?

This probably was the last straw for many of the followers of Jesus and they gave up on Him. For some time, there had been growing dissatisfaction with things. He had seemingly promised a better life, but things had pretty must stayed the same over the last three years. Although Jesus claimed there was a better way, and that He had God's blessing, they did not see that anything was better and after all, He was just a carpenter's son.

It is curious that Jewish Leadership did not pick up on the reaction of Jesus' disciples and followers to His answer about giving Caesar his taxes. This could also have been what convinced Judas that Jesus was not going to be the one to lead the next Zealot revolt. One line of thought on Judas is that he believed that Jesus would eventually realize that peaceful coexistence with the Romans was not working and then Jesus would change into the Messiah riding to the rescue as the Jewish people envisioned.

The followers of Jesus continued to want Jesus to change their world. They did not understand that Jesus was not about changing the world but about them changing themselves. Even with Jesus saying, "Your faith has made you well," when someone was healed, they could not see the part they needed to play in making their lives better. It was not that the Jewish leadership would change their ways and the Romans would disappear, but rather having a spiritual connection to God would give them a better perspective of the world around them. It did not occur to them the life the carpenter's son was living the better way to live.

Jesus was trying to get the Jews to forget trying to change the Romans and Jewish leaders. Instead, He wanted them to change themselves *from within*. Rather than continuing to give the Romans and Jewish leaders power over their lives, He wanted them to reclaim their right to decide how they lived and what was important. The taxes were not going away. Each Jew had the choice of accepting the reality of the taxes but, they did not have to allow the taxes to govern how they lived. Instead, live in God's blessing and enjoy the beauty of all of God's gifts.

During Holy Week, all four gospels describe one instance after another of Jesus trying to get the disciples to recognize the difference between living as they were and the benefits and wonders of living humbly with God, as Jesus was. The successful experience they'd had of healing and teaching, when He sent them out on their own, was not enough to convince them that they could continue the work they had done on their own, thereby continue and expanding Jesus' ministry.

There is a paradox. On one hand, Jesus' followers are discouraged and falling away. On the other hand, the Jewish leadership was still afraid that there may be some truth to his ministry. He could upset their lifestyle either by convincing the Jews that the Jewish leadership was not needed to have a good relationship with God, or his calling into question the Jewish religious laws could start a revolt, which would finish the world as they knew it. Either way, He had to be eliminated.

Jesus was not central to the activities of the Jews who came to Jerusalem from their surrounding home countries for the Passover. Even when He was crucified, it was a minor part of that day's overall activity. The Roman and Jewish leaders' fear that their treatment of Jesus could start another revolt, caused them to deal with Jesus as quickly and quietly as they could. For the Roman and Jewish leaders, the significance of Jesus' death was that it eliminated potential serious problems, not the least of which was, for the Jewish leaders, the serious threat it posed to their lifestyle. This was much different than what is described in the Bible and much different than the significance of Jesus' death has today.

THE LAST SUPPER

The Last Supper started Jesus down the road to His crucifixion. Everything was moving in that direction. Judas had collected his thirty pieces of silver and agreed to lead the high priest's men to Jesus.

The story of the Last Supper is similar in the synoptic gospels (Matt. 26:17-29, Mark 14:12-16, Luke 22:7-13). They all have Jesus proclaiming that one disciple, Judas, had betrayed Him and that they would all scatter when He is captured. Peter claims that he will be steadfast, however; Jesus said, "I tell you, Peter, the cock will not crow this day, until you three times deny that you know me." Mark has Jesus saying that Peter will deny Him three times before the cock crows twice (Mark 14:30).

> During the meal, He took bread and broke it and gave it to
> them, saying, "Take; this is my body." And then he took a

cup blessed it and gave it to them, saying, "This is my blood of the (new) covenant, which is poured out for many. The meal closely follows. Matthew 26:26-28

He took bread, and blessed it, and gave it to them, and said, "Take; this is my body." And he took a cup, and when he had given thanks he gave it to them, and they all drank of it. And he said to them, "this is my blood of the covenant, which is poured out for many." Mark 14: 22-24

The story of the Last Supper in John 13:1-38 includes the betrayal by Judas and Peter's denial, but its description of other activities during the meal is different from the synoptic gospels. It does not include passing the bread and cup found in the synoptic gospel, but it does describe Jesus washing the feet of the disciples, much to Peter's discomfort. Jesus explains the importance of foot washing. If He, as their Lord and Teacher, washed their feet, they should wash one another's feet, for as their teacher He is also their servant.

Foot washing in that time was more than a symbolic gesture. The roads and paths were dirt and either muddy or dusty. A person entering a house would bring in what was on his or her feet. The foot washing then was a welcoming of the guest as well as keeping the house free of the dirt on the feet of the guests. Today, farmers often take off their boots or shoes they wore in the barn or field before entering the house.

All four gospels have Jesus clearly declaring that His time on earth was coming to an end. John, however, has Jesus telling the disciple several things between the last supper and His going to the garden of Gethsemane that are not in the synoptic gospels (John 13:1-31, 14:1-17:26).

Leave it to Thomas in John 14:5 to plainly state the problem the disciples were having. Thomas said to Jesus, "Lord we do not know where you are going; how can we know the way?" Jesus responded with these words:

I am the way, and the truth, and the life; no one comes to
the Father, but by me. If you had known me, you would
have known my Father also; henceforth you know him
and have seen him." Philip said to him, "Lord, show us
the Father, and we shall be satisfied." Jesus said to him,
"Have I been with you so long, and yet you do not know
me, Philip? Do you not believe That I am in the Father and
the Father in me? John 14:6-10a

This is a clear and simple summary of Jesus' three-year ministry. His
lifestyle and ministry were a demonstration of the Father in heaven.
Jesus was living in the likeness of God. It is not a statement of the Father
looking like Jesus, but rather a statement of the two-way spiritual connection between God and Jesus.

Jesus describes Himself as being one who has dedicated His life to living
in harmony with God. Jesus and God were spiritually connected and
at one with each other. Jesus was atoned with God in all that He had
done and will do. All things that were a top priority before He began
His ministry had become a second or lesser priority to Jesus as He har-
monized His life spiritually with God.

This short exchange between Jesus and the disciples clearly identified the failure of the disciples to recognize the spiritual connection
Jesus had with God. No matter what Jesus said, or what He did, they
remained oblivious to the possibility that they too could have a similar connection with God. Jesus' core message that He taught, demonstrated, and lived was lost to the disciples until well past Jesus' death.

The evil ones—think Jewish leadership—did not want the people
around who were living with a direct spiritual connection with the
Father. Those who had the connection with the Father would provide
the example of the difference *between living with the Father* and *living
under the Jewish religious leadership with its rules and taxes.* Jesus surely
hoped and prayed that when the poor Jewish people no longer had
His living presence in their midst, they would remember how He had
lived, what He said, how He related with the Father, and how His

relationship with the Father enabled Him to help people see that they too could live in the presence of God.

The lack of understanding of this message by the Jewish people was ever-present. So, once again Jesus was confronted with the inability of the disciples to allow their spiritual being to supersede their practical earthly being. They had not been able to reconnect to their spiritual being that they had when Jesus sent them out and they were so successful in their healing and teaching. Without the disciples making the spiritual connection with the Father, there was little hope that the Jewish people could make the spiritual connection.

Jesus had set the example of living in God's promise, which they had not been able to grasp. Jesus proclaims the following:

> This is my commandment, that you love one another as I have loved you. Greater love has no man than this, that a man lay down his life for his friends. You are my friends if you do what I command you. No longer do I call you servants, for the servant does not know what his master is doing; but I have called you friends, for all that I have heard from my Father I have made known to you. John 15:12-15

Once again, being friends with God comes up. This is a much clearer description of what being a friend of God means. The conversion between God and Abraham about what to do with Sodom and Gomorrah was two friends talking, with God being patient and respectful and Abraham reverence and persistent. Jesus spoke of friendship being the total commitment of a friend to a friend and sharing between friends from the soul, holding back nothing. I have always marveled at Abraham's friendship with God and whether anyone could have such a friendship with God. Jesus stated that we can have such a friendship with God and defines what it would look like by His life. The relationship that God offers each one of us centers on love and acceptance as we are, which is expressed as God's freely given grace.

All four gospels have Jesus going to the Garden of Gethsemane where Judas and his group of people go to arrest him. In John 17:1-26, prior to going to Gethsemane, Jesus prays the High Priestly Prayer, which starts out with him glorifying God and stating that He had done God's work and recognizing that His time had come. He then prays for His disciples, that after He is gone, they will remain at one with the Father as He had been at one with the Father. He also prays that the disciples can lead the world to know the Father as He has known the Father.

ARREST AND CRUCIFIXION

Jesus went to the garden, a place, called Gethsemane and told the disciples to watch while He went off away from them to pray. After praying, He can back to where the disciples were and found them to be asleep. He was chastising them when Judas came with people from the chief priest, scribes, and elders to arrest Jesus. Peter cut off the ear of a high priest's slave. Jesus rebukes Peter and heals the slave's ear. Knowing full well that He is going to a pain filled death Jesus still rebuked Peter's use of force to protect Him.

Some say that He knew there were too many soldiers to fight, but if that was all it was, then there was no need to repair the damage Peter had inflicted. Jesus' simple act of kindness came from His belief in God's love and grace. Jesus' relationship with God did not include hurting others or fighting or use of force to win. Either His message of God's love and grace would, on its own, withstand the chaos and the inhumanity that He would endure, or it is of no use, regardless of any value it has given.

John records Jesus being led away to Annas, the father-in law of Caiaphas, the high priest, and then to Caiaphas for a trial. The synoptic gospels have Jesus going directly to Caiaphas for trial. The trial was short and just a formality. Caiaphas asked Jesus, "Are you the Christ the Son of the Blessed?" and Jesus said, "I am and you will see the Son of man sitting at the right hand of Power and coming with the clouds of heaven." That was all it took for him to be condemned to death.

While the trial was going on, Peter was standing outside the area where the trial was being held when a woman recognized him as a disciple. Peter denied being a disciple and was again recognized as a disciple, which he denied a second time. As Peter was leaving the area, the crowd recognized him again and for the third time, he denied being a disciple and, "Immediately the cock crows the second time" (Mark 14.66-72, Matt. 26:69-75, Luke 22:57-62, John 18:17-27).

While there are some differences in the four gospels' stories of the events from the time Jesus was arrested to when He was brought before Pilate and sentenced to be crucified, and regardless of which story is followed, Jesus received terrible treatment by the guards, as was the normal procedure for people who were in a Roman prison and condemned to death. The violent treatment of prisoners under Roman rule is extremely difficult for us to comprehend today. The whipping with whips that tore His skin and muscle to the bone and other rough handling of the prisoners was calculated to inflict the maximum pain without killing the prisoner before the prisoner died. Crucifixions were but one of several cruel methods available to the Romans for killing people. Jesus was not the first nor the last to die by crucifixion.

The courage Jesus showed in His acceptance of being arrested is difficult to fathom without including His understanding of the blessing God had given Him. The strength of Jesus' total commitment to God cannot be fully understood without a good appreciation of the terrible and painful treatment and death that Jesus was willing to endure, which the Bible does not describe very well. Unfortunately, the Bible, as written today, with Jesus saying that His time has come and He will die and be raised in three days, does not adequately convey the totally inhuman treatment He would endure before He died.

There are possible reasons for the description in the Bible of His terrible treatment and death being so brief and shallow. Remember that the Bible was not written for the twenty-first century. It could be that treatment of people condemned to die was so well known that the gospel writers did not feel the need for a more detailed explanation. Everyone so condemned were treated that way so why would anyone think Jesus would be treatment differently? Remember that at the time of His death only a few, if any, people thought He was at one with God, and it was only after the word was out that He had raised from the dead did the idea that He was divine begin to gain some traction, with strong help from Paul. The point is that there was little to set Him apart from other people who were crucified or otherwise killed by the Romans.

A second reason for the description of the treatment of Jesus being so brief is that the original copies of the four gospels did cover His treatment more completely, and in more detail, but through the many translations of the copies, the description became what it is today. As the emphasis became more on Jesus being the Son of God than that He suffered the same treatment of condemned men of his day did not have a strong impact.

The Jewish leaders could not kill Jesus, but the Romans could. So, after Jesus had been condemned by the Jewish religious leaders, they took Him to Pilate so he could sentence Jesus to death. Pilate did not sound convinced that Jesus should die, but the Jewish leaders kept pushing Pilate to condemn Jesus.

There was a custom that a prisoner would be released each year at the Passover and Pilate approached the crowd and asked them whether he should release Jesus, or a prisoner called Barabbas. With the Jewish leaders, who were standing in the front of the crowd, yelling for Jesus to be crucified and Barabbas released, the crowd went along. So, Jesus was condemned to a painful death.

We have no information on the size of the crowd, whether it was 50 people or 500 people. Whatever the size, in all probability, only a small proportion of the crowd were followers of Jesus, simply because the followers of Jesus were a small portion of the crowd in Jerusalem for Passover. Also, with the arrest of Jesus, many of His followers may have started returning home. So, when the Jewish leaders, the ones who had the power to make their lives worse than they already were, were yelling for Pilate to crucify Jesus, the majority had no reason to say any different.

The four gospels tell the story of the crucifixion of Jesus with some variations between the gospels; however, they all convey some sense of the pain and suffering Jesus endured during His crucifixion. On top of all that had been done to Him, nails were driving through His hands and feet to fasten Him to the cross and then the cross is dropped, not carefully lowered, into a hole to hold it up. It is hard to tell how long He was on the cross; however, the synoptic gospels make it three hours. They also have the curtain in the temple tearing in two upon Jesus' death. In John 19:30, John has Jesus saying, "It is finished" as He bowed His head and His spirit left. Luke 23:34 states that Jesus said, "Father, forgive them; for they know not what they do." And then in Luke 23:46, Jesus says, "Father, into thy hands I comment my spirit." Mark and Matthew both have Jesus saying, "My God, my God, why hast thou forsaken me?"

See John 18:1-19:42, Matthew 26:47-27:61, Mark 14:43-15:47 and Jude 22:47-23:56 for the stories of Jesus arrest, trial, crucifixion, and burial.

Pilate gave Joseph of Arimathea the body of Jesus, who took the body and bound it in linen cloths and laid Him in a new tomb that had not been used by anyone. From this point each gospel tells the story from a different perspective that leads into different stories of Jesus' appearances to his followers and disciples.

JESUS RISES FROM THE TOMB

All four gospels have Mary Magdalene going to the tomb early the day after the Sabbath to anoint Jesus' body. Matthew includes the other Mary; Mark includes Mary, mother of James, Jesus' brother, and Salome; Luke includes Joanna and Mary the mother of James and other women, and John has Mary Magdalene going by herself and seeing the tomb empty. She ran to get Peter who then brought other disciples who looked and then went home. Matthew and Mark have one angel saying that Jesus has risen and to tell Peter and the disciples that He is going to Galilee ahead of them. Luke and John have two angels at the tomb.

Mark's gospel ends with Mark 16:9. The angel said that Jesus had risen and that, "He is going before you to Galilee; and there you will see Him, as he told you." They fled out of the tomb, afraid. Other texts add to Mark 16:9-20 that describe events after Jesus had risen, which are like those in Luke.

Matthew shows Jesus meeting the eleven disciples in Galilee with Jesus instructing them. Them. "Go therefore and make disciples of all nations, baptizing them in the name of the Father and of the Son and of the Holy Spirit, teaching them to observe all that I have commanded you; and lo, I am with you always, to the close of the age (Matt. 28: 19-20). These verses are late additions. The main problem is that the trinity did not show up until the second century, after Jesus' death.

Luke tells a story of two men walking toward Emmaus, talking about the events of the past couple of days, when Jesus, who they did not recognize, joined them, and joined their conversation. As they approached the village with darkness approaching, the two asked Jesus to stay with them. He did remain long enough to bless and break bread, which finally showed them who He was. The two men immediately returned to Jerusalem, and finding the eleven, described their experience with Jesus, who appeared in the group. Jesus showed the group His hands and feet and ate some food. He then taught them and gave them the promise of His Father, and led them to Bethany, blessing them then parting from them. They went back to Jerusalem full of joy and continually blessed God.

John recorded events of the disciples, except for Thomas, in a room with a closed door, fearful of the Jewish leadership when Jesus appeared. The disciples were glad to see Jesus and Jesus greet them with, "Peace be with you," and breathed on them, and said, "Receive the Holy Spirit. If you forgive the sins of any, they are forgiven: if you retain the sins of any, they are retained." When the disciples told Thomas, he did not believe them, but eight days later the disciples, *with Thomas*, were in the house behind closed doors when Jesus appeared again. Jesus asked Thomas to see His hands and touch his side. Thomas exclaimed, "My Lord and my God!" After this, John described events involving Peter and some of the disciples when they went fishing and Jesus appears. John closes by saying that Jesus did many things that were not recorded and, if everything that Jesus did was recorded, the world could not contain all the books. (Compiled from Matthew 28:1-20 and Mark 16:1-8 with Mark 16:9-20 added from other texts, additionally Luke 20:1-26 and John 20:1 to 21-25 for the return of Jesus after His crucifixion.)

Now What?

The problems before the disciples were many. First, they were at a loss as to how to make sense out of what had gone on over the past several days and even their last three years wandering the countryside. They had followed a man whose presence enabled the sick to be healed and who described a totally different lifestyle. There was no doubt that Jesus had been a very special person, so how could they possibly continue what Jesus had started? How could they duplicate and build upon the experiences they'd had over the last three years?

Matthew 28:18-20 tells how the disciples had lost their leader, the center of their world. He'd had a way about Him, had people believing His message of eternal life, but also had left them without any information on how to effectively use the authority He had given to them.

In addition to that was the continued hostility of the Jewish leaders. The disciples simply were in no condition to take on the Jewish religious leadership. As strong as Jesus was, He could not overcome the leadership of the Jewish religion. So, if He could not do that, what chance did they have? Thus, the week that began with acclamation and joy ended in disillusionment and despair.

While all that the disciples and the followers of Jesus saw and heard was great, it was only after Jesus' death that the apostles and some of the Jews began to emulate Jesus in how they lived and what they did. His impact on these followers was so great that they continued His ministry, which unfortunately became a worldwide religion.

Jesus' thirty-year-life is worth celebrating, not because Paul decided His was divine, but because of Jesus' insight into the value of having a personal spiritual relationship with God and His demonstration of what a God-centered life could look like. Jesus went from one town to the next, skillfully preaching about a new way of relating to God without upsetting the Judaism leaders enough to be arrested. That by itself was an amazing feat. The value of Jesus' three-year ministry is beyond any other three-year period of mankind's existence.

Chapter 9

CHRISTIANITY'S DEVELOPMENT

INTRODUCTION

S oon after the death of Jesus, the story about the relationship between God and mankind as told in Geneses 1:1-31, as demonstrated by Jesus living in a spiritual relationship with God was relegated to minor importance by the followers of Jesus, and, replaced by Jesus' resurrection which gave them their belief in immortally through their living at one with God.

Jesus' belief in the personal relationship the Jews and Gentiles could have with God may have come from His understanding of the relationship between Abraham and God. That was a relationship based on God choosing Abraham and Abraham choosing God and their mutual trust and friendship, and Abraham's reverence for God. These choices were confirmed in the Covenant between God and Abraham, and were accepted by Abraham's tribe, the Hebrews. God agreed to be with the Hebrews for all time and make their descendants a great nation if the Hebrews would have God as their one and only God.

While Jesus welcomed Gentiles in His ministry, the Gentiles' lack of understanding of the background of Jesus' ministry, especially His answers to the Pharisees and scribes, limited their ability to fully appreciate the value of Jesus' ministry. This certainly could have been a contributing reason for the Gentiles not embracing Jesus' ministry as being the most valuable part of His life.

STARTING ANEW

The eleven despondent and disheartened disciples were amazed and glad three days after His crucifixion when Jesus had risen. Even Thomas came around to believing that it was Jesus. Unfortunately, their joy was short-lived for Jesus left, this time for good, with the instructions to, "Go therefore and make disciples of all nations" (Matt. 28:19). So, once again they were left alone to fend for themselves. All they had to guide them was their memories and recollections of Jesus' teachings, healings, and His discussions with them.

So why did Jesus' disciples, now called apostles, and their small core group of followers stick around and continue to keep the Jewish leaders worried? What was it about Jesus that earned His memory such loyalty?

He awakened Jews to the healing power that comes with having a spiritual connection with God. He lived and demonstrated God's unconditional love and forgiveness. He did not tell them what to be or how to believe, but rather His call for them to repent was a simple statement of how they could improve their lives by changing their priorities and live in the fullness of God's blessing. Jesus' life and teachings, and the healings that happened in His presence described and demonstrated what living in God's blessing could be. He talked *with them* rather than *to them* in language they understood. He gave them a look at how life could be living spiritually connected to God. Even though they still did not know how to live as Jesus did, they believed in Jesus' ministry enough to stay with it.

This was the inauspicious beginning for the apostles, in their new relationship with God, as they slowly worked to get their act together, as described in the "The Acts of the Apostles." The Acts of the Apostles was written by Luke, apparently as a continuation of the Gospel of Luke. Luke wrote both books as reports to an official.

The starting point for the apostles, and the small group of Jews who believed in Jesus' ministry, was accepting that the one person who'd kept them together was gone, not to return. They were at wit's end and in deep despair with no place to turn for assistance and guidance. The shock of Jesus' tragic death had overwhelmed them.

No matter how they looked at their situation it was difficult for them to see how to make sense out of the loss of their leader and their source of inspiration for the past three years. The one person who they'd believed was living in the blessing of God, had been cruelly taken away from them because he was showing that God cared for each one of them, regardless of their station in life or what other people thought of them.

With the death of Jesus, many of his followers reverted to their lives before they heard Jesus or dispersed into towns and areas outside Jewish lands. However, a small group of Jewish followers of Jesus remained.

The continued existence of the apostles and followers of Jesus was uncertain and filled with many struggles and much conflict. It is extremely hard for anyone today to imagine the difficulty these people had in knowing what to believe and faithfully follow. Simply escaping the wrath of the Roman masters, finding enough to eat, and escaping imprisonment for failure to faithfully follow the dictates of the Jewish religion was difficult enough, without trying to make sense out of Jesus' ministry. The feeling of loss and despair had to be overwhelming.

Sometime after Jesus' death, the apostles went back to Jerusalem, with Mary, mother of Jesus, His brothers, and some women to an upper room, which seems to have been their meeting place in Jerusalem. As they struggled to make sense out the events of the past few weeks, they took time to select a replacement for Judas, which they did by lots. The twelfth apostle was Matthias (Acts. 1:12-26). All biblical references are to the RSV Bible. If nothing else, this small act showed that with even their bleak future, they still believed in Jesus and His ministry. They were in this room on the day of Pentecost.

PENTECOST

Pentecost is a Harvest Festival that also marks the day that the Law was given on Mt. Sinai. It is fifty days after Passover, or about seven weeks after Jesus' crucifixion. Because of it being Pentecost there were many people in Jerusalem from Palestine and lands outside of Palestine, that included an unknown number of followers of Jesus.

It was during the Feast of Pentecost, that the apostles and Mary, her sons, and friends were all in the upper room for prayer and counsel. They were struggling without their leader and did not know what to do next. With their despair, the people in the upper room were not in a celebrating mood. However, it seems that there remained some sense of purpose in their lives. This sense of purpose was important enough for them to stay together and sort out how to move forward. There remained the fear of the Jewish religious leaders, who certainly would not be pleased to find that killing Jesus did not end his movement. The apostles needed to better define how to continue Jesus' ministry and to prepare for the inevitable conflicts with the Jewish religious leaders.

While they were in the room, they had an "aha" moment of recognizing that Jesus' strength and singleness of purpose had come from having a spiritual relationship with God, which was still available to them. Having such a relationship freed the apostles and other followers of Jesus from their fears and worries and strengthen them to withstand persecution from the Jewish religious leader and freed them to be at peace with themselves.

Acts 2:1-47 describes the moment of recognition that Jesus' ministry and His life exemplified living in the spirit with God and in God's grace. It came to them as a sound coming down from heaven and a great rush of wind filling the house, and tongues of fire appeared on each of them, and they, filled with the Holy Spirit, spilling out into the crowd, and began speaking in other tongues.

There is disagreement about whether they were speaking incoherently or in a foreign language that was recognized by some of the people in the crowd. Acts 2:6 states that the apostles were speaking in the language of people in the crowd.

The explanation in Acts of the profound change in behavior of the people in the room leaves little, if any, doubt in the magnitude and significance of the change they experienced. This describes the apostles and others sudden realization that they could have the same freedom in their spiritual connection with God as Jesus had, by committing to being guided solely by God as Jesus was.

The freedom that came with this realization released them from the overwhelming worries that had so weighed them down. They no longer needed to worry about their daily needs or what the Jewish religious leaders would do. Neither their daily needs nor what the Jewish religious leaders would do could disrupt their direct spiritual connection with God. So, just as Abraham was a friend of God so now, they were friends of God.

They came pouring out of their building. Their excitement and joy from their newfound freedom could not be contained. It overflowed to those around them. They realized that God was with them.

Some accused the people of being drunk with wine. Peter spoke to the crowd of the truth of the people's actions that they were witnessing. Although Acts 1:12-14 includes women in the group in the room, in Acts 2:14-16 Peter, in his address to the crowd, speaks only of men.

In the short time from the last supper to Jesus' crucifixion, they had gone from looking forward to a bright future to despair and hopelessness. What better way to explain the sudden awaking of the followers of Jesus to the wonders and glory of Jesus' ministry than to joyously proclaim their renewed trust and belief in God? Acts chapter 2 closes with the combination of the apostle's excitement and joy, and Peter's explanation of what the apostles were experiencing resulted in many people joining the apostles.

While the first creation story provided the foundation for Christianity, the awakening of the apostles and followers of Jesus during the Pentecost was the beginning of Christianity. This is when the apostles began realizing that the core of Jesus's life and ministry was Jesus' total and clear relationship with God. The spiritual pathway between God and Jesus was grounded in Jesus declaring that God was first, above all else. There was nothing in their relationship to dim or obstruct its clarity.

This beginning gave the apostles and followers of Jesus the support for their belief in Jesus' ministry they needed for them to spread the story of Jesus' life and his ministry throughout the Greek and Roman areas outside of Palestine. Without this awaking during the Pentecost, the apostles and their followers would not have been energized to spread the word of Jesus' ministry. And so, this joyous realization that God was still with them planted the seeds of Christianity.

As a case in point, sometime later, Peter and John were on their way to the Temple when a lame man asked for alms. Instead, Peter healed the man and he walked. The lame man went with them to the temple and, as they were speaking to the crowd, the priests came and arrested Peter and John and brought them before the Jewish authorities. When asked, Peter and John explained the healing of the lame man was through the ministry of Jesus. The leaders threatened them and released them (Acts 4:1-21). The spirit of Jesus most surely must have been smiling.

So, even with the shock of Jesus' crucifixion, Jesus' life and ministry did take hold in the apostles and followers of Jesus, it just took time and patience for Jesus' ministry to become an integral part of the apostles and the early Jesus followers' lives.

THE *WAY* MOVEMENT

Long before Jesus began his ministry, Jews had dispersed throughout surrounding Greek communities and had established Jewish communities within the Greek communities. When Jesus' followers dispersed out of Palestine, they would join or at least be in contact with the existing Jewish communities. However, the members of the Jewish communities would have been reluctant to insert the followers of Jesus' new worship service ideas into their existing worship services. At some point in this dispersion process, one of the early names for the followers of Jesus throughout Palestine and the Greek communities was the Way (Acts 9.2).

Over time, the followers of Jesus were having some success spreading the word in Palestine and Greek communities and they were beginning to get organized and establish their own services and meeting process. There was very little guidance other than the memories the followers of Jesus brought with them.

Acts describe one of the first examples of the new services placing additional requirements for people to follow Jesus. The Way group in each community took care of their needy members; however, only in Jerusalem did the Way members decided on a type of communal living that required all possessions to be considered common property that would be distributed according to need.

A Jerusalem couple, Ananias, and his wife Sapphira, sold some land and held back some of the proceeds rather than giving all the proceeds to the community. In the meeting with Ananias and later with Sapphira, Peter asked them why they were lying to the Holy Spirit. Simply being caught in their dishonesty may not have been enough to kill either one of them; however, telling them that they'd lied to God was enough for them to die from fear and shame (Acts 5:1-11).

Different communities set different rules, none of which were ordained by God; however, if Ananias and Sapphira had lived in a different community with different rules for supporting the needy. Their gift may have been welcomed without question or comment.

Instead of picking up the relationship offered by God and lived by Jesus, the Christian leaders quickly began establishing control and setting limits, like what the Jewish leaders had done.

Jesus had been gone for only a few months and the heart of His ministry was being forgotten. Already the apostles had set requirements that people must meet to join with the Way. As a guiding principle, giving everything to the group may be a good way of gaining acceptance by the group; however, it has little or nothing to do with having a spiritual relationship with God. As a directive or requirement, it placed being accepted by the group ahead of establishing a spiritual relationship with God. It also created fear. Acts 5:11 states, "And great fear came upon the whole church, and upon all who heard of these things." Jesus' ministry was about Gods' love—not about being fearful. God's eternal grace includes the forgiveness of failures.

Falsely declaring theology and rules that were established by church members as having come from God has caused much pain and suffering over the centuries. Blaming God for man-made requirements has been detrimental to non-Christians' acceptance of God's message of love and forgiveness for all from the time of Jesus' death to today.

So, in a short time after Jesus was gone the apostles had forgotten Jesus' admonishment that the last will be first, that leaders are servants to all. The seeds of Christianity's failure to stick to Jesus' ministry have been planted and unfortunately have grown to unimaginable size and strength.

I am not aware of any organization, Christian or otherwise, that has received permission from God to determine with whom He will and will not have a spiritual relationship. The spiritual relationship between God and a person is solely established and maintained by that person and God. Also, one person's spiritual relationship with God will not be the same as another's spiritual relationship with God. Organizations can advocate and support a person's spiritual relationship with God; however, an organization will not have any part in a person's spiritual relationship with God.

All the organizational, theology, and ritual development does not change the fact that the only way a person can live in the likeness of God is to have a clear, uncluttered, personal spiritual relationship with God.

Anyone with a clear spiritual relationship with God can recognize the fallacy in thinking that belonging to an organization is required to have a relationship with God. Jesus' relationship with God was established without regard for the Jewish religion with its priestly rules and governance. For someone who is struggling with, or is unsure about, having a spiritual relationship with God, an organization can look like a way to be connected to God. And it very well can be the catalyst for a person becoming connected to God; however, each person is still required to make his or her own connection with God. A person's relationship with God is strictly between God and each person, without a third party being included in the relationship.

The perceived need to get organized and then to live up to the requirements of the organization will continue throughout the history of Christianity. It has become more important than Jesus' message to the Jews. Jesus was telling each Jew that becoming God-centered would not change the world around them, but it would change how each Jew would think about, and approach living in his or her world. Jesus' message was to each person; however, the Christian message, beginning with the Way's message, has been centered on the requirements of each Christian group.

As the apostles continued to preach and the number of disciples continued to grow, the Jewish priests became concerned and had the apostles arrested. They were brought before the high priest and the party of the Sadducees. When the apostles did not agree to stop preaching and continued bringing in new members into their group, the council was ready to sentence them to death when a highly respected Pharisee teacher, named Gamaliel, stood up and told the members to be careful.

He pointed out that on two previous occasions when an itinerate leader who had acquired a following was killed, his followers soon disappeared, so the council should leave the apostles alone for, if their activities were the undertaking of man, it will soon fail, but if it is of God, it cannot be overthrown. The leaders might even be found opposing God. The apostles were beaten and released (Acts 5:12-42). The priests and Sadducees understood some of Gamaliel's message but not all of it.

It is of interest to note that Jesus related well with what the Pharisees professed to believe, but Jesus was incensed with how they lived. If the Pharisees had lived in the faith they professed, Jesus very well may have supported the Pharisees, who would no longer be part of the privileged class and would have supported the poor and disadvantaged. As we will see it was a respected Pharisee who became a trusted leader of the Gentle followers of Jesus.

Jesus' relationship with God became a major point of disagreement within the Way. The Jewish followers of Jesus thought of Jesus as a prophet as Peter explained in a sermon to some Israelites as described In Acts 3:11-26.

Starting with verse 17, Peter tells the Israelites to repent and be guided by God. The term *Christ* in the sermon is either a late addition or Peter was using it in a context that differed from the standard understanding the Israelites had for Christ. The thrust of the sermon was to tie Jesus to the linage of highly revered Jewish forefathers, Moses, and David. The footnote for verse 22 states, "Jesus is the successor to Moses as was David." The Jewish prophets were held in high regard, but not considered to be divine.

Early in the development of the followers of the Jesus movement, the Jerusalem Church members were the leaders of the movement. Noss explains their thin margin of error:

> Two factors seem to have saved Jerusalem Church from annihilating persecution: First, the apostles were followers of a dead leader and might be expected to lose their fervor

with the passage of time; and second, the apostles obviously kept all the provisions of the Jewish law. (Noss, page 618)

The Jewish Way members were walking a thin line of not upsetting the religious leaders too much.

As stated earlier, long before the time of Jesus, Jews had dispersed out of Palestine into the other parts of the Roman empire and formed Jewish communities in their home countries. Over time Judaism communities acquired some characteristics of the religions and cultures of their new home countries. In the same fashion, the Way members that dispersed to these countries developed their ideas about Jesus' ministry, which were diverse among the different groups and different from the ideas of the Jerusalem Way members.

Very early ugly splits developed over different requirements in different Way groups, which had little to do with Jesus' ministry. Acts 6:1 refers to the two main Way groups within the followers of Jesus as the Hebrews, or Jewish-speaking members, and the Hellenists, or Greek-speaking members. The Hebrews were led by James, the brother of Jesus. Most of the apostles were with James. They believed that they must please God and follow the laws of Moses. They thought of being followers of Jesus, or members of the Way, as a subset of the Jewish religion, with the members continuing to go to the temple. Jesus, after all, did not denounce Judaism, just the leaders of Judaism for using their leadership to enhance their position in the Jewish community and enrich themselves.

The other main group, a collection of outlying groups, the Hellenists were associated with Peter and were less inclined to follow Judaism and were breaking away from the strict requirements of Judaism. They believed that following Jesus' ministry did not require following Judaism. Their decisions about what to use instead of the Judaism requirements went in several directions.

The Hellenist Way members in the Geek communities, which was made up of Israelites and Greek-speaking members, were primarily outside Jewish religious influence. These groups were more liberal and not tied to the Jewish religious rituals. They were formulating their own ideas of the relationship they could have with Jesus and how they would demonstrate their faithfulness to Jesus' ministry.

An early problem arose that highlighted the differences between the Hebrew and Hellenists groups. The Hellenists members complained that their widows were being neglected in the distribution of food. The apostles decided to solve the problem by appointing a seven members committee to disturbed food (see Acts 6:1-7). Stephen, a Hellenist, was selected as a member of this committee. Acts 6:8 describes Stephen as, "a man full of faith and of the Holy Spirit, did great wonders and signs among the people." The footnote explains that names of the seven men were Greek. Either Stephen was a Jew, who originally was from a Greek country or a Greek who converted to Judaism. He may have been part of the group that returned to Jerusalem after Jesus' crucifixion.

Apparently, Stephen was also vocal about his ideas that the rituals, sacrifices and the law were no longer needed. In doing so Stephen incurred the displeasure of Hebrew members, who claimed he spoke, "blasphemous words, against Moses and God" (see Acts 6:11). Stephen was called before the Sanhedrin. He was condemned to death and cast out and stoned to death. A young man named Paul witnessed and consented to the stoning death of Stephen (see Acts 6:8-8:1a).

The death of Stephen sharpened the divide between the Hellenists and the Hebrew groups and caused many more of Jesus' followers to disperse away from Palestine and the reach of the Hebrew Way members. As the Way members dispersed and became part of their new communities, they either joined existing Way groups or started new Way groups. They became part of the growing number of people interested in this idea of a new and different relationship one could have with God.

The Hellenist and Hebrew groups continued to develop a religion centered around each groups' idea of Jesus' ministry. Each group had a different idea of who Jesus was and how to incorporate Jesus into their religious theology. Differences also developed within the Hellenist groups in addition to the general thinking that Jesus was not a prophet.

As the number of non-Jewish or liberal members increased, they were slowly getting the upper hand. More Greek than Jews were joining the Way. The Greeks' more liberal approach to following the ministry of Jesus was more appealing to the new members than having to strictly follow the Jewish law. While some members of the Jerusalem Church, Hebrew Way members, were willing to compromise, an extremist element was not interested in compromising and formed an exclusive group called Ebionites or Nazarenes.

It was soon established that a person was either a Hebrew Way member or a Hellenists' Way member. It was not good enough to simply emulate Jesus by helping each person, as an individual, establish a spiritual relationship with God. The rules that each group established took precedence over simply having a spiritual relationship with God.

The requirements the two groups were developing did little or nothing to guide a person to receive God's blessing. The Hebrew group requirements were based on Judaism; however, the Hellenist requirements were new and being developed on the fly. If anything, requirements for both groups did little more than set barriers that kept a person from establishing a relationship with God.

The word, "church" comes from a Greek word for, "group" or "gathering." It did not refer to a building, room, or meeting place, as it often does today. In this book, the Way Church or Christian Church refers to the people rather than a building.

As the conflict between the Greek and Jerusalem Church members continued, Peter was called to tend to a woman named Tabitha, who had died. Upon arriving, Peter cleared the room and after praying, called for Tabitha to rise. She opened her eyes, took Peter's hand, and arose (see Acts 9:36-43). So, once again an apostle demonstrated what could be done when the spiritual connection with God was present. It still seemed very difficult; however, to keep the blessing of God, without including the manmade requirements, which were central to all the daily and organizational issues of the groups.

At some point in the development of the Hellenist Church, the new members were from several countries. While many of them spoke Greek, they would also speak their native language. The term *Gentile* will be used of the non-Jewish or Hellenist Church and Jerusalem Church for the Hebrew Church.

Next, the book of Acts describes converting a Roman centurion named Cornelius and his family to be followers of Jesus. Cornelius and his family may have been the first Gentiles to be converted; however, since the timing of this and other events is uncertain, it is difficult to say Cornelius' family was the first Gentiles to be converted, or how their conversion fits in with the time of Paul's conversion.

This story is told in Acts 10:1-43. There are some interesting points in addition to Cornelius' family being admitted into the Way fellowship. Cornelius as a Roman centurion had been friendly with the Jews and worshipped one God. Through a series of visions Peter and some friends went to Cornelius' home. Before Peter left for Cornelius' house, he was offered food which he refused because he thought the food was unclean but, he was told that what God made was clean, so Peter ate.

Peter was also concerned about "how unlawful it is for a Jews to associate with or to visit any one of another nation; but God has shown me that I should not call any man common or unclean" (Acts 10: 28). The Judaism laws that defined that was unclean had been violated twice, a serious afront to the Jews.

Cornelius knew Peter was coming and had rounded up his family and close friends to receive Peter. When Peter arrived, Cornelius bowed down at Peter's feet in worship, "But Peter lifted him up, saying 'Stand up; I too am a man'" (Acts 10: 26).

When Peter began the service for Cornelius' family, Acts 10: 44-46 tells us that the Holy Spirit fell on all who heard Peter's words, meaning

Jews and Gentile alike, and they began speaking in tongues and extolling God. This indicts the Cornelius and his family spoke Latin. Upon seeing the Holy Spirit fall on all in the house Peter Baptist them.

The admission of a Roman Centurion, Cornelius, and his family into the Way illustrates the differences between Jerusalem Way members and the Gentile Way members. The Jerusalem Way members were not happy about having a Gentile Way member who did not know the importance of keeping the Mosaic Law (Acts 10:1-48). When Peter was criticized for associating with the unclean (Gentiles) he responded, "who was I that I could withstand God?" (Acts 11:17).

It was bad enough that Gentiles were being accepted without knowing the Jewish history or reading the Jewish manuscripts, but now they were adding insult to injury, Cornelius was the enemy of the Jews, an unwelcome Roman soldier.

This was an early example of the liberal Gentile Way Church overshadowing the Jerusalem Way Church. Although the Jerusalem Church was still considered the center of the Way movement, events were happening that the Jerusalem Church was poorly equipped to stop or understand. Neither the Jews nor the Gentiles could accept that God did not favor one group of people over another. The unwillingness to accept God being available to all, the idea that Paul would strongly push a few years later, was one of the causes of the Jerusalem Church's demise.

During the continuing disagreement between the Jerusalem Way members and the Gentile Way members, a man named Paul entered the Gentile Way. Paul is often referred to as the "second founder of Christianity." His arrival was a new force in the Gentile Church. He would tilt the balance of power toward the Gentile Church and gave it vision and organization, and substantially improved the growth of the Gentile Church.

Paul's arrival was most fortunate for the Gentile Way Church. Paul brought his thorough knowledge of the Jewish laws and historical writings, some of which became Old Testament, and his strong belief in God. Paul raising Jesus' status from being a prophet to being divine, strengthened the Gentile followers of Jesus' movement and led to the demise of the Hebrew followers of Jesus movement. Paul's organizational also skills provided the foundation for Christianity to survive during very difficult times.

PAUL

Dating events during this time in Jewish history are approximant. The article, "The Apostle Paul and His Times: Christian History Timeline," Janet Meyer Everts, found under the Google search of Biblical Paul at www Christianitytoday.com/history/issues/... gives Paul's birth in AD 6, his conversion in AD 33, and his death in AD 64. Other references give somewhat different dates for these and other events; however, I use the dates in this article for Paul's activities to provide a general timeline for his work. Paul's conversion apparently happened around the time of the conversion of Cornelius and his family.

Paul was born in Tarsus of the Benjamin Tribe. His father was a Roman citizen, which meant that he was a Roman citizen. At his circumcision, he was given the name, Saul, apparently in honor of the first king of the Jews. His Roman name then was Paul. He learned to be a tent maker; however, at an early age he was sent to Jerusalem to the school of the famous and highly respected Pharisee, Gamaliel. Paul's attendance at Gamaliel's school resulted in him spending his early life into his early adulthood learning to be a Pharisee and, as an adult, to become a respected Pharisee with a thorough knowledge and understanding of the Hebrew-Jewish history and the available scriptures. Paul had a strong commitment to God.

He was an exceptional person both before and after his conversion. He was an intense man of action who, when he saw a problem, he solved it. Paul was highly intelligent, very persuasive, and certainly creative, he was one who could see new possibilities and not be afraid to pursue them. He did everything with strong purpose and total dedication.

That is, he did things in full measure. There was little equivocating. Things were black or white with little grey area. He also brought with him in his conversions to be a follower of Jesus, his extensive knowledge of Israelite history and Judaism.

Paul was well-schooled on the Judaism principles and accompanying rituals, rules, and writings that had been developed over centuries. From the comments of other Pharisees and the Jewish leaders and his own research, Paul surely knew enough about Jesus to have a sense of his teaching and healing.

Paul believed that Jesus' ministry violated the core value of Judaism and that the followers of Jesus were undermining the relationship the Jews had with God. Paul became fiercely opposed to Jesus' followers. While Paul certainly was not the only Pharisee opposed to Jesus' followers, he was the one who decided to do something about them.

Paul, the respected Pharisee, was given the authority to find and arrest the Jewish Way members, to take them to Jerusalem for trial and execution. Paul quickly became a feared opponent of the Way. As later events showed, Paul was not a cruel person who would delight in causing others to suffer. His work weeding out the Jewish members of the radical movement that followed the dead Jew named Jesus was driven by his need to eliminate competition to the existing Jewish religious structure.

As Paul traveling throughout Palestine, he had plenty of time to think about his job and the people he was persecuting. Paul witnessed the trial of Stephen and his subsequent death. The evidence that Stephen's faith in God and his commitment to the ministry of Jesus was so strong that he was willing to suffer "on to death," by stoning would surely have been on Paul's mind as he traveled from one town to the next.

He continued to encounter people who, like Stephen, placed their total trust and faith in God's care on to death, as demonstrated by Jesus. What Paul was observing was causing him to have second thoughts about his commitment to Judaism and his life as a Pharisee. The more he saw of the Way members the more he became aware of the discrepancies between what the priests and Pharisees said and how they lived, which Jesus so eloquently described in Matthew 23:1-36. At some point, his questioning of what he was doing led him to no longer being able to dismiss the discrepancies between what he said and what he was doing as being of little consequence.

PAUL'S CONVERSION

It is most assuredly true that without the conversion of Paul, the Way groups would not have survived as they did to become the Gentile Church. Either the Gentile Church would not have been able to get out from under to control of the Jerusalem Church, or the chaos of competing theories and leaders from the dynamically different Gentile Way groups would have weakened the Gentile Church enough that it would have been overwhelmed by pagan religions or remained a minor religion. With Jerusalem retaining control of the Gentile Church and continued its partial separation from Judaism rather than totally breaking away from Judaism, the remnants of the Gentile Church that did not revert to paganism or join the Jerusalem Church would become insufficient to continue as a separate church. Even with the Gentile Church members, the Jerusalem churches would still be a sect of Judaism, which is eventually what happened to the Jerusalem Church, when the Gentile Church gained control of Christianity.

It seems that Paul's ideas were well reasoned, and logical, which he explained simply and clearly. His education to become a Pharisee included a thorough study of Judaism with its laws and rituals, which also gave him insight into the difference between the Pharisee teachings and the Pharisee actions, and more importantly, the differences between Judaism and Jesus' ministry. It was these differences that led him to give up being a Pharisee to become a believer in Jesus' ministry.

It was while he was on the road to Damascus that Paul finally realized what he had learned to become a Pharisee was wrong, and the rule and ritual-driven Judaism he worked so fiercely to preserve and protect from the Jesus heresy, was inferior to Jesus' message of a personnel spiritual relationship with God. With this realization came the weight of all the pain and suffering, and the deaths he had caused the Jewish followers of Jesus.

How could Paul explain such a drastic, major conversion of his attitude toward the followers of Jesus? How can he explain that he was not just declaring his sudden change in attitude as a way of getting close to the Jewish Way members to capture and take them back to Jerusalem to be put to death? There were very few ways for Paul to explain his "Aha!" moment so he would not be ridiculed or put to death.

Paul described his "aha" moment of needing to change his life, as it happened while he was on the road to Damascus. He described it as a bright light from heaven, his being knocked off his horse, and a voice saying, "Saul, Saul, why do you persecute me?" When he asked, "Who are you, Lord?" he heard, "I am Jesus, whom you are persecuting; but rise and enter the city, and you will be told what you are to do" (Acts 9:1-6).

Paul's experience on the road to Damascus so transformed him that he could not adjust to it at once. His out-of-the-world experience invalidated all he believed to be true. His misunderstanding of God's message was now confirmed.

That he opened his eyes but could not see and he was led to a house in Damascus where he stayed for three days, without sight nor did he eat or drink, certainly indicates the magnitude of his decision. The Bible tells us that Ananias, a disciple of Jesus, received instructions for the Lord to go to the house to lay hands on Paul. With great reluctance, Ananias did so, which opened Paul's eyes and Ananias then baptized Paul.

Being baptized by Ananias freed him from the burden of his past, which gave him a new life and new freedom. Separating the clutter of his past from his new line of thinking was needed so Paul could hear and take to heart God's message.

The struggle that both Paul and Ananias had in accepting God's guidance was not new. Moses and Jacob went through it, and Abraham struggled to stay true to God's guidance, although Paul's struggle may have been more profound.

As a critical part of his conversion, Paul had to decide who he was and what would be his relationship with God. The change he would have to make would take away all he had worked to achieve and put him in the uncomfortable position of having to depend on the people he had prosecuted.

To complete his changed life, Paul had to give up the life of a respected Pharisee with its accompanying privilege, wealth, respect, and authority—a status he had worked much of his life to obtain, for a life of following Jesus' ministry with no earthly side benefits.

Paul's conversion was the crucial first step in the development of Christianity. Without Paul's leadership, Christianity would be much different than it is today, if it had survived at all. The celebration of Paul's contribution to Christianity overshadows recognition of the magnitude of the change Paul's conversion made in his relationship with God as well as the changes he made in Christianity.

He decided to make the massive change in his life to become a believer in Jesus' ministry without knowing how it would play out. There was no guarantee that following God's directions would result in Paul surviving his meeting with the Way members or having survived that, being allowed to become part of the Way group. While all ended well for Paul, when he made his momentous decision, he had no way of knowing how it would end or how much it would change his life.

Discerning how accurately Paul describes what happened to him on the road to Damascus is not critical to Paul's story. Paul's description of his experience has been accepted as being true, and there is little or no evidence to dispute his story of what he saw, felt, and heard.

Seeing a bright light, being knocked off his horse, and getting chided for prosecuting the followers of Jesus certainly could have been his physical and mental reaction to his profound realization that the people he was prosecuting were the very people who had the relationship with God that he wished to have.

I think it is important to recognize that Paul was being asked a question rather than being told to change. It was still Paul's decision. By following directions, Paul showed he had changed his priorities.

The full story of his change and his acceptance by Way members in Damascus is described in Acts 9:1-22. Slightly different versions are found in Acts 22:4-16, 26:9-18, and Paul's account in Galatians 1:13-17.

I wonder what Paul would have done if the Pharisees had lived as they said they believed. Regardless of all the possibilities that raises, it is reasonable to think that Paul would not have been on the road to Damascus looking for Jesus' followers to arrest nor would Paul have given the Way group the help they needed.

START OF PAUL'S NEW LIFE

Since the Old Testament was not assembled until AD 100, there is no way of knowing what was available to Jesus, the apostles, or Paul, or how much of what was available was included in the Old Testament. Paul and Jesus both believed in Hebrew-Israelite historical writings, but Jesus' interpretation of these writings was different than Paul's interpretation.

It was Paul's passion and desire to be God-centered that gave him the determination and will to give up what he had and make the tremendous changes that allowed him to become a leader of the Way people who he had very recently been working to destroy.

Paul confirmed his new belief in what was required to follow God when he renounced being a Pharisee and became a follower of Jesus.

The freedom he later expressed in his writings and sermons came from his release from the burden of the rituals and rules of Judaism.

It would have been very difficult, practically impossible, for Paul to block out the extensive education and training he had received in Pharisee school and his experience as a Pharisee. The processes he used to think through problems worked for him as well after his conversion as they did before his conversion. However, after his conversion these processes would be tainted by his Pharisee schooling and experience. Although these processes were tainted, they enabled him to finally see the fallacies and deceptions of the leadership of Judaism.

Specifically, his organizational skills and intelligence were important for establishing a foundation for, and growth of, Christianity.

To gain the trust and acceptance of the leaders of the Way movement he had to change how he lived and what he believed, and he certainly had to admit the errors of his way as a Pharisee. Even with the help of Ananias, gaining the leaders' trust and acceptance was a daunting task. It simply was not human nature to accept, at face value, the claims of conversion to a totally new and different life, such as Paul presented to the Way members. Added to their suspicions was their memory of the disastrous results from Paul's prior trips to areas where Jewish Way members lived. It surely was very hard and worrisome for the Way members to accept the new Paul.

The Bible tells us that the leaders of the Way in Damascus were amazed at what Paul brought with him; however, they were still hesitant to accept him. Paul's wealth of information about the Jews' relationship with God along with his energy and enthusiasm were undoubtedly important to Paul being accepted.

Paul's acceptance certainly came with reservations. Some Way members reluctantly accepted Paul and some Way members only permitted Paul to stay with the Way group. With Paul's track record, gaining the acceptance that he did obtain certainly was an amazing accomplishment.

After the tremendous change in his life, and once he was accepted by some followers of Jesus, Paul went off to Arabia to be alone and think through what had happened and how to proceed with his new life. He had a void to fill. His life's work as a Pharisee was gone to be replaced with new beliefs and actions for his new relationship with God.

After about three years he returned to Damascus to resume his relationship with the Way members. Although Paul was accepted by some of the Way members, there was enough push back that the situation was dangerous, and his life was threatened.

He went to Jerusalem from Damascus to meet with the apostles. As one might suspect, the Jerusalem Way members hated him, based on what they knew about him. They were waiting at the gates into Jerusalem to kill him. Instead of approaching the gates, the disciples lowered Paul over the wall into Jerusalem in a basket (Acts 9:23-31). Also see 2 Corinthians 11:33 which shows Paul telling about leaving Damascus by being let down through a window in the wall because King Aretas wanted to catch him. It seems he may have entered Jerusalem the same way he left Damascus.

The Jerusalem Way members were initially afraid of Paul; however, Barnabas convinced them that Paul's conversion to a disciple of Jesus was real (Acts 9: 23-30). Barnabas was a Levi from Cyprus who was a leader of the Way and apparently was a link between the Gentile and Jewish Way members. Barnabas is another person in the Bible who is not given his just do. Convincing the Way members to accept Paul, their feared enemy, required Barnabas to pull off a masterful performance, that gave the Way members the level of comfort necessary for them to allow Paul into their group.

Paul's presence in Jerusalem; however, created enough conflict that he left Jerusalem and went to his hometown of Tarsus. He taught in the area around Tarsus for several years, some references say eight years, until Barnabas came to get him, and they traveled to Antioch to help develop the new faith there. Paul remained for a year to teach a large company of people and to strengthen the church. While Paul was in

Antioch the followers of Jesus in Antioch were called Christians for the first time. (See footnote for Acts 11:19-26.) Before long, the term Christian was used to identify all followers of Jesus.

At this point, many of the Christian leadership in the Gentile communities were still Jewish. Faithfully keeping the Mosaic Law may still have been critical to the Jews in the Gentile Christian Church leadership; however, the only complaint about not following the Mosaic Law came from the Jerusalem Christians members.

Paul's acceptance by both the Gentile and Jerusalem Christians did not mean that all the reservations the Christians had about Paul had been removed. Certainly, part of the reservations came from Paul's personality of forcefully presenting his faith in God. There were Christians who disagreed with Paul and his theology throughout Paul's ministry.

Paul was truly an amazing man. He was able to convince the Gentile Way leaders, who originally were terrified of him, that his conversion was true and real. He was a new man, who no longer supported the Judaism ritual, rules, and structure. He was the new wine that needed a new wineskin, His complete transition from a dedicated and feared Pharisee to being recognized as a dedicated Way leader was a tremendous accomplishment. Paul's leadership would change Christianity forever.

PAUL'S STRUGGLE WITH ISSUES

Paul had to sort out his next move. Paul believed that his calling was to be more than a leader who repeated the same message that the other church leaders were saying. It seems that his struggle to define Jesus was central to his calling to have a new and different message for the Church.

There is no clear picture of when Paul developed his thinking about who and what Jesus was. The decision to be a follower of Jesus was the start of his process of defining his relationship with the Gentile

Christians, and more importantly, his relationship with God, and deciding who Jesus was and what Jesus' role would be in the Gentile Church. He began putting his thoughts together while he was in Arabia. From that beginning, he built his theology to what it became over the next few years.

For the Jews, who knew Jesus' ministry and life, Jesus had been accepted as a prophet, in line with the Jews' historical prophets, which had served well for accounting for Jesus' successes among the Jews.

Paul knew that the prophets were people with a special relationship with God. That relationship gave them clear insight into God and clear understanding of the relationship that God could have with the Jews. Paul also knew that the positive impact the prophets had on the Jews and that the reverence the Jews had for the prophets were unique to the Jews and would not have nearly the same meaning to the Gentiles.

Paul had some idea of what Jesus had accomplished during his three-year ministry. Paul knew that Jesus was a remarkable man with exceptional ability to live a God-centered life. Not only could miracles happen in Jesus' presence but being with Jesus had changed the disciples by giving them a glance of what they could do with a clear spiritual relationship with God.

Paul recognized that Jesus was a prophet whose direct relationship with God was more encompassing than he had seen anyone else have. Paul concluded that Jesus' relationship with God was unique. Paul did not recognize any other Jewish prophet or anyone else in the Old Testament who had a relationship with God such as Jesus had. Even if Paul knew about the success the disciple had healing and teaching, or that Peter had healing a lame man and raising from the dead a lady named Tabitha, their relationship with God did not rise to the relationship Jesus had with God.

Another example of God's direct relationship with the Jews, which Paul may or may not have known about, was the apostles' experience during Pentecost. God had spoken directly to the apostles and those who were with them in the upper room, apparently their meeting place. Acts 2:2-3 describes the experience as a rush of a mighty wind filling the house and they were all filled with the Holy Spirit. That the words, Holy Spirit, are capitalized seems to indicate Luke wanted to make sure the passage was read as God connecting directly with the people in the upper room.

Although Paul believed the Gentiles could have a spiritual relationship with God just as the Jews could, Paul was convinced that without the Gentiles knowing the Hebrew-Jewish history, Jesus as a Jewish prophet was not saleable. Paul did not think the impact the prophets had on the Jews could be duplicated with the Gentiles. Even if the Gentiles had a working knowledge of the Old Testament, Paul believed it would have been very difficult for Gentiles to appreciate how important the prophet's role was in the life and history of the Jews or how prophets could fit into their religion.

Paul's realization that the Gentiles and Jewish followers of Jesus had a stronger relationship with God than those who followed the Law—read the Pharisees—had to have been a profound discovery for Paul. This recognition alone could have released Paul from the bondage of the Law.

Paul's understanding of Jesus' message was more complete than the Jews'. Paul recognized Jesus' relationship with God was special and hard for the Jews to grasp. Paul's understanding of Jesus' message was a breakthrough. Paul realized that love was central to Jesus' spiritual connection to God. Love was more than the fulfillment of the Law. It was central to the spiritual freedom of Jesus' relationship with God. It threaded through all that Jesus was and all that he did.

Paul and Jesus had grown up under the same complex and punitive religious system. What each one took out of that experience was a critical part of who each one was and how each one met and related to the people and surely played a part in who each one became.

Jesus's appeal to the people He met came from His caring, compassion, and His demonstration of God's love. Prior to his conversion, Paul's appeal came from his organizational skills, his knowledge of Jewish history, and his drive to accomplish his intended objective. Through his conversion, Paul was able to recognize and accept God's love.

Paul's attendance at Gamaliel's Pharisee school led him to be an excellent Pharisee. He was an intelligent and able Pharisee who could process information and come to a clear and definitive conclusion. He retained this ability when he converted to following Jesus. However, he was not able to totally remove himself from all that he had spent a major part if his life to learn and use. Realistically, it would have been next to impossible for Paul to wipe away all that he had learned in Pharisee school, which could have limited how much of Jesus' relationship with God he could recognize and accept as being available to all people.

Paul was a practicing Pharisee until his conversion in his thirties. Paul, the Pharisee, was getting in the way of Paul, the Christian. That Jesus' relationship with God enabled people to change their lives was more than the Pharisee Paul could recognize as being possible.

For the Jews who knew Jesus and saw Him as He grew up to be a carpenter, Jesus' relationship with God came from His reading of the manuscripts that were available to Him, His interaction with His extended family and people in Nazareth. His observations of hardships of the Jews that came from the Jewish and Roman leaders gave Jesus the reason for His ministry, and most importantly, His recognition that even with all that they were contending with, a direct relationship with God was available to the Jews. It was extremely difficult for the Jews to turn away from what they had been taught to recognize that a personal spiritual relationship with God was available to each one of them. This simple idea was one that Jesus could not get the Jews to accept as being true for them but was recognized by Paul, after his conversion, as being true for all people.

Jesus spent his time observing the struggles of the Jews and the short-comings of Judaism. Jesus clearly saw the core message of God's love for the Jews that thread through the creation story, and God's promise to Abraham, the Ten Commandments, and the Jew prophets; a love that is offered to all people and is received by those who follow and trust God.

Although Paul's grasp of Jesus' ministry was greater than the apostles and the early Gentile disciples, it was not strong enough for Paul to put Jesus' message of love central to Paul's ministry. As we shall see Jesus' birth, divinity, and death will be most important in Christianity.

MAKING JESUS DIVINE

We will never know the process Paul went through to recognize Jesus as being divine; however, his recognition of Jesus' divinity did not happen in a vacuum. There were several factors that affected his decision. Paul brought intact the religion of Jesus in the vehicle of a religion about Jesus (See Noss, page 620). Jesus lived His relationship with God for all to see, and Paul picked up on Jesus' life being integrated with His relationship with God. Love was central to His relationship with God and the people He met and knew.

The concept of Jesus's ministry that Paul developed during his early time as a Way member was different than the concept Jerusalem Way group had of Jesus' ministry. In his sorting through all the information from his life as a Pharisee and since his conversion to following Jesus, he came to two spiritual realizations that were central to his faith. They were a 'freedom of the spirit," and the "Lordship of Christ Jesus" (Noss, page 621).

Paul realized that the spiritual freedom in Jesus' ministry did not exist in Judaism. Paul realized that Jesus' relationship with God was without ritual and the requirements of Judaism, which led Paul to declare his long-held belief that the Law was the only way of living in God's favor was wrong. He realized that the good in the followers of Jesus was more deeply felt than in the followers of the Law. Becoming a follower of Jesus came from within a person, being heartfelt rather than being based on the external requirements of the Law. Love replaced the need for requirements such as the ideas of the clean and unclean, and circumcision and dietary requirements.

Paul's freedom of the spirit was close, if not the same as the central idea in Jesus' ministry.

Even knowing some Gentiles had become followers of Jesus, Paul wanted the message of Jesus to be recognized by all Gentiles. It had to be different than, and stand out from, the pagan message. How could Jesus' message to the Jews be equally true for the Gentiles? The Gentiles already had the gods of their mythology. There was no good place to insert Jesus into their mythology, and God was not about being inserted into a religion. The story of Jesus had to resonate with the Gentiles more than the pagan stories that they already knew.

The Jewish followers of Jesus, known as the Jerusalem Christians, thought of Jesus as a prophet, like the prophets Isaiah and Elijah. Paul did not think that Jesus being a prophet would measure up to the gods of the pagan religions of the Greeks and Romans.

Another issue leading to Paul's decision that Jesus was divine may have been that Paul was uncomfortable with things he could not logically explain or having loose ends. For Paul, it was not possible for a carpenter's son from the village of Nazareth in the backwater area of Galilee who, on his own, without an education such as Paul had received, developed a special relationship with God. All the pieces had to fit in somewhere and some pieces were missing. There had to be more to it than what Paul could see.

A third issue, which I believe was very important, was his Pharisee education which, continued to be a part of who he was. After much thought, Paul decided that for the Gentiles to recognize Jesus for his wonderful teachings and work, Jesus would have to be divine.

Paul's decision was not made in a vacuum. Paul's world was a troubled world with one or more pagan religions embedded in each nation. To gain new Christians, Paul had to draw Gentiles away from the pagan religions they were following. A divine Jesus place him in the same status as the Greek and Roman gods. For Paul, this allowed Gentles to accept Jesus as their God in place of their existing gods and opened Jesus' ministry to the Gentiles.

Paul's philosophy of Christianity became the basis for his teaching and for much of the church's theology. Paul may or may not have believed that God created us in His image and wanted us to live in His likeness; however, he determined that only Jesus lived in a close spiritual relationship as would the son of God, which he did not think was available to the Jews and Gentiles. Even though Paul had seen the strong faith in God that Stephen and other followers of Jesus had, Paul believed that Jesus did things that people could never do. Paul certainly evaluated what he knew about Jesus and his followers through his Pharisee training and experience that required there to be someone as the leader above everyone else, which fit his divine Jesus like a glove.

Paul believed a divine Jesus made Christianity available to Jews and Gentiles alike. Paul wanted to spread Abraham's relationship with God to all mankind and believed only a divine Jesus could do that.

Paul's divine Jesus was his answer to having the Gentiles look to Jesus for more guidance than they were receiving from their pagan religion; however, at some point, Paul decided Jesus was more than the Gentile and some Jewish Christians believed Him to be. Paul thought there was more to Jesus' life and ministry than His loving relationship with God and His desire for Jews and Gentiles to live in God's blessing. Paul changing his emphasis about Jesus from simply being divine to being the one true God for all mankind. This placed Jesus well above the gods of mythology worked. The Lordship of Christ Jesus was successfully marketed to the Gentiles.

By declaring the "Lordship of Christ Jesus," Paul decided that Jesus was like God, who came to earth as a human to teach about God, who was to die a horrible death, to rise in His victory over death to be with God as Lord of life and death. Paul declared that Christ existed in the beginning and created everything, known and unknow, that follow his own creation. The first eighteen verses of the Gospel of John have a similar description of who and what Jesus is.

Paul's divine Jesus was a god in His own right. Paul's definition of the divine Jesus made Jesus little or no different from God. Jesus became a god that the Christians went to for guidance and salvation. In Christianity, it seems God can be second to Jesus and it is sometimes hard to determine whether the term Lord refers to Jesus or God.

Paul's declaration of the "Lordship of Christ Jesus" created a major conflict with the Jewish followers of Jesus. Having Jesus be divine was not a major leap of faith from the prophet Jesus; however, Paul's interpretation of Jesus' relationship with God was a radical change from what the apostles and Jews believed Jesus' relationship was with God. Their belief came from Jesus' actions and messages, such as they could have God's blessing by living a life centered on God.

Paul's divine Jesus did not sit well with Jerusalem followers of Jesus, as well as the Jews who were not followers of Jesus. Nothing about Jesus fit the Jews idea for Him to be divine. The idea that God would send Jesus to earth as a baby conceived out of wedlock did not fit. That Jesus struggled as a human only to die a horrible death did not fit. And then for Jesus to go back to heaven, leaving His disciples and followers in a quandary about his message did not fit. The Jews expected much more of a divine person than Jesus's ministry provided. Paul's entire idea about who and what Jesus was, simply went against the Jews perception of their relationship with God.

For the Jews, He was clearly a prophet, and making Him divine was an afront to their relationship with God. Prophet Jesus' terrible death, while tragic, could have been thought of as being like the death of John the Baptist; and therefore, more acceptable.

Mythology was an integral part of the Greek and Roman religions, which was an important part of their lives. Paul's message that Jesus was, "a god in human form, who was killed and returned to his godly form," resonated with the Greek and Roman people. Paul's message was an ideal fit with what the Greek and Roman people already believed, but not for what the Jews already believed.

Although some Gentiles were converting to follow Jesus before He became divine, Paul believed it would have been difficult to convince enough Gentiles to follow the teachings of a little-known Jew who talked to some Jews about their relationship to God for Christianity to be a viable religion.

Although Paul's thinking was in response to the major issues of that time, his thinking has remained embedded in Christianity. Paul's Jesus has been instrumental in setting Christianity on a path of growth and wealth and continues to be the theological basis for Christianity.

There is no question in my mind that Paul's leadership gave the Gentile Church the needed guidance and direction for it to survive the turmoil of its early time; however, I do have issues with Jesus' birth and cruci-fixion being the most prominent events in the Christian calendar. The glorious celebrations of Jesus' birth and death exceed the celebrations of any of Jesus' messages in His ministry. The strong support in Jesus' ministry for establishing a personal spiritual relationship with God has been lost in the theology of Jesus' crucifixion, His rising from death, and being the Savior.

Jesus' ministry was about living—not about dying. That mankind has sinned (missed its mark or been less than it could be) has been a problem since before Adam and Eve. Making the point that we have sinned a main part of the Christian message detracts from the positive message that Jesus proclaimed. The underlying messages of Jesus' min-istry were of God's love and that the Jews could improve their lives by making God central to their lives, as Jesus' life demonstrated.

Paul's explanation of Jesus' divinity had an additional benefit, one that provided a stabilizing force for Christianity. Noss states:

> This was important in the development of Christianity, for here Paul saved it from an extreme-that of non-ethical mysticism-as dangerous to its balance and truth as the legalism from which he had earlier rescued it (Noss. Page 623).

It is certainly true that Paul's conclusions put Jesus into a format the Gentiles knew; and therefore, it made transferring allegiance from pagan gods to Jesus easier. The rapid growth in the Gentile Church after Paul made Jesus divine attests to the success of Paul's decision. For Paul, a divine Jesus was a better answer than convincing Gentiles of Jesus' amazing feats without Jesus being divine.

MESSIAH

Paul surely knew there would be problems if the Gentiles called Jesus *the Messiah*. Paul believed that by making Jesus divine he would avoid the problems that he knew would come with calling Jesus the Messiah. The ancient idea of an Israelite Messiah, a great Prince of Peace, who would come from the seed and lineage of David, began showing up during the time of the Prophet Isiah, something after the split of David's kingdom into the north and south kingdoms. With the arrival of the Romans the Messianic concept, which closely follows the Zoroastrian concept received greater eminence.

By recognizing Jesus' divinity, which was a status equivalent to, or higher than the Romans' and Greeks' gods, Paul believed he was making Jesus available to the Gentiles without getting into the Messiah issue. The Jews' concept of the Messiah was that the Messiah would gather the God-centered living and dead to be with God forever. The Messiah would come down from heaven, with the end of the world, when trumpets would sound accompanied by angels.

In the time of Roman rule, the Jews strongly believed that a Messiah would come to save them from the terrible woes of the Romans and their oppressive religion and marginal existent. The idea that God would intervene to save the deserving Jews did have some strings attached. To be included as one of God's own, the Jews would have to live in the blessing of God before the Messiah came down.

So, there were at least two reasons for the Jews to change the way they were living. First, Jesus believed that God intended for the Jews to live a life in spiritual harmony with God. With such a life, death would be a minor occurrence. Being in spiritual harmony with God requires that the Jews place their personal relationship with God first above all else. Jesus' examples throughout His ministry made this point. Matthew 6:25-34 provides some examples of this theme in His ministry. Without placing God first above all else their continued worrying about their daily needs for existence were blocking them from being one of God's own.

Second, the Jews who were God-centered would be ready for the Messiah when He came and the worry about being selected would be gone. Jesus was convinced that living with God-centered faith would give the Jews the spiritual strength and peace of mind to remove the stress, uncertainty, and hopelessness of their lives. Being God-centered would not cause the Romans or the Jewish religious leaders to change their ways or go away, but rather would put all the Jews' daily needs and concerns in perspective and would have them in control of their lives, and they would be ready for the coming of the Messiah.

Compounding the difference between Jerusalem and Gentile Christians was the idea that Jesus was the Messiah, an idea that was accepted by the Gentiles, but was totally unacceptable to the Jerusalem Christians. For the Gentiles, the Messiah was a Savior rather than a messenger from God. For the Jews, the appearance of the Messiah would mean that the righteous had been collected and time had ended. Neither of these things had happened and Jesus did not come from the clouds accompanied with angels. Jesus did not fit the Jews idea of who the Messiah was or what His purpose was.

The few Jews who knew of Jesus' teachings and saw the healings, did not considered him to be the Messiah nor was He a factor in the lives of the many Jews who had not heard or seen Him. Rather than being the Messiah to those who heard Jesus, he was considered a breath of fresh air in the stifling atmosphere of the Judaism rules and rituals, and Roman occupation. While they loved His ministry, that did not qualify him to be the Messiah.

While Paul probably did not intend for the divine Jesus to be one and the same as the Messiah, but that is what happened. Christians took the concept of the Messiah being a messenger to the Messiah being the divine Jesus. By associating the term *Messiah* with the divine Jesus, the Gentile Christians had taken a major piece of the Jews' religion and history, and arbitrarily assigned it a new meaning.

The Jews were adamant that Jesus was not the Messiah and became more so as the Gentile Christians tried to convince them otherwise. The Jewish Messianic idea had been around since the time of the Hebrews and may have originated with Zoroastrianism. That the Gentile Christians changed the definition of the term *Messiah* and took it as their own was a serious affront to the Jews and their history.

The Jews' Messiah concept was an integral part of who they were. Paul knew and well understood the Jews' concept of the Messiah. It seems that the Jews' and Paul's expectations of the Messiah were similar. This different definition of who Jesus was continued to be the major unsolvable difference that separated the Jerusalem followers of Jesus from the Gentile followers of Jesus.

It was while the gospels were being written that Paul's idea of Jesus being *more* than a gifted teacher was developed. Even with some believing him to be a prophet, there is nothing that would make the Jews think that Jesus was the Messiah or divine. If this idea had been raised at the time of Jesus' birth or during His life before He started His ministry, it seems likely that His birth and His young life would have received better treatment by the Jews. All four books do agree that Jesus' family lived in Nazareth and Jesus spent most of His first thirty years at home in Nazareth but say little else for this period.

PAUL'S MINISTRY

Paul strongly believed that his story of Jesus must be available to all Gentiles. While I have not found a connection, the source for Paul's belief of incorporating Gentiles into following Jesus could have come from God's covenant with Abraham as described in Genesis 12: 1-3, that God would make Abraham a great nation.

Paul did not think Jesus' ministry was a sellable concept to many Gentiles. Paul believed that describing living in the likeness of God without a divine Jesus would be a hard sell, even though some Gentiles became members of the Way before Paul developed his idea that Jesus was divine. Some Gentiles were taking Jesus' ministry to heart and changing their life priorities by putting God first and having faith and trust in God like Jewish Jesus followers did.

There is much about Jesus and his message that is worthy of being followed regardless of a person's religion. Paul recognized that Jesus's ministry was true for all people and that he needed to, "as we say today," package it so that it would relate well to the Gentiles.

It is unfortunate that Paul's one idea that Jesus is the divine Son of God caused so much tension between the Gentile Christians, and Jewish Christians, and non-Christians that it continues to be a source of disagreement and intolerance between Christians and Jews.

The disciples did not grasp Jesus' core message of following God's guidance until after Jesus was crucified. Neither did the people who heard Him teach and saw the healing that happened in his presence, nor the Pharisees, priests, and scribes who followed Him trying to find a reason to arrest him. Jesus' ministry was not based on Jesus being divine but rather was based on having the Jews live as God would live. Jesus' life demonstrated that the Jews could live in the likeness of God. Jesus' ministry was not about whether He was or was not divine. It was about the Jews living in their chaotic world with God's guidance and blessing.

Paul also failed to recognize the significance of the death of Stephen and the willingness of the followers of Jesus to be put to death for their belief in Jesus' ministry.

Paul's message, that all people could live in a spiritual relationship with God can be found in Jesus' message about following God's guidance. From the little we know of Paul's life after his conversion, it seems likely that Paul was living in the likeness of God.

By declaring Jesus as being divine, Paul had created a way, in addition to what was already in place, for Jesus's ministry to be acceptable for all people. Paul gave Jews, Greeks, and Romans all an approach, establishing a relationship with God. Unfortunately, all too often Christians, regardless of the denomination or sect have not been able to easily accept people with different beliefs than theirs.

In AD 47, Paul and Barnabas went on Paul's first mission trip to Cyprus and Galatia. Other missions would follow; however, upon their return from this mission trip differences between the Jerusalem Christians and the Gentile Christians had become so severe that they could no longer be ignored.

Paul was in complete disagreement with the Jerusalem Christians. In AD 49, Paul and Barnabas went to Jerusalem to confront the Jerusalem leaders, primarily Peter, James, and John. Ground rules were established during this meeting for Gentile membership in the Christian Church.

The apostles felt that Jesus' message should remain tied to Jewish law and Jewish history. Even before Paul was involved, a conservative group of Jerusalem Christians that included former Pharisees had been creating problems regarding the Gentile Christians' lack of following Jewish law. The Pharisees were having difficulty giving up what they had learned in Pharisee schools.

Paul believed that God was for all people and the Gentiles could have a spiritual relationship with God without following the Judaism requirements. Paul had observed the strong faith in Jesus the Gentiles had without having to follow the Judaism rites, and he argued for accepting Gentile Christians without requiring them to adhere to Jewish law and history.

Although change was hard for the apostles, they reluctantly gave Paul their cooperation based on his being called to work among the Gentiles. The apostles' cooperation came with some requirements that the Gentiles would have to meet that primarily concerned preparing and eating meat. The important part of the agreement was that it released the Gentiles from being bound by the actions of the Jerusalem Christians and removed the need for Gentiles to read and know the Israelite manuscripts that became the Old Testament.

For Paul, this was a great victory for the Gentile Christians and increased the flow of Gentiles into Christianity. It also seems that Jerusalem Church saw the agreement as relieving them of having to deal with Paul's thinking. However, to the determent of both sides, this agreement became a critical factor in the continuing differences between the Gentile and Jerusalem Christians. The sum and substance of Paul's ministry was the Gentile Christians, with little knowledge of the Old Testament, quickly outnumbered the Jewish Christians, who rather quickly lost relevance.

This agreement began the process of the Gentile Christians formalizing the rules for membership in the church that were different from the rules for membership in the Jerusalem Church. No longer being tied to Judaism and free of the need to read and develop an understanding of the Old Testament removed a burden from the Gentile Christians, but it also removed a chance for them to better understand the meaning and importance behind Jesus' stories and parables. While the Gentiles knew they would have to change the way they lived, they felt that the Jews were expecting too much. With their divine Jesus, the Gentiles did not think the Old Testament was needed. Jesus would be their connection for having a spiritual relationship with God.

Even with the agreement Paul had obtained with the Jerusalem Christians for the Gentile Christians, Paul still had problems with the Gentile Christian leaders. There were several different ideas about who Jesus was and what he accomplished. Paul encountered resistance to his ministry in Damascus and during his mission trips.

It was not a foregone conclusion that Paul's thinking would prevail. His ministry did provide an alternative to some of the extreme thinking within the Church leadership. We will never know for sure, but it seems reasonable to think that Paul's energy, passion, perseverance, and persuasiveness ruled the day, and his ministry became the basis for much of the Gentile Church theology.

It seems evident that some of the Gentile Christians, who were involved in organizing the Gentile church groups prior to Paul's arrival, were still not comfortable with a former Pharisee being the prominent Church leader, who was providing much of the information, direction, and structure for the Church. Paul was getting enough push back in both Damascus and Jerusalem to convince him to leave both cities. Even though Paul's thinking and ideas became the central theme of the Christian Church, the other ideas were still around.

Paul continued his mission trips in AD 49 through AD 57, traveling in the area around the eastern end of the Mediterranean Sea. Acts 14-18:28 describes Paul's trips and activities, including founding churches in Corinth, Thessalonica, and Beroea, as well as supporting Christian communities in the cities he visited.

It was Paul and others who traveled outside the Jewish communities who had the difficult task of telling the story of Jesus. They had to explain three key ideas. Their first task was explaining the story of Jesus.

Jesus, the poor itinerate carpenter who was so sure that He understood God's message to the Jewish people that He willingly risked everything to demonstrate that the Jewish people could live as God intended. Matthew 10:5-6 and 15:21-28 describe Jesus' ministry as being solely for the Jews. While, on occasions, Jesus ministered to Gentiles, his ministry centered on having the Jews receive their guidance solely from God. Jesus wanted the Jews to be ready for the judgment day when the world, as they knew it, ended and God selected the righteous to be with Him.

Paul's success was limited by the non-Jews lack of knowledge, or at best minimal knowledge, of the Old Testament writings and Jewish history, both of which were central to Jesus' message and the Jews' understanding of his message. Paul made up for this lack of knowledge by stressing that the divine Jesus was sent by God. The divine Jesus made it easier for the Gentiles to switch their allegiance from their pagan gods to God.

The second task was to convince the Gentiles that each person could personally relate to God and/or divine Jesus. That God or Jesus were available to each person without a priest interceding was new and different. It changed the relationship a person had with a deity from servant-master to a personal caring friendship between a person and either God or Jesus. The simple and direct relationship that Jesus told the Jews they could have with God became less simple and less direct when Christianity became involved. The main issue is that a person could have a personal relationship with either God or Jesus without gaining permission from a priest or religious leader.

In other religions, a person had to go to the religious leader or priest to receive information from a god. The idea of establishing a personal caring relationship with God would have been a new and startling idea for people to accept.

Over time the simple idea of Jesus' ministry, that one could go directly to God, has been minimized and has become complicated. Some Christian denotations have inserted intermediaries between its members and God. Contrary to Jesus' belief that people have this God given opportunity, the leaders of some denotations believe that humans could not just talk to God as they chose. I continue to be surprised by the number of people who don't feel they can talk directly to God.

The third task was to convince people of the Jews' firm belief that the end to the world, as the people knew it, was close at hand and only the chosen few blessed by God would survive. This was an easy sell. The idea that the end of the world was to happen soon was not just a Jewish idea.

Paul had a better grasp of Jesus' message than other Christian leaders. His work to convert Jesus' message to the Jews to a message for all mankind was certainly a profound and successful accomplishment. His belief in his new understanding of his relationship with God was stronger than the prestige he had as a Pharisee.

IMPACT OF PAUL'S MINISTRY

Because early Christian leaders could not comprehend that a carpenter's son from a small village like Nazareth in Galilee had a mystical and wonderous life like Jesus', they accepted Paul's divine Jesus and built an organizational structure for Christians to follow. While they may have professed to believing that everyone was created in the image of God and could live in the likeness of God, their actions exposed their lack of belief that everyone, on their own, could have a life as Jesus had.

Having said that it was through the work of Paul and the other leaders that Christians grew in number and spread out through the Roman Empire. The Roman leaders were not sure what to do with them. They did not worship the emperor but obeyed the Roman laws. They were pacifists unwilling to fight to defend the Roman Empire. They kept to themselves and met secretly at night. This led to their persecution.

The perplexity of the Roman leaders is expressed in a letter Pliny the Younger, governor of Bithynia (in Asia Minor) wrote to Emperor Trajan, Pliny reports:

> ...that when he found Christians who persisted three times over in saying they were Christians, he ordered them to be executed; "for," said he blandly, "I did not

doubt that, whatever it was they admitted, obstinacy and unbending perversity certainly deserve to be punished!" (Noss page 626)

Christians were publicly put to death as early as AD 64. This had far-reaching effects, both on the Christians and the public at large, in shaping the feeling that the Christian religion was to its adherents not only worth living by but dying for as well. (Noss page. 626)

Jewish Christians who had fled Palestine, as well as the Gentile Christians, believed in Jesus on to death. The persecutions continued sporadically until the early 300s. If the persecution had been continued on a steady basis, the Christian movement may have been completely wiped out. It is worthy of note that the message the early Christians were getting from Jesus' ministry was changing how they lived. They were making their relationship with God important above also else, onto death.

The strain that Christianity placed on the communities they were in is exemplified by an experience Paul had in the Roman city of Ephesus. It seems that a silversmith named Demetrius was upset that his and the other silversmiths' business of making silver shrines to the goddess Artemis was in decline. Greek mythology had Artemis as the goddess of chastity, virginity, the hunt, the moon, and the environment. Demetrius declared that not only in Ephesus but throughout Asia, Paul was pulling away people by telling them that gods made by people were not gods. Demetrius created enough anger that a riot resulted. Things were getting out of hand when the town clerk quieted and dispersed the crowd.

Paul wanted to speak to the crowd but was dissuaded by friends from doing so. The disruption to the economy based on supporting the existing gods that resulted from the Christian concept of one God for everything, was a real threat to the communities and the acceptance of Christianity. The difficulty was that Christianity required giving up worshiping all the gods and the associated activities that had been an integral part of the entire lives of the people in these communities (July/August 2016 BAR, Archaeology Gives New Reality to Paul's Ephesus Riot by James R. Edwards and Acts 19:23-41).

At the time of Paul's death in the latter part of the AD 60s, it was not yet apparent that his work and letters would have such a profound effect on Christianity. There were other leaders contributing to the ultimate success of Christianity. Early Jewish followers of Jesus, such as the apostles, the writers of Mark, Matthew, Luke and John, and the writers of the non-Pauline Epistles, brought with them their belief in the life and ministry of Jesus and were major contributors to the early Christians and were instrumental in the development of Christianity. Although some of the leaders weren't in agreement with Paul's theology, it was Paul, with his appreciation of the unique Jesus, who set the path for Christians to follow and established the core of much of the Christian theology of today.

Paul prevailed and was instrumental in spreading Christianity throughout the Roman Empire. He may very well have assisted in spreading Christianity into other places outside the Roman Empire. He also laid out the basic organizational structure of the church, as well as incorporating in the church literacy his ideas on celibacy, divine grace, and salvation.

His work increased the gap between Jesus the man and Jesus the divine. The revisions to the religious writings during this period are demonstrated in the differences in the description of Jesus. The description in the Didache as a prophet and teacher does not come close to the superhuman being of the Epistle of Barnabas (see chapter 10). The superhuman Jesus is at the central theology of much of Christianity today. The original description of what constituted the Messiah was strictly a Jewish concept. By making Jesus divine, Paul opened the way for early Christian leaders to change the Jewish description of the Messiah by making Jesus the Messiah, thus eliminating much of the criteria a Jewish Messiah must meet.

The early manuscripts, some of which became part of the New Testament around AD 400, were what the Gentile Christians used to understand Jesus' message of hope and God's love for them. When these early manuscripts., were being written, Paul was active in the non-Jerusalem church affairs, and his theology was being accepted as church theology.

It is reasonable to think that Paul was in touch with some of the apostles and the writers of the Gospels and letters, who were well versed on Paul's ideas about the divinity of Jesus. Even with their Jewish background, the apostles and the writers of the Gospels could not help but see the success the Gentile Christians were having in recruiting new members. The total lack of any reference to Jesus being the Messiah in the early Jerusalem Church writings makes it likely that Paul's theology was added to or included later in the manuscripts that became the Gospels and other early documents. It would have been difficult for the apostles and their followers to stand firm against the success of Paul and not incorporate Paul's theology into their writings.

Gentiles had joined the Way movement before Paul decided that Jesus was divine; however, some believe that the rate of gaining Gentile members would not have been enough for the Way movement to be sustainable without a larger-than-life standard-bearer that people could look to for guidance. We will never know if Christianity could have survived without the driving force of Paul and his decision that Jesus was divine.

Paul certainly understood that Jesus' divinity created a radical change in the way Gentiles viewed Jesus from the way Jews viewed Jesus. Because that change became the basis for Christian theology, with little or no variations it still existed today as a barrier to mutual acceptance of the different relationships Jews and Gentiles can have with God.

There were unintended consequences with recognizing Jesus' divinity, one of which was separating Jesus from mankind. Paul created new problems centering around the Christian's relationship with Jesus and God. Jesus being divine separated Jesus from all people and placed

Jesus on a level like the level of God. He became something unique to himself, something that is not available to anyone else.

By recognizing Jesus' divinity, Paul created a pathway for Christianity to elevate Jesus to a position of being a god between God and man. Some ministers refer to Jesus as Lord or God, which puts Jesus' life and ministry beyond the reach of mankind. In other words, by placing Christ at the beginning of time and making Christ's time on earth as Jesus, a part of the overall creation of all things, everyone would have to be a "Christ" to emulate Jesus. Since Paul describes Jesus, as the Christ, as the Lord of life and death, Jesus' scheduled time on earth, between His birth and death, fills a minor role in Christ's existence. With Paul's description of who Jesus was, God's role in creation is changed and not clear.

A divine Jesus decreases our relationship with God. It was Abraham who showed how to have a personal, direct relationship with God. Jesus believed the Jews were, "made in the image of God," and could live in the likeness of God. Jesus told the Jews and demonstrated to them that they too could live in the likeness of God, as people made in the image of God.

Suffice it to say that Paul's concept of how Jesus fit into the relationship between God and mankind did sharpen the differences that existed between the two groups. Paul's concepts brought Gentiles into the Church, without requiring circumcision, or reading the early Jewish manuscripts, some of which became the Old Testament. For Paul, everything starts and ends with the divine Jesus.

Paul's ministry continues to be with us. His concept of who and what Jesus was remains central to today's Christianity, as it was for the early Christians.

Chapter 10

EARLY CHRISTIAN STRUGGLES

THE DIVIDE BETWEEN GENTILE AND JERUSALEM CHRISTIANS

L ove is the foundation for the relationship between each person and God. It was difficult for the Jews and Gentiles to base their lives on God's love while they could not have a loving relationship with each other. Christians still have a way to go in our relationship with Jews.

There is no question that the apostles and other Jews in the Jerusalem church were influenced by their Jewish religious background. Jesus simply did not fit the description of what the Messiah should be or how He should arrive. In short, even in the small number of people who believed in Jesus, there was little thought that He was the Messiah. The people of Nazareth, who drove Jesus out of town had reasons to be suspicious of the claims made about His accomplishments and certainly would not have been thinking of Him as the Messiah. During Jesus' first thirty years, nothing happened that would you will see Him to be considered the Messiah.

Equally true, the Gentiles were influenced by the pagan religions they had known all their lives, with the interplay between humans and the gods. The mythology, mystery, and magic that surrounds the gods of their pagan religion was what they expected from this new religion.

The reported activities of Jesus and His being risen from the dead certainly met the criteria established by the pagan religions.

The Jerusalem Christians followed Moses' laws, attended Judaism rites and requirements. They believed that Jesus was normally conceived, and grew up to be an exceptional man, who as an adult was a prophet and teacher, who wanted the Jews to be ready for the coming Messiah at the end of the world as they know it. Jesus closely followed the teachings of Judaism. His argument was with the Judaism leaders, not Judaism.

The Gentile religion was built on Paul's idea that Jesus was Christ, a divine being who possessed the nature of God. He was the Son of the unseen God. As such, He lived as a human, to die, and rise after three days and ascend to heaven.

During the first 100 years after the death of Jesus, the split between the Jewish Christians who thought of Jesus as a prophet and teacher, and the Gentile Christians who thought of Jesus as a superhuman sent by God, became so strained that it could not be repaired.

The church in Antioch was started in about AD 40 by mostly Jewish Christians who fled Jerusalem after the death of Stephen. As Greek members joined the church, Jewish and Greek members ate meals together and worshipped together. Some members of the Jerusalem church who strictly adhered to the Jewish understanding of Jesus' ministry arrived in Antioch under the leadership of James, the brother to Jesus, were upset and demanded that the Gentile and Jewish members stopped eating together. Paul was outraged and argued with Peter and denounced Peter as a hypocrite. (Galatians tells of this conflict.) This was the first major argument in Christianity.

Apparently, the conservative Christians from Jerusalem did not agree that the mixing of liberal Jewish and Gentile Christians was part of the deal that was made with Paul. Although James countered the actions of the extreme group of Jerusalem Christians, the damage had been done and James could not get Jerusalem church members to expand their thinking enough to keep them from losing relevance in the development of Christianity. Equally unfortunate, the inability of Christians to expand their thinking continues to exist in Christianity.

Pauls' reaction to the Antioch church members giving in to the Jerusalem church members gives a good indication of Paul's thinking on how the Jews and Gentiles could work together. He was not interested in having the thinking of the two church groups create separation. He apparently thought that the need for the Greek members to think of Jesus as being divine did not mean that the Jewish member had to think Jesus was divine. For Paul, the message of Jesus' ministry and life could be as clear to the Jews with Him being a prophet as it was to the Greeks with him being divine.

I earlier wrote about the different ideas the Israelites and the Gentiles in the various Greek communities had about how to present Jesus to the Church members. For example, Paul had started a church in Corinth around AD 49. Paul's letters to the church in Corinth indicate that the church members were having ethical and leadership problems that were endangering the church.

Early Gentile Christians were putting together their theology as they worshipped Jesus. The people that came from different areas and pagan religions were bringing different ideas about what Christianity should look like. None of these differences rose to a level of acceptance that would keep Paul's theology from being the standard for Gentile Christianity.

These differences within the Gentile church family were in addition to the major unreconcilable difference between the basic theology being developed by the Gentile Church and the theology of the Jerusalem Church. Some of the differences within the Gentile Church were called heresies when the Catholic theology was developed and remain today.

The official split between the Jerusalem and Gentile Christians was inevitable.

The Jerusalem council of the apostles marked the beginning of the separation of Jewish and Gentile Christianity. Both Churches agreed on some essentials such as the second coming of Christ, the resurrection of the dead and the inauguration of the kingdom of God. Paul himself believed that it would happen in His lifetime (Thess. 4:15-17).

However, the churches saw some things differently. The original Judeo-Christian baptism and the breaking of bread were transformed in the Gentile Church under the influence of Paul. Baptism was tied to Jesus' death, burial, and resurrection. The communal meal was upgraded to a sacrament. These differences led to increasing anti-Jewish thinking in the Gentile church.

There are two writings that reflect the different thinking in the early church. The Didache or Doctrine of the Twelve Apostles summarizes the Mosaic Law for use as a guide for new church members. It holds none of Paul's idea of Jesus being the Son of God and referred to Jesus as a servant or child. Jesus is expected to reappear soon and collect the members of his church to the kingdom of God. The Didache may predate some of the New Testament.

The second writing is the Epistle of Barnabas, which was not written by Barnabas, is an early expression of Gentile Christianity. It is anti-Jewish. The major point of this letter is that the covenant between God and the Jews was voided because it was never approved by the Jews. This goes back to the golden calf affair. The letter claims that when Moses smashed the tables inscribed with the Ten Commandments, a new covenant was made with God that was sealed by the blood of Jesus. The letter also states that the Son of God became human so that people could look at him and stay alive.

The first and second-century Christians were having difficulties discerning the meaning of Jesus' teaching and the miracles and then figuring out how to present it to the people. I think that it is important to recognize that the Jerusalem church did not look at Jesus as the Messiah but rather as a servant and teacher who would come back to gather the dispersed believes and take them to the Kingdom of God.

286

This is in line with Jesus' teaching in Mark 8:34-38 and Mark 9:33-37, that the first shall be last.

The underlying message of the Epistle of Barnabas was that God could not have both the Jews and the Christians be special people blessed by God. Although only God can decide who He would bless, the Christians were deciding for God who He would and would not bless. This idea is unfortunate for God did not give the Christians or anyone else the authority to decide who He would bless.

The friction between the Gentiles and Jews apparently went deeper than how each viewed Jesus. The underlying thinking of the Jews required full knowledge of the Old Testament and the belief that the predictions of the Old Testament had been filled by the prophet Jesus. The Gentiles, on the other hand, did not think that their lack of knowledge about the Old Testament should hinder their ability to follow Jesus without being included as a Jew.

> This was the situation that confronted Paul. He addressed it by saying that each side was partly right and partly wrong and by pointing out that there was a common basis that could unite both into a single church. The Jews were right to emphasize their ancestry and their traditions because these things pointed towards the coming of Christ. Correctly understood and applied, these traditions gave Jews a great advantage in living the Christian life. But Gentiles were also right to insist that claiming descent from Abraham meant nothing if those who did so did not also believe what Abraham believed and did not relate to God in the same way as he had done—by faith.
>
> Faith, says Paul is the key theological principle that unites both Jews and Gentiles because it is by faith that we are justified, or made right with God. (ACCS, Book VI, pg. XVIII Edited by Gerald Bray and Thomas C. Oden General Editor xviii)

I think Paul believed that the benefit of having Jesus be divine would outweigh the resulting problems. I also believe that Paul thought that Gentiles and Jews could worship together and develop strong bonds within the church by celebrating their common faith in God while accepting and learning from, their differences as the Antioch Church did for such a short time.

The issue as to whether Jesus was or was not divine is not about Jesus' relationship with God and the Jews. It is about the Jews, Gentiles, and Paul's relationship with God and Jesus. Our perception about who Jesus and God are does not affect who they are. God and Jesus are not changed by what Jews and Gentiles think. God gave us our freedom to make our own decisions. God will rejoice with us when our decision result in good and will support us when our decision turn out to be bad. God loves and sticks with us regardless of what we do. Jesus' patience with His disciples certain is a good example of God's patience with Jews and Gentiles alike.

There is an assessment of the events in Jesus' three-year ministry that requires more study and discussion than simply accepting the heart felt truths described in the Gospels as being true beyond question. The intent of writers is not in question. It is the circumstance of the observation of an event or the telling of a story that can cause a difference between the Gospel description and the actual reason for the Gospel writing.

CHRISTIANITY'S OPPRESSION OF THE JEWS

Paul believed that Jesus was the example of God, not what God looked like but, the spiritual being of God. This theme, which came from Paul's belief that Jesus was divine, became the basis for the Gentiles understanding of Christianity. However, this theme distorted Jesus' ministry and began the process of getting away from the Jesus message.

At the time of Paul, many of the Christian leaders were Jews, who had at least a general knowledge of the Jewish manuscripts, some of which became the Old Testament. This was not enough; however, to provide the Gentile Christians more than, at best, minimal knowledge of the Old Testament writings. As a result, the Gentile Christians did not understand what the Jewish followers were saying and why they were taking the positions they were taking. The Gentiles did not recognize that their uncomprehending position that Jesus was divine, without exception was placing the Jews in the impossible position of having to deny who they were. This met that neither group could establish a common basis that they could use to build a common understanding of Jesus' ministry or to develop a compatible belief structure.

The oppression of the Jews began with the early Christians solving two theological problems. These two ideas about Jesus are clearly described in the Didache and the Epistle of Barnabas. Jesus, the Prophet, and teacher of the Didache became the spiritual being of Paul and apostle John or, one of John's disciples, and of the Epistle of Barnabas.

The additional theological problem that needed to be solved was justifying the decision that Jews had lost God's blessing. It was not enough for the Christian Church to declare that the Jews failed to see the total reason of Jesus' ministry and existence, as describe by Paul, but rather the Christian Church felt it needed to discredit the Jews for thinking that they were blessed by God.

The idea that the covenant between God and the Jews was not renewed after Moses broke the Ten Commandants tablets was wrong. The Lord continued to guide Moses and Israelites and God renewed His covenant with the Israelites. Even with their failings, the Israelites were still the people chosen by God to be a great nation, who shall bring God's blessing to all people of the world. See Exodus 32:1-35 for breaking the covenant and Exodus 34:1-35 for renewal of the covenant.

Early Gentile Christians' solutions were counter to Jesus' core message of love. Both remain problems today and have served as the reasoning used to oppress the Jews.

Added to the reasoning that the Jews were no longer God's chosen people was the determination that the Jews killed Jesus. Geza Vermes also pointed out that:

> Half a century after Barnabas, the bishop of Sardis, Melito, declared that the Jews are guilty of deicide: "God has been murdered... by the right hand of Israel." (BAR Nov/ Dec 2012 the article by Geza Vermes pg. 78.)

I have also wondered how the Christians who said the Jews were no longer chosen by God explained the relationship between the Israelites-Jews and God that continued to love and protect long after Moses broke the tablets. The Jews continued to treat God as their God, and God continued to treat the Jews as blessed people. And how does Jesus, a Jew, who showed what being spiritually connected to God meant and looked like, fit into the Christian destructive relationship with the Jews?

It would have been well if the early Christians had recognized their debt to the Jews. It is not too late for Christianity to do so today. Asking and receiving God's forgiveness has no expiration date.

Starting with Jesus being a Jew, then the Pentecost event that kept the story of Jesus' ministry alive, was between God and the Jews. And then it was the spreading of Jesus' story by the Jews that dispersed out of Jerusalem and into Roman and Greek cities. Then the impressive group of early Jewish leaders of the followers of Jesus, such as Peter, John, Barnabas and of course Paul, and all the Jews supporting early Christianity that contributed to the continued existence Christianity. The simple question is, how would Christianity have started and survived without the input and guidance from the Jews?

So, even if the Jews killed Jesus, which they clearly did not, the guidance, leadership, and steadfast support that was given to the early church by the Jewish followers of Jesus more than makes up for any failings of the Jews during the last days of Jesus' life. There is nothing anyone can do to void God's forgiveness.

With all that was owed to the Jews who believed in Jesus' life and ministry, the decision by the Gentile Christians to go their separate way, by degrading the Jews was a terrible and oppressive way to build a religion that professes to believe in God's love.

Blaming the Jews for Jesus' death as an important feature of Christianity has always troubled me. I do not believe that using the perceived failures of others provides a firm foundation for one's faith. Equally so, I do not believe persecutions regardless of the justification given, represents any of the values of Jesus ministry.

I have always wondered how the Romans escaped blame. It was the Romans who tortured and crucified Him. The fact that Jesus, who was viewed as a potential troublemaker, scared the Jewish religious leaders enough for them to wanted Him dead does not relieve the Romans of being the ones who did the killing.

There is no question that the Jewish leadership wanted Jesus dead; however, it is also clear that the Romans had the option to release Him or kill Him and chose to kill Him. The four gospels described Jesus being executed by Pilate and an outside source, the Roman historian Tacitus, confirms it. Unfortunately, blaming the Jews for killing Jesus remains a key point upon which the destructive relationship with the Jews has been built.

The added burden of being responsible for the death of Jesus, a responsibility, that unfortunately, was given to the Jews by the Gentile Christians, just added salt to their wounds. The failure of the Gentile Christians to accept that the Jews will continue to think of Jesus as a prophet and making the Jews responsible for Jesus' death are blemishes Christians continue to carry today.

So, the apparent need to take over the Jews' relationship with God seems to have been the driving force for using questionable reasoning to justify their decisions. Granted, the Jerusalem Christians that demanded the separation of the Jewish and Gentile Christian in the Antioch church may have started, or at least clarified, the fight for primacy, there was no requirement for the Epistle of Barnabas to continue it. There is nothing in the Bible that justifies such actions, nor is there anything in the Bible that would keep both the Jews and Gentiles from being special. Jesus demonstrated that God's relationship is with individuals, regardless of where he or she is from or what group he or she has joined.

And what does being chosen by God mean? Jews have dispersed over the world and have endured hardships and persecution but have persevered through the centuries. Even with being despised and ruthlessly treated by Christian communities and nations, they have benefited their communities and their nations. Through all the mistreatment they have received, their continued steadfast commitment to God has been their demonstration of what it means to dedicate their lives to God and how their commitment to God sustained them through terrible times. No other people have suffered as much for as long a period in their commitment to living in the blessing of God as have the Jews.

EARLY CHRISTIANITY

Early on, the framework for the belief structure for Christianity had been established. The belief that Jesus was the Messiah had become the central belief of Christianity, with some variations and exceptions.

Christianity was like the man who builds his house on sand and rains and floods, and the wind comes and the house falls (Matt. 7:26). Surely, the ravages of hatred for, and indifference to, the Jews weaken the ability of Christians to demonstrate God's love to others. Christians had, and still have, lost track of Jesus' teaching of God's forgiveness and grace. One should not underestimate the truth of Jesus' statement from the cross in Luke 23:34, "Father, forgive them; for they know not what they do." What is not to understand about that statement?

While good things were accomplished, there will continue to be disagreements and terrible actions, in the misguided effect to strengthen and expand the reach of Christianity, all of which will often be contra-productive and destructive and will be a complete distortion of Jesus' ministry. It can be reasonably argued that the early success in oppressing the Jews led to the future oppressions of the Jews by Christians, which needs not to be continued.

In their own ways, both the Jerusalem Christians and Paul and the Gentile Christians were trying to make sense out of what they believed God required and what Jesus demonstrated. The Jewish Christians were trying to fit it into the existing Jewish religious structure. Paul and the Gentile Christian leaders, on the other hand, were trying to have Jesus' life and ministry make sense to the followers of the Greek and Roman pagan religions. In doing so, both lost the simple and direct connection Jesus had with God. Unfortunately, all their efforts were putting new wine into an old wine skin.

Being spiritually connected to God will bring God's grace and blessings, and an accompanying peace of mind. Unfortunately, instead of concentrating on the lessons in Jesus' life, both the Jerusalem Christians and the Gentile Christians concentrated on getting organized and setting requirements for membership. This strong emphasis on organization and rules remains today.

Apparently, the prevailing thinking of the Christian Church leaders was that a relationship with God could not be as simple as described in Genesis 1:1-31, that there was more to living in a relationship with God than the simple message of Jesus' ministry. They apparently thought It was unrealistic for a non-divine Jesus to live as He did. They could not conceive that any person could emulate Jesus' life, or that the message of Jesus' ministry was more important than His birth and death, and the rituals, rules, and theology they came up with. Just like the Judaism priests, it was inconceivable to the Christian leaders that living by the message of Jesus' ministry was all that was needed to guide a person to live in God's blessing. They thought that there had to be more to it than that.

The problem was not the Christian organizations, but rather the structure, ritual, and theology that are central to the organizations. Structure, ritual, and theology did not come from God, but rather came from the need of the early leaders of the Christian organizations as it does today.

The bells and whistles they came up with were what they thought were needed to get God's attention, while all they really needed to do was to tell and show people that there was a God who loved them. God only required that they believe in Him and stay spiritually connected to Him, and that His grace was for all who believed in Him and ask for it.

A major deviation from Jesus' ministry was establishing an organizational structure, with an order of importance and authority that came with it. In other words, it established an organizational pecking order. While Jesus certainly was the disciples' leader and the one the people came to hear, He viewed the position of leader differently from being the one in charge or the boss. In Mark 10: 43-44 Jesus said, "whoever would be great among you must be your servant, and whoever would be first among you must be slave of all." This idea quickly became lost in the making of the organizations.

While Christian organizations can be a good source of information, a person who is not dependent upon a Christian organization and is not limited by its requirements has greater freedom to live in his or her spiritual relationship with God.

Apparently, the Antioch church members worshiped in fellowship without concerns for where they we from or their history. The Antioch Church members thought of themselves as "we" rather than "us" and "them" until the Jews from Jerusalem came and strongly objected to the two groups eating together. What a wonderful opportunity it would have been to allow the church fellowship to grow with members continuing to find common areas of agreement while retaining the two different opinions about who Jesus was, which would represent two different paths toward reaching a spiritual relationship with God.

However, that is not how Christian theology was developed. The need, above all else, to have an organization, with all its structure, rituals, and theology, and for everyone to think the same started early in Christianity development and remains strong today.

As more Gentiles joined Christian Church, the different Christian communities were becoming divided over issues—other than who was eligible to receive Jesus' message about God's relationship with mankind. And then, what did the eligible people need to do to be allowed to receive this information?

For the Jerusalem Christians, the requirements were straightforward, follow the Jewish laws. It was not that straightforward for the Gentile Christians. They were in the process of making their own rules regarding their relationship with Jesus and God. Sadly, the Gentile Christians have never been able to establish a common theology that is generic enough to accept all people who have a personal relationship with God or who are looking to have such a relationship with God.

The issues pertained to who could be part of the Christian community, and the restrictions that were imposed could, and surely did, keep people from joining the Christian communities and enjoying the support of a community in their search for a personal, spiritual relationship with God. With all they had heard of Jesus' ministry, the Christians still could not get away from the need to establish rules and requirements that must be met to be accepted to be a member.

The Christians were already setting boundaries separating themselves from others and from each other. Early Christianity was made up of specialty shops that required doing certain things to be included rather than as supermarkets that one and all can enter. While Jesus' ministry was for the Jewish people to have a God-centered relationship, He did not turn others away. Jesus allowed all to come to him, regardless of whom they were or where they came from. There was no organization a person had to join or ritual one had to follow to be part of Jesus' followers or to receive Jesus' blessing; however, there was one thing each person needed to do for God be part of their lives. Each person needed to be God centered. Being God centered is a decision that was totally up to each person. If a person did not pay attention to God, God could not be in that person's life.

Unfortunately, Christianity is still made up of special shops, with each shop's false promises that following that shop's rituals and theology will lead to having a God-centered life.

The Old Testament that was included in Jesus' ministry, was lost to the Gentiles. Without having the Old Testament as background for Jesus' ministry, the Gentiles were at a disadvantage in understanding the message of Jesus' ministry. We know that in some form, Jesus knew the first five books of the Old Testament (the Law or Pentateuch) and some of the books of the Prophets, because he refers to them when talking with his followers. The Jews accept that these books, as well as the other Old Testament manuscripts that were available, along with the religious beliefs and the guidance of His parents, were the basis for Jesus developing His belief and faith in God. His understanding of the covenant the Jews had with God came from these sources.

God's relationship with the Israelites was direct and without fanfare and centered on immediacy. The sense of the impending end of the world came from the Israelite reading of the Old Testament manuscripts and similar thinking in the neighboring countries. Much of what the Israelites inherently learned from Jesus, came from their common history as stated in the Old Testament. Without this, the Gentiles had to come up with their own basis for their spiritual relationship with God. This new relationship with God is still a work in process.

The idea that the early church decided that Jesus was divine did not change Jesus' message. Jesus did not have to be divine for His message to apply to all mankind. The simple uncomplicated relationship Jesus had with God got lost in the thinking that there was more to Jesus' ministry. Christianity is still missing the simplicity of Jesus' ministry.

As the early Christian churches were formed and grew in membership, they used what was available as their source of information and for daily guidance, such as the Epistles and Gospels. The Old Testament was also an important source of information for the Jerusalem Christians, but not so much for the Gentile Christians.

When the Christians began to see themselves as being separate from Judaism, they did model their services after synagogue services. The services were open to all, church members and the curious. The service consisted of readings, prayer, sermons, and singing. A second service, for church members only, was a meal which all present shared, and a brief ceremony recalling the Last Supper. The Greek name for the ceremony was "Eucharist" (the giving of thanks). As the church membership grew and the common meal became impractical, a ceremony was held at the end of the regular service with the non-members leaving the service.

Over time the process of being accepted into the Christian fellowship became formalized. Various rules were introduced, not all at the same time, some of which remain in church services today. The use and definition of the rules varied from one church to the next. The early rules, some of which became rituals, were to have the new members give up their pagan gods and morality and commit to having faith in Jesus. This was also when the churches were developed organizational structures with boards of elders, bishops, and deacons.

With or without a divine Jesus, the manmade rules, theology, and structure that religious groups and churches established play little or no part in God's guidance. While the original intent for the rules, theology, and structure was to provide direction for people to follow to become connected to God, they often become, at best a poor attempt to please God, and at worse, they are self-serving.

As it turned out Paul was asking too much, in expecting there would be tolerance for each other's beliefs. Unfortunately, this lack of tolerance precluded the Jews and Gentiles from learning from each other, nor were they able to form bonds based on their relationship with the same God. This gap between the Christian and Jewish communities is not as big a problem as it has been in the past, but it remains a problem today.

When the Epistle of Barnabas was written in the 120s C.E. the apostles and original leaders of the Christian Church would have passed the church leadership to the next generation. With new leadership and more Gentiles joining the Christian Church, the lack of knowledge of the Old Testament became more pronounced. Also, the disagreement about who and what Jesus was, became more deeply embedded in the differences between the Jerusalem and Gentile Christians, and within the Gentile Christians.

It apparently wasn't recognized that it was the Jews who dispersed from Jerusalem and spread the word of God's commitment to mankind. And it was the Jews, including Saul of Tarsus, or Paul, the developer of the basic Christian theology, as well as many of the original members of the followers of Jesus in Greek and Roman cities who kept alive the embers of faith in Jesus' ministry. How would Christianity have started without the Jewish members providing guidance, direction, and their lives to keep the faith in Jesus strong enough to survive the persecutions by the non-Christians?

Having a relationship with God that Jews believed was *acceptable to God* was the basic problem the Jews have been struggling with ever since the time of Abraham, with at best, sporadic success through their existence. It seems that the disciples, the crowds that followed Jesus, Paul, and both the Jerusalem and Gentile followers of Jesus saw the relationship that Jesus had with God as being worth emulating. The differing degree of success each group had should not be used to judge to intent of each group.

Whether or not we believe that Jesus is divine is not important to receiving God's grace. God's grace is unlimited and unconditional, extending to all things large and small. The grace of Christianity is limited and conditional, tempered by such issues as fairness, equality, theology, and the happenings of yesterday, as defined by the person or persons passing judgment. This has nothing to do with God's grace.

Jesus' opening statement to His ministry clearly said what his core mission was, "Repent for the kingdom of God is at hand" (Matt. 4:17).

Jesus believed that the end of the world, as they knew it, was at hand and He wanted the Jews to return to God before it was too late. With or without believing that the world we know is about to end, the heart of Jesus' message was for the Jews to make their relationship with God their priority above all else.

Whatever information the followers of Jesus had about His ministry, whether it was oral stories or parts of the writings that led to the gospels, it was enough for them to recognize Jesus' core message of love and have life changing faith in Jesus. This message they would carry on to their death.

The prevailing ideas in the Old Testament, that we are made in God's image and that we can live in the likeness of God was central to Jesus' ministry. The Sermon on the Mount, disciples going out to preach and heal, and the healing in His presence exemplifies living in the likeness of God.

Jesus' ministry with the Jews and other people He met was centered on them establishing a personal spiritual relationship with God and for them to be guided by their relationship with God. Jesus' comments about His time with them being short have been taken by many people to mean He *was divine*, and He would be going back to heaven. However, it also could have meant He knew that the Judaism leaders were about to close in. He knew he could dispute the Judaism leaders only so long, and three years was a long time. Jesus wanted the Jews to be guided by God without regard for His relationship with God.

Jesus' disciples and the people who followed Him, and that He met as He went from town to town, were excited about His message without any thought that He could be the Son of God, the Messiah, or divine. Jesus did not set Himself apart from the people He lived with while He was growing up and developing His relationship with God. Everything Jesus did and said came from Jesus choosing to stay connected to the Jewish people while He demonstrated His commitment to God and lived in the blessing of God.

All through His ministry, Jesus demonstrated how Jews could live at one with God. He told Jews to change and be God-centered. He repeatedly told a person who was healed that it was that person's faith that enabled the healing. Healing did not happen when the person to be heal lacked faith (Mark 6:5-6).

Jesus' interactions with the people around him were person to person, not God to person. It supported His belief that each person could have a personal relationship directly with God just as He had. Jesus did not think He needed to intervene on the behalf of a person for a person to be connected to God. He repeatedly wanted Jews to realize that it was through their faith in God that their life would be improved.

When Jesus sent the disciples out on their own to heal and preach, they showed what God-centered people could do, which gives credence to the idea that the Jews and Gentiles could live in a close spiritual relationship with God as Jesus had. God was, and is, available to all who make the commitment to live a God-centered life.

After Jesus' death but before Paul declared Jesus to be divine, there is equally strong evidence what people could do through their faith in God. For example, Peter through his faith in God, healed a lame man (Acts 3:1-10) and raised a dead woman in Joppa, (Acts 9:36-43) just as the disciples did when Jesus sent them to heal and preach. (Mk 6:7) And there was the faith the Roman Centurion, Cornelius had in God who with his family and friends were blessed by the Holy Spirit and baptized by Peter and accepted into the Gentile Church (Acts 10:1-43).

In short, there were several instances of Jesus and his disciples, as well as the man mentioned in Mark 9: 38, healing the sick. It seems there is strong evidence that having a spiritual relationship with God was improving people's lives

Additional stories of the disciples and later the apostles, healing people both before and after Jesus' death are told in Mark 6:7-13, 9:38-41 and Acts 3:1-26, 9:36-43.

Jesus using everyday activities, such as farming, carpentering, and sheep herding, in His ministry. Because of the extensive use in these same activities in both the Jew's and Gentile's world, Jesus' ministry would relate as well to the Gentiles as it did to the Jews. I think the Gentiles would have understood Jesus' message just like the Jews did who'd heard Jesus for the first time in the Synagogue in Capernaum.

Enough early Christians seem to have obtained a level of spiritual connection with God that they concerned the Roman leaders, who could not understand what guided Christians and perceived them as a threat to the Empire. As a case in point, the Romans did not understand why the Christian's belief was so strong that the Romans could not bring them back to believing in the Roman religion. Undoubtedly, some of the Jesus followers, who Paul saw were doing profoundly better than the followers of the Law, were Gentiles.

THE REALITY OF JESUS' MINISTRY

The original relationship the Jews and Christians had with God was based on love, the foundation upon which the strong friendship and respect Abraham and Moses had for God and God had for them. Jesus loved God and was committed to live in God's guidance, which was the basis for His trusting, respectful friendship with God. Jesus' entire ministry was based on God's love.

He wanted the Jews to meet foe as a friend, with love rather than anger, fear, and hatred. He risked everything knowing that the result of His ministry would most likely result in His untimely death.

Jesus revived a person's trust and faith in God that changed that person; however, each person's relationship with God remained between God and that person.

Unfortunately, the heart of Jesus' message of love, as embodied by respect, having high positive regard for other, forgiveness, and fully living with our God-given abilities, has lost relevance to our reliance on Jesus to save us from ourselves.

God does not pick sides and neither did Jesus. Jesus accepted the people as they were and appreciated those who reached out to Him. He served as the catalyst for them to receive God's love.

Jesus' ministry was as true for those who believed He was a prophet, as it was for Gentiles who believed He was the Messiah, as His ministry is for all people today. God has not changed nor has His willingness to have a relationship with all who want a relationship with Him.

The phrase Jesus used so often, "Your faith has made you well" has been overshadowed by the importance of Jesus being divine. Jesus wanted Jews to have a personal faith in God. Jesus wanted the Jews to believe and to be faithful to God and to have their faith in God be first in all they did.

Jesus repeatedly showed, with His parables and His interaction with Gentiles, that God loves all mankind. If Christianity had picked up the core message of God's love rather than making the core message be about structure, organization, and requirements, Christianity would look much different than it does today.

When Jesus awoke a person's trust and faith in God, healing resulted because the change that happened was in the relationship between that person and God. When Jesus was not accepted in Nazareth, there was no healing because of the Jews' lack of trust and belief in God regardless of Jesus' faith in God.

The broad range of actions and teaching used to describe Jesus' relationship with God can serve as a guide to each person's relationship with God, but it is still up to each person to have a God-centered relationship with God. It surely is true that shedding the misconceptions and the religious rituals and teachings and creating a clear, uncluttered channel for a spiritual relationship with God can be hard work.

Having a clear channel to God allows a person to put aside all the concerns, worries, and problems associated with daily living. Without a clear channel to God, the daily issues retain their prominence and interference with a person's relationship with God.

Having a relationship with God is not the goal. Our relationship with God guides each one of us to live our gift of being made in God's image toward the goal of living in the likeness of God.

The message of the first creation story; that we are made in the image of God and that we can live in the likeness of God, has not changed. Placing spirit fulfillment ahead of material fulfilment, is living as God intended. Regardless of what friends and neighbors think, respecting and worshiping God in all that one does is following Jesus' example of living in the likeness of God.

There is no indication that God changed His mind and decided that mankind "wasn't made in the image of God" after all. As far as God was concerned, the Jews and Gentiles both could live in His blessing. All that was required was for each person, regardless of what group they belonged to have a spiritual bond with God and to live a God-centered life. God really does not care how a person relates to Him; however, the relationship needs to be clear and uncluttered.

SUMMARY

Anyone who wants to have a spiritual relationship with God must have his or her relationship with God be above all else, otherwise, there was no relationship. God is not involved in manmade circumstances. All manmade requirements for having a relationship with God are not part of a spiritual relationship with God. Anyone, regardless of his or her religion or nationality, can establish a relationship with God and live in God's blessing.

Jesus certainly set the example that one could establish and keep a spiritual relationship with God; however, Jesus' message always was that each disciple must establish his or her own spiritual relationship with God. Being made in the image of God gives that ability to each one of us. We live in the likeness of God when we live in our spiritual relationship with God.

Why did God bother to create us in His image, if He did not think we could handle it? What are we missing that would keep us from having a direct relationship with God? The God of the Old Testament was a God who helped men who were spiritually connected to Him and believed in Him, such as Abraham, Jacob the son of Isaac, Joseph the son of Jacob, Moses, David, and the Prophets. Jesus is in great company following in their footsteps.

Jesus or a priest, or a family member, or friends could not change a person to have a God-centered life. Jesus' message that each Jew or Gentile is the only one who can establish his or her relationship with God is as true today as it was in Jesus' time.

Regardless of what Christianity has made of Jesus and His ministry, Jesus clearly stated His purpose as being to get the Jews to change their priority to living a God-centered life. He wanted the Jews to be the light to the world through living in their faith and trust in God, that is, living in the likeness of God.

Jesus lived His God-centered faith in all that He did. Jesus met the complex and troubled world of His time head-on. His interaction with the people and His ministry was guided by His understanding of what it meant to live in the likeness of God. With His successes as well as His disappointments, including His heart-wrenching failure to convince the Jews to change, He continued to live within His spiritual connection with God.

Jesus' three-year ministry never reached more than a small percentage of the Jews. However, the message of Jesus' ministry and His life was strong enough to withstand the concerted effort of the leaders of Judaism to stop Jesus and eliminate any evidence of His existence. The Pharisee Gamaliel said it best when he said, "... for if this plan or this undertaking is of man it will fail; but if it is of God, you will not be able to overthrow them" (Acts 5:38-39).

Since Jesus' ministry was of His relationship with God, the priests and Pharisees could not get rid of His ministry by killing Jesus. It is important to recognize that when the religious leaders arrested the apostles and were ready to kill them, Gamaliel spoke, cautioning the assembled leaders to think through their actions. Gamaliel was talking about the followers of an itinerate carpenter, whose followers had accepted as being a prophet, and whose teachings were believed to be of God. Gamaliel's comments resulted in the apostles being released.

The love and trust in God that is in Jesus' responses to the three temptations were in His core message to the Jews, to be true to God in all that you do. Many of the early Christians got this message for, as the Roman officials discovered, the Christian religion was not only worth living by but was worth dying for as well. Being a Christian then was a personal decision, one based on his or her belief in Jesus' message. Their choice was to either put the emperor first and live, or to adhere to his or her belief in Jesus' message and kept God first and die. They chose to die.

The most important information we can use from Jesus' life is His three-year ministry, not His death. Jesus' ministry was about getting the Jews to live a God-centered life before the end of the world came. He did not teach and provide healing for three years so that His death would be the one thing people remembered about Him. Instead, celebrating His ministry and His God-centered life seems to me to be more appropriate without taking away from celebrating that He rose from death.

Jesus' ministry came from His understanding of God's Covenant with the Jews and His experiences as He grew up, which included the example set by His father, Joseph, readings of the available Old Testament documents and His conversations with His mother, His rabbi, and John. From all this, He recognized the simplicity of the relationship God wanted with the Jews and the freedom such a relationship with God would give the Jews.

The trials and tribulations the Israelites described in the Old and New Testaments define the harsh realities of the Jews' life during and before the time of Jesus. Jesus' life and His ministry showed the Jews a better life through living in the likeness of God.

God's love is the greatest gift He has given each one of us. It is given without demands and with only one stipulation, that we make our relationship with God our top priority. God does not expect perfection; however, He wants us to believe that we are made in his image and that we can live in His likeness.

Jesus survived for three years by explaining and living a spiritual connection to God. Jesus' life and ministry were simple and direct. What you saw and heard was what you got. The organizational structure, and the myth, mystery, and magic that has been added to Jesus' message.

Unfortunately, the story of Christianity continues along the path of being in control and having financial wellbeing ahead of living in the likeness of God.

Chapter 11

THE GROWTH OF CHRISTIANITY

LOSING SIGHT OF JESUS' MINISTRY

As we continue to look at the Christian movement, a movement that was about to experience drastic changes, it is time to look back on the improbability of a carpenter's son, from an out-of-the-way part of the Jewish land, being the catalyst for the start of a worldwide religion. Who would have thought that Jesus, who never had a large following and who was unknown to the majority of the Jewish population, and whose one purpose was to change the way Jews lived within their covenant with their God, would be the central piece of a religion that has affected millions of peoples, worldwide over 2,000 years. Christianity has grown from a small group of struggling followers of Jesus to a middle east religion that became a force in the affairs of, first the Roman Empire and the Greek culture. And today it continues its amazing accomplishment by being a worldwide force however misguided it may be.

Jesus was not about starting a new religion. Jesus objected to the rituals and regulations that became the Judaism religion of His time. His ministry was about the importance of having a personal relationship with God. Jesus strongly objected to Judaism's theology, and its trappings of structure and rules, all of which took precedence over the ancient manuscripts that described living in God's guidance.

Jesus' ministry was about giving the Jews an alternative to the Judaism of His day. Jesus did not want the Jews to follow the dictates of the Judaism priests. Instead, Jesus wanted the Jews to live spiritually connected with God, and to think of God as a friend, a Father, and a benevolent granter of forgiveness and grace. The relationship between God and Jesus was one of trust and caring. It was Jesus' choice, not God's directive, to live in God's likeness. This was the choice Jesus wanted the Jews to make.

Jesus wanted Jews to live his message of living each day in the likeness of God, in Jesus' day, not at some future date or after death. This simple idea of living in the image of God was set aside in the Christian leaders' push to develop the Church theology and give it organization and structure. So, the simple idea that we are made in the image of God was replaced with processes and procedures that must be followed, including acceptance by the Church membership, before a person could be considered a Christian. Apparently, Church leaders believed the Bible's statement in Gen. 1:27, "So God created man in his own image, in the image of God he created him; male and female he created them. 28 And God blessed them ..." was insufficient to draw in new members to the Church.

And adding to the apparent inadequacy of the message in Gen.1:27-28, the core message of Jesus' ministry, and simply following in the footsteps of Jesus was viewed as being anything but simple, nor was it considered doable. With nothing to go on except the memory of the apostles, and friends and followers of Jesus, the information the church used was not of one voice, but rather was what each group of Christians heard and thought of Jesus' ministry.

Continuing from chapter 10, over time the process of moving away from Jesus' ministry continued as the various theologies and requirements of Christianity increased and became more complicated, the idea of establishing a direct spiritual relationship with God became less part of the Christian message. Unfortunately, this is still true today.

Regardless of which group of Christians were followed, as Christianity grew larger, stronger, and better organized, it lost the simplicity, beauty, and power of Jesus' message, which today is still worth being studied and followed. Jesus showed us what following God entailed. However, within twenty years of His death, His followers were well on the way to losing his example. Throughout the history of Christianity there have been people who tried to go back to Jesus' core message—with mixed results.

By the year AD 100, Christian literature separate from the Old Testament and in all probability designed to serve as new Scripture, that became the New Testament was being established. The change from the first to the second generation and decreased expectations of Jesus' quick return made writing of a scripture necessary.

The apostle's approach of following the laws of Moses and staying connected to the Jewish religion did not appeal to the people in the non-Jewish communities, which was where the church membership was growing. Early in the second century, the Jewish Christians were no longer a factor in the Christian Church. The Jewish Christians had, for the most part joined one of the early Christian groups, returned to Judaism, or joined other religions. This is about the same time that, with Christianity losing sight of Jesus' ministry, a destructive process began of fighting over who was right and the most powerful.

The 5,000 manuscripts that existed before and while the New Testament was being established attest to the many different ideas about how to follow Jesus to have a relationship with God. Over time, as the early Christians searched through the diverse ideas for following Jesus, they came to several conclusions. While the different conclusions were pared down, they would have been further reduced if they were just about having a God-centered relationship.

This is somewhat understandable with the recognition that Paul received approval for Gentiles to join the church without studying the Old Testament. When the early Christian leadership included both Jews and Gentiles, the Jews, who would have been knowledgeable of the context of the Old Testament would have worked to keep the Old Testament in Christianity. However, as the leadership became more Gentile and less Jewish, the knowledge of the Old Testament would have also decreased. Apparently the Gentile leadership did not recognize how important the Old Testament was to Jesus' ministry.

The impact of the decision to have Gentiles join the church without studying the Old Testament was coming home to roost. Many of the ancient manuscripts that become the Old Testament provided guidance to Jesus in His relationship with God and His ministry. Jesus 'message to the Jews was that they could have a personal spiritual relationship with God. Their relationship would be just between God and each person, without the interjection of any of the requirements of the Jewish religious leaders. The Jews came to believe and trust Jesus because of what He said and did.

Jesus' message that the Jews could have a personal spiritual relationship with God was missed by Paul. Without recognizing this key message of Jesus' ministry Paul was not able to make Jesus' ministry relevant to the Gentiles by itself unless Jesus was divine.

Once Paul's idea that Jesus was divine was accepted, the message of the Old Testament was replaced by the divine Jesus, the Christians' Savior. Therefore, Gentile Christians had little need to read and understand the Old Testament, so they would not tie the message of the first creation story to Jesus' ministry. The need to have more Christians superseded the need to have Christians who knew the basis of Jesus' ministry.

The value of Jesus's life and His demonstration of living in the likeness of God was lost in the continuing theological arguments and the magnificent buildings, expensive jewelry and clothes, beautiful paintings, and other forms of wealth and power that has become integrated with Christianity.

While early Christians were deciding how to fit Jesus into their developing theology, there continued to be serious differences about how to describe Jesus and his ministry. As the different ideas became more clearly stated, they became more pronounced and firmly supported. The failure to come to some consensus was a problem that, after 2,000 years, remains in Christianity today.

Some of the apostles, such as Peter and John, who, as disciples never fully grasped the significance of Jesus' ministry while He was alive, were finally beginning to recognize the message in Jesus' ministry and were changing their lives; however, in the second century, the aging apostles slowly dropped out of the picture with the continual spreading of the liberal approach.

The idea that if each person lives within Jesus' ministry, he or she would be living in their spiritual relationship with God never received much consideration.

The decision to make Jesus' life and ministry central to Christianity was pretty much mitigated by the long, and sometimes bitter, discussions about Jesus' ministry.

Equally so, early church leaders evidently felt that the message of the opening thirty-one verses of the Bible could not be taken at face value. It really was not true that the Jews and Gentiles had received God's gift of being made in His image, after His likeness, along with His gift of the world, without an operating manual or strings attached. They felt that it was all a myth, something not to be considered in the operation of Christian Churches.

Jesus' teaching about living in a God-centered spiritual relationship and enjoying God's blessing was being replaced with a variety of theologies, rules, and rituals that minimized Jesus' messages. Also, they apparently did not recognize the close connection between Jesus's ministry and the Old Testament.

Breaking away from the rules and rituals of Judaism was a good thing; however, the value of this move was neutralized by the adoption of Christianity's rules and rituals some of which were modeled after the Judaism rules and rituals.

The broad range of requirements for membership in the different Christian groups came from the structures and theologies of the early churches, which have been carried forward in the different rituals and theologies of Christianity today.

Probably the most damning actions of the early churches have been the continuing need to be in control. The continuing contest for which brand of Christianity is best has been going on since the beginning of Christianity and continues to be very destructive within Christianity resulting in costing many people their lives without much, if any, good to show for it.

The early Church leaders apparently did not see any other clear direction for the Church. Starting with Paul and continuing through the development of church theology the Church leaders never considered that the Jews and early Christians could have a direct, uncluttered relationship with God. This one omission remains the main theme of Christianity today.

Paul provided the Gentile Church with organizational direction and gave them a divine Jesus. Even with similar beginnings of the Greek-speaking churches within the overall Christian fellowship, it did not take long for the church leaders from the different areas, or districts, to have differences regarding core theology and how to deal with the outside forces against the church. The theology of each organization placed additional requirements that were supposedly necessary to receive God's blessing.

There were several early Church leaders who shepherded Christianity through the difficult times of its development into the Christian institution that covered the European, North African, and Middle Eastern countries. Unfortunately, early in its development, the competing ideas about Christianity and Jesus' message of forgiveness were dealt with harshly.

Even with the input from Paul, the early Christian movement did not have a single approach to following in Jesus' footsteps. There was not even agreement regarding who Jesus was.

FIGHTING FOR CONTROL

The early Church continued to be sporadically persecuted by the Romans as well as having strife within the Church. At some point after AD 150, as Christianity was growing and organizing, they began developing its procedures and theology. The word "Catholic" was first applied to the Christian Church in its meaning of *universal*. One group, who was apparently better organization and more aggressive, adopted the term Catholic for itself. This group worked to do away with those of different ideals and theology, while also fending off the enemies outside the Christian movement. It began developing doctrine and an ecclesiastical organization.

The groups other than Catholics were called heretics. The attempts by the Catholics to eliminate other groups was a very destructive process within the church.

That each Christian group needed to be in control goes against Jesus' teaching that stressed, *If anyone would be first, he must be last of all and servant to all.* The need to be in charge is not compatible with Jesus' idea of leadership and parrots the thinking of the Judaism leaders who went to great lengths to retain their status and control in the Jewish communities.

What the Christian leaders did not believe or chose to ignore was that religion is manmade not God-made. God did not, and does not, require a person to belong to any religious organization or denomination. Jesus' example is that each person can establish a spiritual connection with God and live a God centered life. Religious groups can help people develop his or her relationship with God, but the group will not connect a member with God. It is up to each person to make his or her own connection with God. God can not cause a person to be spiritual connected with Him. Each person must make his or her own decision to be connection with God.

In addition to the interior struggles of the Church, the persecutions by the Roman Empire continued to be the major outside threat to the church. It remained so until later in the 300s. While the Roman persecution was terrible and martyred many Christian leaders and members, many of the Christians continued to refuse to bow to the demands of the Romans, even knowing that it would result in torture and death. This dedication to an idea about a dead person was baffling to the Romans.

Even with the early Christians' dedication to God, Christianity was in danger of being destroyed. If the persecutions had not been sporadic Christianity may very well have been wiped out.

The Romans and Greeks had their own religions that were an integral part of their society and government. The Greeks were more amendable to Christianity because they could see how Christianity fit their mythology better than Roman mythology.

The Romans were concerned with the Christians' lack of respect for the Roman way of life and the Roman Emperor. In general, the refusal by the Christians to compromise on issues of faith set them apart from other groups which made them suspect to the Roman leaders. For example, in the outer reaches of the Empire, where the Christians were strong, the enemies of Roman were just across the borders ready the strike. The Romans believed that the Christians' pacifism would hinder the Romans' efforts to defend the border.

As the church continued its struggles during the time of the interior turmoil and persecution from the Romans, the Catholic Church continued to develop its doctrine and to declare itself to be the strict authority regarding what was and was not holy. It should be no surprise that the Catholic—or universal church—was not universally accepted by all Christians. Other Christian groups did not agree with the Catholic Church and its claim of having all the right answers.

Unfortunately, the intolerance for different doctrines and viewpoints of different groups has plagued Christianity from the very beginning.

Several other groups came up with their own theology, that discounted and/or rewrote the basic Catholic doctrine. Any doctrine that deviated from the Catholic doctrine was called a 'heresy' by the Catholic Church. The threat to the Catholic Church by the heresy groups was serious enough to cause the Catholic Church to develop a consensus about Catholic theology.

One heresy doctrine was the Gnostic (of knowledge) doctrine. This was a doctrine that held that the world was evil, and the true God lived far removed from the world, and He had nothing to do with making it. The god of the Old Testament was spiritually inferior and that humans were evil, who could only become good through acquiring wisdom of the mind which could lead them to eternal life.

They believed that spiritual beings, male and female, including the pre-existing Jesus, existed between the world and God. This brings up the idea that there is a place somewhere between heaven, where God resides, and the world.

A Roman, called Marcion deviated somewhat from the Gnostic doctrine. He also discounted the Old Testament and claimed that the true God was good as revealed by Jesus. The people's souls could be redeemed by following Jesus and St. Paul.

There were groups that followed other doctrines in addition to the Gnostic and Marcon doctrine. The intolerance of the differences has led to conflicts and the killing of thousands of people. And while people of the different Christian religions kill each other much less often than they have historically, the lack of acceptance of different viewpoints, starting with the ongoing persecution of the Jews, is still a hindrance to Christians having a personal relationship with God.

The inability of Christianity to allow people, within and outside of Christianity, to have different ideas about God and His creation results in an unworkable relationship with God. How can one expect to receive God's blessing while he or she is not accepting, without reservation, all of God's creation?

We continue to justify eye for an eye as being necessary to do away with evil. Forgiveness is sparingly earned, if granted at all. Granting forgiveness does not mean ignoring past acts for which forgiveness is needed, rather forgiveness can include admonishing that the act not be repeated.

God's forgiveness knows no bounds, it is unlimited. The story in John 7:53-8:11 about the woman caught in adultery, ends with Jesus telling her, "Neither do I condemn you: go, and do not sin again." As Jesus so often did, in simple language, He gives an encompassing message. In this case, it is a message about forgiveness.

No one was refused acceptance by a Christian group or was killed because of Jesus' ministry per se. Much, if not all the condemnations, fighting and killing has come from how different groups interpreted Paul's divine Jesus and of what Jesus said and did during His ministry. The theologies and procedures developed by these groups were at best inaccurate and usually wrong. That the Christian leaders did not make the message of Jesus' ministry the primary message of Christianity caused major divisions within Christianity that continue to exist today.

Another source of conflict was the groups of people of different backgrounds and cultures. These groups worked to retain as much of their culture as they could while following the Roman requirements enough to placate the Romans. As Christianity spread throughout the Roman Empire and surrounding areas, adding the Christian theology compounded the conflict between the Roman and cultural requirements.

Complying with Christian theology while placating the Romans and retaining cultural customs was an ongoing concern. The converts in each area were still of that culture. So, while their new Christian beliefs required substantial cultural changes in some areas and noncompliance with Roman law in other areas there could not help but be changes to Christianity to bring it into the existing culture and to placate the Romans. On one hand, Christianity required that worship gods other than God be discontinued; however, in the third century, a consensus developed that Jesus' birthday was December 25, in part because it coincides with a pagan festival celebrating the god Saturnalia and the winter solstice. This put Jesus' birthday outside a time in the fall that was thought to be closer to His actual birthday.

To better understand the turmoil within Christianity, the world in which the Christians lived was in a constant state of conflict. The constant bloody wars and disruption of the movement of people throughout the area surrounding and in the Roman Empire could certainly be used to support the Gnostic and similar doctrines. With the Roman Empire in decline, there was no stabilizing central force, no way was found to end the chaos and brutal existence.

In Christianity, there was a broad range of doctrines being develop and followed, which added to the confusion. God's simple message of *believe in Me and I will support you* was nowhere to be found in men struggling to be in control of other men.

Back to the heretics that bothered the Catholics, the first Christian leader to propose a program for dealing with the heresies was Irenaeus, the bishop of Lyons in Gaul (France). Between AD 150 and AD 175 a creed was written, that became the Apostles Creed, to oppose the Gnostic and Marcionite doctrines. Using the Apostles Creed along with the authorized or "canon" version of the Old Testament that was set around AD 100, and preliminary versions of the manuscripts that would become the New Testament, did strengthen the position of the Catholic Church and, to some extent, slowed down the various heretical movements.

A second measure was to establish an authentic, *canon* New Testament scripture. While the New Testament was virtually set at the end of the second century (Noss page 634), it was St. Athanasius to be the first to name the twenty-seven books of the New Testament in AD 367 (Introduction, New Testament, RSV). The canon version was set in AD 400 in the West and later in the East (Noss. Pgs. 633-634).

However, these documents and various actions against the heresies did not eliminate the heresies or keep them from causing problems in the future.

Also, the relationship between the Christian Church and the Jewish people continued being hostile and destructive.

It seems that throughout the existence of Christianity it has never been enough for someone to be accepted into a Christian fellowship simply because he or she had in spiritual relationship with God.

THE NEW STATUS–STATE CHURCH

As Christianity continued to grow and become stronger, it was becoming a serious challenge to the pagan religions and a greater concern for the Roman leaders.

The Roman government was concerned about the survival of the Empire with the non-Roman people, that the Romans considered to be barbarians, being located along the Roman border opposite the pacifist Christians. The Christians did not conform to the Roman thinking and could not be counted on to fight when needed. They were becoming a society within the Roman society and that was scary and unacceptable. So, they continued to be persecuted.

When Emperor Decius returned from the endangered frontier, the weakness due to the Christians caused him to issue an order in AD 250 that all citizens of the Empire must get a certificate from the government that he or she had sacrificed to the empires' image. Failure to have such a certificate meant death. There were conspicuous martyrs from the ensuing persecutions. Some Christians complied and others bribed government official. The prosecutions soon ended. When the lapsed Christians came back to the church they were not welcomed by the faithful Christians, which created schisms.

As emperors came and went the persecutions started and stopped.

The Apostle's Creed answered some of the concerns; however, heresies continued to exist. By this time Jesus was generally thought to be the Christ, but not by all Christian groups, and for those who thought Jesus was Christ, disagreements within the Christian leadership continued in other areas, such as, whether Jesus was a finite or eternal being.

The persecution of the Christian Church continued sporadically until the situation improved when a young Roman Emperor, named Constantine, came to power. It has been written that as a young man he had seen a cross in the sky with the message that, "under this sign, he will be a conqueror"; however, he apparently did not become a Christian until after he completed his conquests, and he was on his death bed.

Constantine began changing the situation when in AD 313 he, jointly with another contender to be Emperor, granted freedom of religion equally to Christians and other religions. This stopped the persecutions but not the internal strife in the Church.

In AD 323, when Constantine became the sole ruler as Emperor of the Roman Empire the situation further improved for the Christian Church. Constantine wanted Christianity to be a uniting force within the Roman Empire. The persecutions stopped and he strengthened the Catholic Church. He restored the lost properties and increasing its holdings, sometimes at the expense of pagan religions. He frowned on heretical sects as being detrimental to the unity in the Empire. He made the Christian Sunday a legal holiday and built new churches, often at pagan expense.

Regardless of Constantine's wishes, the controversy within the Christian Churches continued. After failed conciliatory efforts, Constantine called for a council of all the Christian Churches to settle the issue. In 325 delegates from the Churches met in Nicaea and produced the Creed of Nicaea.

There were objections to the Creed. A rider was attached to the Creed listing the objections. Despite the objections about the Creed of Nicaea, it was adopted under pressure from the emperor. The Creed did not solve the doctrinal difficulties or save the peace.

There continued to be disagreements over the Nicaea Creed, even though some churches gave lip service to accepting it. The eastern churches were not in agreement and strongly objected to meaning of some of the terms in the Nicaea Creed. The Roman interpretation of words was much stricter and precise than the Greek interpretation of the same words. The difference in how words were defined and used in the Roman and Greek languages continued and interfered with the development of a common theology for Christianity. The core disagreement centered around Jesus being the Savior and if he was a Savior, He would have to be God.

The need for power and control began very early in the development of Christianity. When Constantine's successors followed in his steps and made Christianity the imperial state religion of the Roman Empire in AD 383, Christianity was given the power and control it had so long coveted and that it retained to a greater or lesser degree from that time forward. The emperors' interest was, however, too much; it amounted to active control.

This time in the life of the Christian Church was very dangerous. Overnight, it went from having to compete with the established pagan religions while being persecuted, to being appointed the chosen religion of the same government that had recently been persecuting it. And that same government gave it all that it needed to be successful, depending on how success is defined. It is evident that rather than the unity Constantine and the emperors who followed him were hoping for, their preference for Christianity highlighted the lack of unity and the unresolved differences in Christianity.

Of all the groups in Christianity, the Catholic theological and organizational development put the Catholic Church in a good position to take advantage of the government's generous offer. Unfortunately, there was a trap hidden in the designation of the Catholic Church as the imperial state religion, both for the Empire and the church.

The pagan religions of the Empire were an integral part of the emperor's authority. They had many gods, and, at the time of Constantine, the Emperor was included as a god after his death. Since Christians believe there is only one God, all the pagan gods were excluded, and the emperor could no longer be considered a god after his death. So, accepting Christianity as the religion of the Empire diminished the emperor's authority. This along with the people being told that what they had believed all their lives was wrong created the seeds for unrest.

After many arguments throughout Christianity, who and what Jesus was has remained unsettled. Finally, a general council met in the year 451 in Chalcedon, in Asia Minor, and formulated a definition of the relation of Christ's natures that became standard Catholic doctrine.

This Creed, as was true for the Nicaea Creed, was readily adopted by the western churches, but the eastern churches were much less accepting of it. So, even though it was no better at bringing peace within Christianity, it became a standard of the Catholic Church.

The copies of the creeds in use today differ from the original creeds. An example is the change in the Nicene Creed. Once again, the Greek use of terms and the Roman use of the same terms were different. The Greek description of Jesus was abstract; however, when translated into Latin it had a firm connation that was different from the Greek connation.

From the very beginning the group that chose *Catholic* as their name, and throughout the persecutions and the turmoil from Christianity being chosen as the imperial state church, the Catholic faithful had continued developing their doctrine. The work of the Catholic group put it in a good position to become the most prominent Christian Church.

The prominence of the Catholic Church did little to improve the situation. The result of all this was that there were church doctrines established outside the Catholic Church, such as the Coptic Church in Egypt and Abyssinian, Jacobite Church in Syria and Armenia, and Nestorian Church, which was started by Nestorius, Patriarch of Constantinople. All three churches exist today in eastern countries, such as Egypt, Syria, Iran, and India.

As if there was not enough chaos, Constantine created an additional problem in AD 324 when he decided to build Constantinople, a new city on top of an old city, as the eastern center of his empire, with Roman remaining the western center of his empire. Having two centers of the Roman Empire along with strife within the Christian Church, with its close ties to the empire, led to splitting the Church into the Roman Catholic Church, with the Pope in Roman, and the Eastern Orthodox Church, with the Patriarch in Constantinople. The complete separation of the western and eastern churches was not finalized until 1054.

The combination of the diminished standing of the emperor and losing the uniting force of the Christian Church when it split in two were contributing factors leading to the end of the Roman Empire. One date for the end of the Roman Empire is AD 410 when Roman was sacked by the Visigoths.

In the west, differences were primarily between the Catholic Church and the other Christian Churches. These unresolved differences, which weren't settled by the Apostles, Nicaea, and Chalcedon Creeds, tended to be centered on the difference between the Eastern Orthodox Church and the Roman Catholic Church that was repeatedly on the winning side of the doctrinal disagreements, with other western churches being minor players in the conflicts. The Roman Catholic Church became the Church for western Christianity, with Roman as its center, and the eastern Christian churches became the Eastern Orthodox Church, with Constantinople as its center.

Going back to Jesus' third temptation, when the devil offered Jesus the world if he would worship the devil, Jesus responded with, "You Shall worship the Lord your God and Him only shall you serve" (Matt. 4:10). With the Christian Church accepting the government offer to be the Empire's Church, an offer which the church may very well have felt it could not refuse, and with the acceptance of the government gifts, the government "the devil" had given the Christian Church earthly power over all who lived and worked within the Empire. God now had competition for the attention of the Church. From this point, both the Roman Catholic Church and the Eastern Orthodox Church will continue to fight, and lose, the battle between serving the people and controlling the people. Unfortunately, when the Protestant Churches came along, they did no better.

The inability to accept all people regardless of the religious belief again caused great turmoil, loss of connection with God, and devastation of the people and their civilizations. The devil was in charge.

While being the official state religion stopped the persecutions and executions and returned the property and wealth that it had lost, as well as adding new property and wealth, it created new problems for the Catholic Church, as Jesus knew it would. Being tied to and beholding to the emperor often took precedence over having a spiritual relationship with God. As such, the Catholic Church could not help but be involved in matters of State, nor could it keep from using its high position for its own purpose. One could compare the activities of the Catholic Church to the activities of the Jewish religion at the time of Jesus and see many similarities.

The efforts of Constantine and the Catholic Church could not stop heresies from continuing to crop up within the Christian Church. There were disagreements within the Church centered on who was Jesus and what was the content of His ministry. By this time, the Church was being led by the fourth and fifth generation of leaders. The twelve disciples, who apparently did not write much until after the death of Jesus, had died, as had Paul, as had the second and third generation of leaders. As the discussions continued and became more complex the opinions became more pointed and more firmly entrenched.

Through its work on developing doctrine and the three creeds, the Catholic Church in Roman had become the stronger Church than the Church in Constantinople. The issues within Christianity primarily centered around the disagreement with declarations by the Catholic Church in Rome that its theology and doctrine were the true statements of Jesus the son of God. Even with its continuing effort, the heresies continued to give the Catholic Church fits. The most prominent church to disagree with the Catholic Church was the Eastern Orthodox Church. The lack of resolution of their differences led to their eventual split.

The main discussions and actions concerning the Catholic Church doctrine that took place in the 400+ years after the death of Jesus centered around solving an unsolvable problem. The Catholic Church simply did not have enough information to solve the problem of whether Jesus was man or God. The Catholic Church solution was to declare that Jesus was both.

And how necessary was it to solve this problem? The message of the "Sermon on The Mount" is not enhanced by the decision of the Catholic Church that Jesus was both divine and human. The Catholic solution to this problem did not enhance what Jesus did and said during His ministry. Jesus wanted the Jews to have a spiritual relationship with God, but he did not expect them to live as He did. He knew that when they established their spiritual relationship with God, they would still be fishermen, farmers, and shepherds.

One major development of this time was establishing the Pope. In Matthew 16:18,19, Jesus told Peter that, "And I tell you, you are Peter, and on this rock, I will build my church, and the powers of death shall not prevail against it." This passage appears to be a late addition to the Gospel of Matthew, from its use of the term *church*, which would not have been a term Jesus would have used, and there is very little evidence that Peter went to Roman; however, that he did was, and remains, part of Catholic doctrine.

Starting in the fourth century the Catholic Churches that served as the seat of a bishop were designated as "Cathedrals." It was not until the twelfth century that the massive architectural wondrous cathedrals were being built. These cathedrals were and continue to be architectural and engineering master pieces that serve as the seat of a bishop and are presented as testimonies to the Catholic Church's faith in, and dedication to God. Unfortunately, the major source of funds for these magnificent structures and their continuing repairs and upgrades came from the poor and tradespeople, who were and continue to be barely getting by.

Matthew 16:18-19 did not become an issue until 440 when Leo I became Pope. The Catholic Church doctrine was that all bishops were equal. Since the center of civil authority was in Constantinople and the western Catholic Church had won the doctrine decisions and had led in developing the New Testament cannon, it was accepted that the Catholic Church in Rome was the leading church, and since Jesus had stated He would build his church on Peter, Leo declared that St. Peter was the first among the apostles and Peter's church would be first amount all Catholic Churches. Leo reasoned that, as the successor to St. Peter, he would be first among the bishops, which carries the title of Pope. Interestingly, when Rome was captured by the invading Visigoths, they looked favorably on the Pope and spared the Catholic Churches, while ransacking and destroying the city and surrounding areas, because they were Christians of a heretical sect. The date of the capture of Rome, AD 476, is the second date that is often used as the date of the fall of the Roman Empire although Constantinople, the eastern capital of the empire did not fall until AD 1453.

Leo's logic conflicts with Paul's Epistle to the church in Rome that indicates Peter did not make it to Rome. As described in chapter 2, Paul's Epistle served as introducing Paul to the church leaders. If Peter had already been in Roman, why would Paul write such an epistle?

Paul knew Peter from his trips to Jerusalem and the dust-up they had in Antioch. If Peter was in Rome when did Mark talk with him while writing the gospel of Mark? As is often the case there are more questions than answers about the development of Christianity.

The development of monasteries did not begin until around the end of the third century. Paul had suggested that men and women practice sexual abstinence, but the idea did not take off until after the Catholic Church became the state religion and the men and women, who pledged sexual abstinence, began living separately from society. Monasteries arose from this movement of people living on the fringes of society. Many hermits became monks and joined a religious order that supported the monasteries. While some monks lived in monasteries, some individual monks living in caves and other out-of-the-way places. Both solitary and communal types of monks spread quickly in Syria and Asia Minor. In the west monasteries were slow to get started but, with the turmoil disrupting society, monasteries became popular. The world outside of the Christian Churches continued to be chaotic and dangerous. In medieval times the monasteries served as safe havens for travelers and a quiet and tranquil escape from the outside world. They were usually respected by different religious orders. One influential hermit monk was Gregory the Great, who was the first monk to be chosen to be pope (AD 590-604). He was the forerunner and model of the powerful medieval pope.

CATHOLIC CHURCH DEVELOPMENT

It is of note that much of the Catholic Church doctrine was developed during periods of great turmoil and chaos in the world around the Mediterranean Sea, which was where Christianity was born and developed. The doctrine that was developed during that time responded to the events of that time in defining the relationship between God and Christians. The strength of this doctrine is reflected in that much of it remains part of Catholic literature today.

One of the greatest personalities of the early Catholic Church was Augustine (AD 354-430), bishop of Hippo in North Africa. He was a brilliant man of many interests, who profoundly influenced the Catholic Church. In his early life, he had a concubine and studied different religious philosophies before he converted to Christianity. It was well that he joined the Catholic Church for his writings became a major part of the theology of the Catholic Church.

His theology and writing were influenced by his study of other religions, as well as by his own life of early riotous living and ensuing guilt, but also, by the fact that the barbarians were attacking the Cities in his area of Africa and in Europe, and evil seemed to be taking over the world. With death, destruction and plunder of whole villages and murder of masses of people continuously occurring throughout northern Africa and the old western Roman empire, the idea that mankind was basically good was not a salable doctrine.

Noss wrote that Augustine's conception was, "God is the one Being, alone absolutely real and absolutely good. He is the source of all other things, and they depend upon him at every moment for their continuous existence. The physical universe especially has only a derived reality and is scarcely worthy of study in itself" (Noss page 645).

Augustine's concept of God does not include Paul's idea that Jesus was divine or that Jesus was involved with creation. Paul had Jesus doing the creating while Augustine left creation in God's hands.

An example of Augustine's thinking is his explanation of the Trinity, a concept that gave the early church leaders much difficulty. The Trinity first appeared in the early second century. It has been a troubling concept ever since. Augustine's explanations were simple and direct even though they did not clarify the idea enough to stop the continuing debate about the Trinity. Other religions thought of the Catholic idea of the Trinity as having three Gods instead of one God. When talking to people of other religions, any gains the Christians obtained in describing having a relationship with one God were lost in trying to explain the Trinity.

The doctrine Augustine developed greatly influenced both the Catholic Church and later Protestant Churches; however, there were other outstanding church leaders during his time who did not agree with Augustine. Issues such as predestination (Gnosticism was not totally dead), original sin, and God's grace, were subjected to discussions and disagreements.

The Catholic Church leaders did not think that God's grace was freely given to all. They believed that some people were beyond salvation and were doomed to eternal damnation. They did not think that people who wantonly murdered and enslaved people and destroyed villages could possibly receive forgiveness from God.

They could not justify the idea of freely given grace and forgiveness, so it became a lost concept. Apparently, in following Paul's thinking, the Catholic Church leaders could not image that God's grace and forgiveness was unlimited.

Continuing the development of the Catholic Church, the collapse of the Roman Empire in AD 476 opened the way for the Visigoth, Ostrogoth, Vandals, and other invaders to have free reign over what was the western part of the Roman Empire. It was the good fortune of the Catholic Church that many of the invaders had been converted to Christianity by members of a heretical Christian sect.

As civilization contended with the collapse of the empire, the favorable treatment given to the Catholic Church by the invades, provided the Catholic Church with a great opportunity. As the only functioning organization in much of Europe and North Africa that could provide services that the former state government provided, the Catholic Church was involved in both the civilian and religious matters until new state governments were formed.

In the seventh century, the former Roman Empire area was invaded from the north and southeast. As these invaders settled and mingled with the inhabitants, new state governments and were formed, and the church maintained close ties to them.

Unfortunately, the power that came with filling in for the state and guiding the new state governments resulted in the church and its leaders acquiring great church and personal wealth. It would be several years in the future before the new young state governments would be able to successfully contest the authority of the church.

In the early AD 600s, an Arabian named Muhammad, started the Islam religion. Muhammad was well versed on Judaism and Christianity. He believed the last judgement was near. The meaning of Allah, the deity, was like the Hebrew El.

The conflicting theologies within Christianity and the obvious power and wealth the Christian leaders and Churches had obtain, very will may have been part of the reason that Muhammad decided to start his own religion. The resulting conflict between Christianity and Islam was and is extremely destructive.

Prior to Muhammad starting the Islam religion, the Arabs had several locate religions. One such religion centered on Mecca, an oasis, that was on an old caravan trade route. Sometime, long before Muhammad, a meteorite fell on the sandy ground of Mecca. The local residences worshiped the meteorite as a gift from heaven. As the fame of the meteorite spread, tribes from across Arabia tribes came each year on a pilgrimage to offer sacrifices and go around the meteorite seven times and kiss the meteorite in the hope that the heavens will bless them. At some point a Kabah, a cubed-shaped structure, was erected in honor of the meteorite and the meteorite was placed in the southeast corner. Muhammad included this ritual in Islam.

Those who submitted to Islam were called Moslems. Muslim is a different spelling of Moslem, the "submitters."

The invasion of the former Roman Empire from the southeast came from the Islam religion. The Moslems quickly overran the area east of the Mediterranean Sea, North Africa, and Spain and put pressure on Constantinople. The Moslems were stopped from going any farther north than southern France by the Frankish King Charles Martel.

Meanwhile, Emperor Leo III and his successors were successfully defending Constantinople.

THE SPLIT INTO THE EASTERN AND WESTERN CHURCHES

Charles Martel's son, Pippin the Short, was made King of the Franks, a Germanic Tribe had converted to Christianity, and gained land in northern Italy for the Pope. His son was Charlemagne (Charles the Great) who continued his father's plan. Charlemagne became King of the Franks in 768, and in 774, became King of the Lombard Tribe who had ruled much of Italy, whose influence had been greatly reduced. Pope Leo III (a different person than Emperor Leo III) on Christmas Day AD 800, crowned Charlemagne the Holy Roman Emperor. He was the first person to rule over an area comparable to the Roman Empire in the 300 years since the breakup of the Roman Empire.

This did not sit well in Constantinople and basically established that the western and eastern parts of the Roman Empire were going their separate ways.

The seeds for this split were sown back in the infancy of the Christian Church. The unresolved issues that came from the adoption of the Roman Catholic Church versions the Apostles' Creed, and later the Nicene Creed and Chalcedon Creeds, and the assembling of the New Testament remained, despite the efforts of Emperor Constantine and church leaders to unite the Christians under one doctrine. The varying interpretations of who Jesus was and what his message was could not be fit into a single doctrine. Today the Eastern Orthodox Churches give more support to the apostles than does the Roman Catholic Church.

The split was finally and completely made in AD 1054 when the pope excommunicated the patriarch of Constantinople and the patriarch responded in a similar fashion. The split in two of the Catholic Churches was complete.

The split was both in the government and church, in both the east and west. The close, almost inseparable, ties between the church and government were strong from the process of waging war and forming new governments and alliances. The leaders of the governments needed the blessing of the church, and the appointing of the Pope and other church leadings were made with the concurrence of the governments.

The differences between the eastern and western churches include several items that boiled down to assigning a level of importance of worship activities and the meaning associated with them. Probably the most prominent difference is the unquestionable belief by the eastern churches that the Pope is not the head of the whole church.

Once a doctrine was established differences were not tolerated, and each difference became a new heresy. The different doctrines began building the walls that strengthen the east and west split in the Catholic Church. As we will see this is not the last time groups of Christians will separate from the "Catholic" Church.

There is an old saying, "One convinced against his or her will, is of the same opinion still." It is unfortunate that the various Christian Churches have not accepted this truism and allowed each other to worship God differently, rather than spending time, money, and lives continuously trying to get all to worship God the same way. Simply stated, different-shaped pegs will not go through one round hole. The ill-conceived and misguided effort to get all people to think and believe the same has been, and continues to be, very destructive today. The loss to mankind has been much greater than any perceived gain that has been achieved from this effort to have everyone worship God the same way. The lengths the Catholic and Protestant Churches have gone to in this regard are most troubling.

TROUBLES IN THE ROMAN CATHOLIC CHURCH

Jesus simply wanted the Jews to be the light of the world by living in God's likeness. Living in the likeness of God means having faith in God and living a God-centered life. Jews who were living in the likeness of God would treat all people with respect and kindness, love, and compassion. living in the likeness of God did not include control of people, magnificent buildings, and exquisite clothes and trappings.

It is unfortunate that instead of following Jesus' example of living in the likeness of God, the Catholic Church used Jesus' ministry as the basis for establishing a multi-million-dollar industry of theology, creeds, magnificence architectural structures, and many land holdings, all to glorify a Jesus that the Catholic Church had developed. The Christianity of Paul was based on the belief that Jesus had the inside track to his relationship with God, something the common people do not have. So, rather than Christians being able to talk to God directly, Jesus became the "go-to guy," the "Savior" rather than the prophet that lived in the likeness of God.

Before the Roman Catholic Church was the Empire Church, its doctrinal concern was centered on interpreting and following the ministry of Jesus. Unfortunately, after the Roman Catholic Church accepting Emperor Constantine's generous "gift" of being the State Church, along with the money and land that came with it, things got complicated. The gift gave the Church additional areas to pursue. The Church now had to support the Empire and had a business to run and political concerns to deal with. It also had to administer, operate, and maintain the great sums of money, and vast sections of land and many buildings it had acquired. In this new role it felt it could not be an unimposing organization of simple means and dress, but rather had to impress people with the status and wealth it had received as God's representative to the people.

Whatever idea the early Catholic Church had about living in God's likeness was lost in the search for worldly powers and religious control and the accompanying wealth and control of the people. The Catholic Church's claim that they were living in God's Covenant was no more accurate than the Jews making the same claim. Was not the Catholic Church mimicking Judaism? Even with all the times the Catholic and

Jewish religions strayed from God's guidance, God remained ready to welcome both Christians and Jews to join Him in His Covenant.

During the Middle Ages, a period from the fall of the Roman Empire in AD 476 to the fourteenth century, also known as the Medieval Period or Dark Ages, the Roman Catholic Church grew in prestige and power, and the difficulties in the relationship between the Church and emperor, or king, became more pronounced. Starting in about the eleventh century the secular heads of states were getting powerful enough to increasingly governing without the assistance of the church. While the kings and secular leaders initially only wanted to take back control of non-religious affairs, they also started inserting themselves into religious affairs. The underlying issue was which one was the most important and had the most power.

The Catholic Church was not able to manage its worldly empire and stay true to its calling. As Jesus said in His answer to the third temptation, "You should worship the Lord your God and him only shall you serve." The interference of dealing with worldly affairs diverted the Church's attention from God. The Church decreased its time with God and problems frequently cropped up from its lack of attention to its relationship with God.

At this point, the power of the Roman Catholic Church was based on control and fear, with little concern for Jesus' ministry. This was a much larger manifestation of how the leaders of Judaism used the Jews' faith in God and their trust in the Judaism leaders that allowed the Judaism leaders to enrich themselves instead of improving the lives of the Jews. The Catholic Church had taken the example of the Judaism leaders to new heights of leadership privilege and wealth.

The bishops and clergies did not always adhere to the rules set by the Pope. This was especially true in the outlying areas that, on paper, were under the Pope's domain. The bishops and clergy were adhering to the wishes of their secular leaders and were marrying and having families rather than being celibate as required by the church. As the secular leaders became sure of their positions and their control of their lands, conflicts with the Pope were unavoidable.

One of the first tests of power was between emperor Henry IV in Germany and a man named Hildebrand who became Pope Gregory VII. Instead of following the decrees of Pope Gregory VII, Henry IV appointed a cleric and undermined the Pope's authority. The Pope excommunicated Henry IV and released the king's subjects from their allegiance to him. After Henry's nobles turned against him Henry relented and the Pope removed his ex-communication.

Pope Gregory VII's great victory was short-lived. Three years later the Pope excommunicated Henry again, and this time Henry marched to Rome and drove Gregory out and set up his own pope. Soon thereafter both Henry and Gregory were dead.

The successors, Henry V and Pope Calixtus II came to a compromise. Bishops everywhere would be chosen by church law, yet the German bishops would be invested, or approved, by the emperor before their consecration. It was also agreed that bishops would be celibate. Some of the reforms of Gregory VII had been achieved.

These conflicts continued off and on. A hundred years later when Innocents III became pope, he declared that he was first among his peers and spiritually superior to all things godly and worldly. When Germany had two people claiming the throne Innocent crowned Otto III to be the Holy Roman Emperor after he obtained large promises from Otto III. When the Emperor forgot his promises, Innocents put a rival in the field and with the help of the King of France replaced Otto as the Emperor. As the conflicts continued within the Empire, Innocents gained greater control and was improving his control of the affairs of state in the Empire, as well as his control of the ecclesiastical affairs of the church. He gained acceptance of the dogma of transubstantiation and the rule that the good standing of a Catholic was conditioned upon periodic confession, absolution, and communion.

At this point, in the thirteenth century, the papacy along with the Catholic Church had reached a new high of religious and secular power. The Catholic Church, which at this point was the major Christian Church in Europe, had been seduced by power and worldly treasures.

Being rich and powerful eliminated the problems of being persecuted, living at the whims of others, and being dependent on others for substance, just to name a few of the problems that ceased to exist. However, this was the exact opposite of what Jesus' ministry was about. Starting with the temptations and going through the beatitudes, loving your enemies, not practicing piety before men, commissioning the disciples before sending them out on their own, and his crucifixion, nothing about Jesus' life and ministry supported the course chosen by the Roman Catholic Church.

So, at the height of the power and prestige of the Catholic Church, it had totally gotten off the track of following the original core message that served it so well in its beginning days. The ministry of Jesus was hard to find in the activities of the church. There was one member; however, who went back to the core values of the church.

Noss points out that, "St. Francis of Assissi (1182-1226) is one of the world's great personalities, as an individual the most winsome of saints, as a world figure Christ in a medieval incarnation" (Noss page 658). He followed Jesus' example of ministering to the poor, sick, and disadvantaged. He lived from handouts and begging for feed. He spent time with the animals in concert with nature, all of which set him apart and distant from the society of his age. He did attract twelve men to join him, and they went to Pope Innocent III for recognition, which was granted.

That must have been a compelling sight of a man of devout poverty needing permission from the rich and powerful head of the Catholic Church to continue the work first demonstrated by Jesus. It would be hard to have a sharper image of how far the church has gotten away from Jesus' ministry than the scene of St. Francis in his poor clothing standing or kneeling before Pope Innocent III, in all his grandeur, requesting permission to live as God intended.

St. Francis continued his work which grew and spread throughout Europe. Others had to intervene; however, to organize and put structure to his organization. Unlike the Catholic Church the Franciscans never lost sight of their mission and continue their work today.

At this point in the life of the church, there continued to be heretical groups working to undermine the Catholic Church. They often were vicious and killed indiscriminately with the intent to bring down the Catholic Church and civilian government. In many cases the followers of the heresies were stronger than the Catholic Church in an area. The Pope's solution to this problem was to appoint judges of the Inquisitions, without local or civilian control.

A group, the Dominican Order, was founded by Dominic about the same time (1170-1221) as St. Francis started his work. Its first purpose was to convert the believers of the Cathari heresy in southern France. Cathari was a religious sect that rejected all things Catholic and in the thirtieth century was strong in Southern France and parts of Europe. It was based on there being two principles, one good and one bad, and that the material world was evil.

In the early thirteenth century, the Catholic Church authorized an inquisition in southern France and Spain to eliminate the Cathari heresy. The Dominican friars were devoted to learning and vowed to poverty. They were sent out through Europe to preach and teach and bring people back to the Catholic Church. They were successful and the Order grew quickly. Unfortunately, they were also chosen by the Pope as Inquisitors, a task for which they were poorly suited. The Dominican Order can still be found in parts of the world.

Another inquisition, the Spanish Inquisition, began in 1478. It was placed under the control of the Spanish Monarchs, Ferdinand, and Isabella. What started the Inquisition were the royal Decrees of 1492 and 1501 that required all Jews and Muslims to convert to Christianity or leave Spain. Many people converted; however, the church suspected that the converts were still following the Jewish and Muslim religions in secret. So, the Inquisition was to ferret out the ones who were continuing to follow the other religions. The primary tools were to have neighbors tell on neighbors who were then tortured and killed.

Being an informant had its own risks. If the informant's information was not what the judge wanted, or if other people, for self-preservation, informed on the informant, the informant would find himself or herself as an accused and being tortured. It was rare for someone to live through being tortured. Confession brought a quick death instead of a slow tortured death.

Going back in the history of Christianity, If Constantine had not made the Catholic Religion the State Religion, and thus intertwined civilian and religious government together, would the heretical sects and other religious groups have been so threatened and, therefore, so strongly against the Catholic Church that the Catholic Church felt it was necessary to go to extreme unchristian measures for its preservation?

My sense is that the Catholic Church would not have been so threatening; however, when people weren't accepted as being a Christian unless they swore allegiance to the theology of the Catholic Church, there still would have been conflicts, but maybe not as severe or as deadly as they were.

The issues were not so much about religious beliefs as about power and control. While the Muslims seem to also have the same need to control all the land and people who were outside their control, and while the defense of one's beliefs is understandable, it surely should not have required forcibly converting everyone to the same beliefs. The death and destruction caused by not allowing religious freedom was and still is appalling, and certainly not what God envisioned, nor is forced allegiance to a theology based on what the church claimed Jesus modeled.

It is well to remember that the people living in David's Kingdom were not all Jews who followed Judaism. And the people who lived in Galilee and Judea during the time of Jesus were not all followers of Judaism or Jesus' ministry. Also, that Jesus ministered to those who came to Him, Jews, Romans, and Gentiles alike, without asking if they believed in His ministry.

Fighting was the unfortunate state of Christianity. Various sects fought with each other and with the Catholic Church to gain dominance as the Christian leading organization. The fighting was oftentimes to the death and oftentimes with government support, but simply could not be justified with Jesus' ministry or God's Covenant with Abraham. Using all means possible to gain control is about as far from Jesus' ministry and life as anyone can get. Mankind has proven to be a slow learner so this problem continues and could become worse in the future.

With the demise of the Roman Empire, the Catholic Church increased the time, money, and energy spent on schools for young men. As the quality of education increased, the level of inquiry and discussion went from rather mundane subjects to law, medicine, theology, and philosophy.

The study concerning the relationship of logic and faith became known as Scholasticism. It was the system of theology and philosophy discussion, based on Aristotelian logic and writings of early Church Fathers with a strong emphasis on tradition and doctrine. It began at the time of Charlemagne in a very simple form. As the weight of these discussions increased, "...the problem becomes in one direction the problem of the reconciliation of science and religion, and, in another, that of the reconciliation of philosophy and theology" (Noss page 659). In time, it became known to be a narrow-minded insistence on traditional doctrine.

One of the most intellectual men of his time was Thomas Aquinas, born in 1227. He was recognized in his day as one of the sharpest and brightest minds and contributed must to reconciling issues around philosophy and theology. He was a Dominican friar and taught in several Catholic schools. Two of his books continue to be used in the Roman Catholic Church. They are *Summa Gentiles* and *Summa Theologica*.

Starting late in the eleventh century, the church was calling for armies, identified as Crusades, to take Jerusalem away for the Muslims, and from time-to-time other non-Christian groups. Raising an army solved a second issue, that of finding something for the second and later sons to do. The first son inherited the position, land, and other property of the father. This led to unrest and serious problems throughout the Christian lands. The promise of adventure, wealth, and a free pass to heaven led many to join a crusade. Over about two centuries there were eight major crusades, with a few minor ones thrown in, that accomplished little other than to briefly capture Jerusalem and for a time, holding land in the northern area of Palestine after Jerusalem was again lost to the Muslims, and to get a lot of people killed.

Two organizations started during the First Crusade to defend and assist the Christian pilgrims in their journey from Europe through Muslim territory to Jerusalem. One was the Knights Templar and the other one was the Hospitallers.

In 1119, The Knights Templar was started as a closed community of devout Christian men who took monastic vows of poverty, chastity, and obedience that provided protection for the pilgrims traveling to Jerusalem. They became a large organization that was well-financed and had well-equipped men who were furious fighters who won many battles. The Templars were endorsed by the Catholic Church in 1129. Their demise started with the fall of Acre in 1291 and Pope Clement dissolved them in 1312.

The Hospitallers were founded in Jerusalem in 1099 to care for the sick and poor pilgrims. They were endorsed by Pope Paschal II in 1113. The Hospitallers maintained hostels in Italian cities for use by the pilgrims. They were well-financed and became a furious fighting force. The Hospitallers along with the Templars were a formidable military force in the Holy Land. When the Muslims recaptured the Holy Land in 1309 the Hospitallers moved from place to place until they went to Rhodes and ruled it as an independent state. In 1530, when the Muslims again caused them to move, the Hospitallers went to Malta.

Today it has no territorial rule, but its sovereign status is recognized by the Holy See and some Roman Christian states.

While both the Templars and the Hospitallers started with noble ideas about serving people in need, they soon morphed their work with those in need into becoming independent military forces on to themselves that far exceeded their original purpose. Both organizations became lost in their new status, as Jesus predicted in His answer to the third temptation.

Between the Inquisitions and the crusades, and later the subjecting and enslaving the Indians of South America and Mexico, the Catholic Church had managed to cause the death of hundreds of thousand people of several races and nationalities all in the name of Jesus, which heightened the stupidity of these tragedies.

The Catholic Church did these things by convincing itself, and the people, that it was the sole arbitrator of who would and would not go to heaven, and by being the most educated members of a community and a country's leadership. Often the priest or bishop would be the only one in the community that could read the official documents, which often were written in Latin. So, what the priest or bishop reported the document said, was it.

The Catholic Church fought hard to keep its places on top of the power structure and did manage to retain this position until the fifteenth century.

There is an old saying that goes something like this, "If you start out with an inaccurate assumption, all the brilliant minds in the world can't bring you to a correct conclusion." This, in a modified form, is the problem the Catholic Church was having.

To continue the ministry of Jesus, who was of the people, the Church decided that it needed rules and regulations, and creeds, theology, and doctrine, and expensive and beautiful church buildings, and glorious settings, robes and furnishings, and an eminent exalted leader drew from a group of learned church leaders.

Aside from all that, the most damaging thing was the death and destruction it caused because of its unwillingness to accept the validity of other people's different relationships with God. One problem with the Church's thinking that only it could determine the relationship people could have with God was that it very closely mimics the Judaism leaders thinking that only they could determine the relationship the Jews could have with God and with the Romans. In other words, the Catholic Church was doing all the things Jesus was against in His answer to the third temptation.

Of all the approaches for following Jesus the Catholic Church could have chosen, I cannot think of any approach that was farther from Jesus' ministry than the one they chose.

When Jesus told the Jews to turn around their lives, having new rules and regulations, and higher and more expensive buildings and garments, was not what He had in mind.

Jesus' message was never complex. It was always stated in the simplest terms. He was talking to shepherds, carpenters, farmers, and laborers, in terms they could understand. This is the simple concept that was lost as the Catholic Church grew and developed methods of ministering to its followers and the non-believers it encountered.

It has always befuddled me as to how anyone, even with no more than minimal knowledge of Jesus' ministry and His simple message could conclude that enslaving and killing people could be derived from Jesus' message and ministry. When one considers that the Catholic Church leaders had much more than minimal knowledge of Jesus' message and ministry, the enslaving and killing becomes inexcusable. Unfortunately, there was more such reasoning to come and not just from the Catholic Church.

There were civilian changes in the works that would adversely affect the Catholic Church. Early in the tenth century, organizations called Guilds were being formed. Merchants, tradesmen, and artisans of similar occupations were joined into Guilds as protection and as a way of controlling the use of the members' services and products. Existing towns served as business and commercial centers and new towns were forming to serve as business and commercial centers as well. As commerce increased the towns grew to become cities, the people's income and livelihood became dependent on the guilds and commerce rather than on the lords and kings. The peasants that worked for the lords and kings were moving to towns to work for the members of the guilds. Having the lords and kings derive income from owning vast tracts of land became less important to the economy. This also made the close ties between a king and the Catholic Church less important to the people.

In the fourteenth century, Europe was entering a period called the Renaissance (French for "rebirth") that lasted through the seventeenth century. The Crusades, along with the new discoveries by Columbus, Magellan, and Marco Polo, the advancements in science, and the migration of artisans and scholars to Italy after the fall of Constantinople in the fifteenth century, coupled with the newfound freedom that accompanied the growth in the guilds, and the expanded opportunity for work other than tenant farming and servanthood, and for new educational opportunities greatly increased the work opportunities available to the common man, as well as giving him knowledge of the world, art, and writings.

There were several positive outcomes of the Renaissance, but there are two that stand out. The first one was the growth of the middle class. It had its beginnings prior to the Renaissance but became much stronger during the Renaissance. The middle class was composed of the common people, who were better educated and who had the time and money to appreciate what the Renaissance had to offer.

The second outcome was decreased control the civilian and religious leadership had over the people and their activities. The relationship between civilian leadership, and commerce and business, was, in general, usually good for both parties. While the king could not survive without the tax income and the commerce and business couldn't survive without the support of the king, the king's control over business and commerce was much less than it had been when the king's income came from peasants' work on the land he owned.

The Catholic Church, on the other hand, was not able to establish a similar financial relationship with the people. The people, rather than continuing to follow the dictates of the Catholic Church, began to question the obvious failures of the church leadership to maintain high moral and religious standards they profess to believe. As a source of new money, the Church instituted the taxation of all transactions and appointments and the sale of indulgences, which were issued based on the assertion by the Pope that he had a collection of unused merits from the saints that he could sell to deserving Church members.

CHRISTIAN REFORMATION

During the middle-ages, the Roman Catholic Church was the largest and richest organization in its part of the world, and certainly among the richest and largest organizations in all the world. It had gotten so far away from the simple message of Jesus that its daily activities were no longer governed by Jesus' ministry.

Although there were alternatives, such as the Coptic and Nestorian Churches, the situation was ripe for changes in the Catholic Church. All that was needed was someone to step forward. The person who gave voice and action to the long desire for a reformation was a German named Martin Luther (1483-1546). He was born in Saxony into a poor family and became a priest through a strict, difficult monastic process, and was ordained in 1507. He became a professor at the new university in Wittenberg. Luther traveled to Roman where he saw the priests and the pope in their expensive clothes, with all the pomp and flaunting of their wealth, instead of living humbly with the humility of Jesus. With his experience growing up and what he was observing, his dissatisfaction with the church was becoming more pronounced.

The final straw for Luther was the arrival of the papal agent, Tetzel, selling indulgences in a neighboring town. Luther spoke out against the selling of indulgences, which led to Luther posting his *Ninety-Five Theses* on the castle church door, primarily taking to task the selling of indulgences. As was the custom, he was expecting a debate on each point; however, he had hit a sore spot that evidently had been festering with the people, for their request for copies overwhelmed the ability to produce enough copies. Not surprisingly, Tetzel attacked Luther as did others. The Pope ordered him to go to Rome for a trial; however, the Elector of Saxony intervened, and the Pope modified his order to an order for him to appear before the papal legate at Augsburg, which he did. The results of his appearance were inconclusive.

Luther had concluded that the Catholic Church had strayed so far from the Bible that it had become anti-Christian. He believed that a community of people who were faithful to the Bible was all that was needed to follow Jesus, whom he believed to be the Christ.

Martin Luther's Reformation was the first of several reformations that have led in the broad range of Protestant Churches, each with its own rituals and theology that exist still today.

Luther's followers grew originally in central Germany and then spread throughout Germany and Europe. The clash between Lutherans and Catholics resulted in religious wars which brought Germany to the brink of chaos. The result was the Peace of Augsburg, which gave equal rights to the Catholics and Lutherans and restored some order.

Luther did not establish a theology or doctrine for the non-Catholic groups. In a short time, other leaders emerged developed their own ideas of what the new religious groups should do.

More radical reformations came In Switzerland. One was Ulrich Zwingli (1484-1531) was a well-educated priest whose sympathies were with the Humanists. He advocated for only following the truths found in the Bible. His position was much different than Luther's position to not give up what is not forbidden in the Bible. Zwingli produced a civil war between Catholic and Reformed forces, which resulted in his death in one of the battles in 1531.

A young preacher in Switzerland, named Farel, began working on religious reform but found it so difficult that he asked a young Frenchman by the name of John Calvin, who had fled France, to join him in his work. Before fleeing France, John Calvin had published *The Institutes of the Christian Religion,* a crystal-clear definition of the Protestant position. These, *Institutes* became the foundation of Presbyterianism, and spelled out several positions regarding the relationship between God and man. Of special interest is his writing on original sin. His idea about original sin goes back to Adam and Eve, with which we are all burdened.

Calvin's reasoning led him to regard living as a serious undertaking. Such things as laughing, enjoying others at parties, card playing, and dancing were the work of the Devil and doomed one to Hell. God required hard work, even though faith not work got one to heaven. Solemn attention to God's work was the way to show one's faith and receive His love.

Once again, God's message, when asked, *forgiveness is freely given,* is lost in the development of theology. The Bible tells us that God was so mad at Adam and Eve that He threw them out of the Garden of Eden; however even though God was mad and punished them, God forgave them and continued to be their God.

Calvin managed to convert many people in Geneva, Switzerland to his way of thinking and Geneva became a refugee for a diverse group of scholars from several countries that did not support the Catholic or the established Protestant organizations. The French Protestants, the Huguenots, adopted Calvin's church organization. It comprised of the members, elders, and deacon, regular services led by the minister who performed the sacraments and met with the elders and deacons. The members chose the elders and deacons, who chose the minister.

The Reformation continued to spread throughout Europe, England, and Scotland to the dismay of the Catholic Church and some of the kings. It was not a smooth transformation and several wars, massacres, hangings, and burnings at the stake occurred from the fourteenth through the sixteenth centuries.

As the Reformation freed people to look at religion on their own, some used their own interpretation of the meaning in the Bible to go further away for the Catholic doctrine than did Luther and his followers. So, there was basically a reformation within the Reformation. One such group was the Anabaptist, which means "re-baptizers." They followed the New Testament in a serious and determined manner. They also believed that infant baptism was insufficient and were baptized again. Because of their separate ways, they were often called Separatists. The Anabaptists were severely persecuted. Eventually, a leader by the name of Menno Simons was able to soften their treatment. His followers in the Netherlands and the United States were and still are called Mennonites.

The Anabaptist was accompanied in its revolt from both the Catholic dogma and the Lutheran approach to the Reformation by the "Unitarianism." Both the Anabaptists and the Unitarians were too radical to be tolerated. Their beliefs included God being one person, there is no Trinity, and that Jesus is the Son of, but not the one God. Jesus became divine by living an exemplary life.

There were other groups that deviated sufficiently from the basic protestant thinking to be considered Nonconformists; however, they were more cooperative than the Anabaptists and not as heterodox as the Unitarians. There was no standard text or doctrine within the Protestant religious community, even though it appears that there was a core group of churches that used similar text and followed similar doctrine.

While all the changes were going on in Europe, England's King Henry VIII was separating England from the rule of the Pope and starting the Church of England, which used many of the worship elements of the Catholic Church. There were some members of the Church of England who did not want to start a new movement, but rather they simply wanted to *purify* the worship service by taking out the Roman Catholic Church elements. The Puritans, as they soon were called, found themselves in trouble with the King. The result of the conflict was that some emigrated to Holland and became Congregationalists and Baptists. Others emigrated to America, in Massachusetts and Connecticut and became the New England Congregationalists. Meanwhile the Puritans in England revolted against the King, which resulted in King Charles I having his head chopped off, and England was a Puritan nation for twelve years.

Another English nonconformist group was the Society of Friends, known as the Quakers. In some respects, they were the most radical group. The Quakers believed God's message was not confined to the scriptures, although reading scriptures is helpful, God's message can come directly to a believer who speaks God's message. They treated all believers as friends, who had the possibility of being an instrument for God's purpose. War and slavery were terrible failures. Their meetings are opened with prayer and medication waiting for someone to be moved to speak by his or her understanding of a message from God. As with other Protestant groups, the Quakers were persecuted. The Quaker religion came to America with William Penn, who had the grant of Pennsylvania from Charles II. He opened Pennsylvania for colonization to all who desired religious freedom. Today there are additional Protestant Churches with different theologies as the basis of their relationship with God.

As the industrial revolution in England becoming a reality, it drew people away from the farms and small craft shops into a new existence, for which they were ill-prepared. Their loss of moral ties led to social ills, the most pronounced being drunkenness. The situation was adversely affecting the wellbeing of the communities and England. As had earlier been the case, the situation needed someone to rise to the occasion. This time it was John Wesley, a student at Oxford. He had a student study group the met regularly for, *methodical* study and prayer in their rooms. They looked to the Quakers and their sense of God's close presence in daily life. They did not want to leave the Church of England, but as they traveled through England and gained followers, they decided to start a new denomination called Methodist. The church grew and traveled to America where it soon became a major denomination in America.

The success the Reformation was enjoying gave the Catholic Church phase to consider the need to rethink its position on Christianity. Interestingly it was Emperor Charles V that pushed the issue and after his efforts to bring about a reconciliation of the Protestants and Catholics, he pressured Pope Paul III to call the Council of Trent in 1545. Over a period of eighteen years, three main statements resulted. The first one was the restatement of the Catholic doctrine that had been developed in medieval times. The second one was to restructure the Inquisition to make it available to all civil authorities in Europe, with the hope that it could rid Europe of the Protestants. The third was the rise of new Catholic orders, the most famous of which was the Jesuits.

The Jesuits were started by a Spanish nobleman, Ignatius Loyola. They bound themselves into a life of strict militia-like discipline, *spiritual exercises* and absolute obedience to their superiors, short of sin. Their definition of sin made it difficult to sin. They were pretty much self-directed answering only to their superiors. They were initially successful in their missionary work, especially in the Americas; however, their methods soon wore out their welcome to the point that their sole purpose was and remains to promote the supremacy of the Pope.

The failure of the Catholics and Protestants to reach an agreement to work towards a common goal and to respect each other led to long periods of turmoil and destructive conflicts, including the Thirty Years War, which was fought mainly in Germany with devastating consequences for the county and its people. The Catholic Church's close, and often inseparable, relationship with civil authorities had slowly weakened its status in the eyes of the layman. The strongest example of this is the rise of dissatisfaction of the Frenchmen that led to the French Revolution, which included violence to the clergy and the turning away from Christianity. When Napoleon came to power, he came to terms with the Catholic Church but retained control of the church.

As the Catholic Church continued strict adherence to the established doctrine, there were two new developments in the nineteenth century. In 1854, Pope Pius IX proclaimed the Immaculate Conception of the Virgin to be a dogma of the Catholic Church. This means that Mary, having conceived Christ while still a virgin, was free from original sin by the immaculate purity in which her parents conceived her. The second dogma was that the Pope was infallible in matters of the church. Both proclamations did nothing to help the relationship between the Catholic and Protestant Christian. It also did not help stem the tide of laymen asking themselves if all the ritual, theology, and doctrine were necessary? This was especially true in the world of science, which for some time had been troubled by having to fit the continuing scientific discoveries and knowledge into the framework of medieval religious thinking that had no tolerance for thinking outside the strict dictates of both the Catholic and Protestant churches. Galileo's experience is a classic example of the Catholic Church's answer to new ideas. The reaction to Darwin's *Origin of the Species* illustrates the Protestant discomfort with science.

In the nineteenth century, the Protestant churches brought Sunday School into the religious structure. The Protestant leaders had for some time looked for of a way to educate young people in the Christian religion. The Sunday School of the nineteenth century has, over the years, seen several improvements that have increased its effectiveness in bring the Christian message to young people.

MODERN CHRISTIANITY- CONTINUES TO LOSE ITS SENSE OF DIRECTION

The basis for the story of Judaism and Christianity comes from the ancient people who developed the first creation story. This story describes their perception of the close spiritual relationship between God and mankind.

The Hebrew Tribe of the Semitic people had several gods they could follow. It was Abraham who chose the god of the mountain, "God All Mighty" to be his God, and it was this God who chose Abraham. The Covent between God and Abraham confirmed the relationship between God and mankind as described in the first creation story.

These ancient people were comfortable enough with their perception of a loving God to declare two basic ideas as the foundation for their relationship with God.

The first idea was that mankind was made in the image of God and could live in the likeness of God. This meant that all mankind was on the same basis with God and that all mankind could live in God's blessing. He did not use different requirements for some nor did He establish the need for there to be kings and servants.

The second idea was that mankind could have a personal relationship with God, which included God freely giving mankind His blessing, forgiveness, and grace with only the requirement being that He was mankind's God above all else. This idea was a new and different way of looking at the gods. Normally the various gods were feared, and only special people could communicate with the gods.

Whether there was or is more than one God, as suggested in the first creation story, is not near as important as believing in the message that our God is the God of Abraham, who is open to having a spiritual relationship with each of us and freely gives us His blessing, forgiveness, and grace, with only the requirement that He is our God above all else.

That we are made in God's image and that we can have a personal relationship with God, serves as the foundation for the stories in both the Old and New Testaments of the Bible.

It is a sad truth that Christians have never been of one mind about what constituted an acceptable relationship with God. The failure to accept that God was not as picky about His relationship with individual Christians as Christians have been about each other's Christian's relationship with God, got Christianity off the track from the get-go, and it has never gotten back on track.

STRUCTURE AND THE THREE M'S

There were many religions in the ancient world that described various relationships mankind could have with the unseen entities that mankind called *gods*.

All these religions incorporated the same main ingredients, the three "M's", Myth, Mystery, and Magic, into their own rituals and theology. These three "M's" remain in Christianity of today.

What can be made of today's Christianity? How did we get from enjoying the simple, straightforward, uncomplicated teachings and life of Jesus, based on the creation story idea that all mankind was made in the image of God, to the Christianity of today, with its specialty shops, that one must obtain permission to join? The unbelievably complex structure of the religious myths, mystery and magic that are embedded in each specialty shop's theology, doctrine, and dogmatic beliefs will continue to cause religious disagreements that all too often will lead to misery and wars.

Regardless of how well the various Christian organizations are or are not working together, the basic question remains, is all the structure, ritual, and doctrine necessary for people to have a spiritual relationship with God?

The requirements of the current Christian churches for acceptance of that Church's theology to become a member, and remain a member in good standing, have nothing to do with Jesus' ministry. He helped people regardless of their religious beliefs or any other requirement—other than they needed help. His work to improve a person's life was given without any strings attached. Examples of His work are healing the paralytic in Mark 2:1-12, and Jairus' daughter in Mark 5:21-43, feeding the 5,000 in Mark 6:30-40, and healing the Syrophoenician woman in Mark 7:24-30 and the centurion's servant in Matthew 8: 5-13.

The three *M*'s and religious structures were not required by God when He made mankind in His image with minimal instructions and requirements. I do not think God, in His wildest imagination, thought that being made in His image would result in the religious organizations we have today, ones that are so far removed from His simple relationship with His friend Abraham. With its many religious doctrines and theologies to follow, Christianity today spends little time living as what God saw as being good.

The similarities between Christianity of today and Judaism, whose leaders' efforts led to Jesus' crucifixion are much greater than the similarities between Christianity of today and Jesus' ministry.

INTOLERANCE

The underlying issue for mankind is the intolerance people have for other people. This is a problem that we have not been able to solve. If God, who gave us everything thing we need to live in the world of His making, had kept control of us He could have required tolerance for all, but our relationship with Him would not be much different than the relationship churches have with their members. Since He entrusted us with control of His creation it is up to us to solve the problem by being as tolerant of others as God is.

Both the ideas that we are made in the image of God and that we can have a personal relationship with God thread through the Old and New testaments and are the foundation for Christianity; however, through the intervention of religion between God and mankind, with its doctrine, theology, and rituals, the idea of simply having a spiritual relationship with God to guide each one of us to live in His likeness has lost much of its strength and has been relegated to being a footnote in Christian theology.

Throughout history, Christians have continually failed to incorporate tolerance for others into their lives. Christian Churches, and Christians on their own, have participated in and supported, actions of intolerance that have caused great hardships, suffering, and death throughout the world. History is filled with the results of Christianity failing to follow the guidance of the Ten Commandants and the teachings of Jesus.

Intolerance was evident in the story of Cain and Abel, and it has been a part of the stories throughout the Old and New Testaments. Intolerance was the driving force behind the Catholic Church's fight against heresies and the fights between Catholic and Protestant Churches and between the different Protestant Churches. Intolerance is central to the theological strife that resulted in Christianity splitting into the Eastern Orthodox Church, centered in Constantinople, and the Roman Catholic Church, centered in Roman. Perhaps the most profound lack of tolerance is the continuing destruction caused by Christian's intolerance of the Jews.

Much harm has been done and will continue to be done in the name of Christianity when people of different beliefs and lifestyles are shunned or loudly declared to be possessed by the devil or are declared to be a danger to Christians. Somehow, Jesus' curing the daughter of a Roman soldier, meeting with the Samaritans, and accepting and curing other non-Jews have been relegated to being insignificant and not germane to Christianity. It seems to me to be extremely difficult for someone to be spiritually connected to God while believing in the doctrines, theologies and structures, and the thinking of many of today's churches.

Consider two events of the last 100+ years. Would there have been a First World War had the Christian Government of the Empire of Austria-Hungary not tried to retain tight control over all parts of its Empire? And after the First World War, could the Second World War have been avoided if France and its allies had not forced an unsustainable burdensome armistice on Germany after the First World War? Surely, in both situations, the governments could have found better solutions than the two wars and the massive death and destruction that came from these wars.

Think of all the effort, lost lives, and misery that could have been avoided simply by allowing different people to have a different relationship with their spiritual entity. I often wonder what Christianity would be if the Jewish and Greek members of the Antioch church had been allowed to continue meet and eat together, even though they had different ideas about who and what Jesus was. If this early simple idea had been allowed to continue and grew, it could have led to a totally different Christianity of unlimited possibilities.

Instead, Christianity has gotten far away from the idea that having a personal spiritual relationship with God is important above all else and accepting the theology of each Christian denomination as being more important than having a spiritual relationship with God. A person's belief in God and dedication to living in the likeness of God is hard to find a tolerant religion or government of today. Both are more concerned with power and control than with allowing each person to have his or her own spiritual relationship with God.

One would hope having a personal relationship with God would foster tolerance for each other; however, people and nations that claim to be Christian maintain such deeply felt intolerances that the people and their governments, and too often churches, are guided and directed by anger, suspicion, and violence against all people who think differently, which has led to many Christian groups taking unchristian actions including hangings, burning at the stake, inquisitions, and destructive wars.

There are Christian Churches and groups that are to be commended for their willingness to tolerate and accept differences found within Christianity and between Christianity and other religious groups.

These are small steps in the right direction that one can hope will be the future for Christianity.

MISGUIDED THEOLOGY

I think it is a gross understatement to say that Christianity is missing the mark.

People of the world see Christianity as just another religion no better, and in some cases, worse than other religions. The central nonreligious teachings of Jesus' have been surpassed by Christianity religious theology.

It is unfortunate that Jesus' simple message became, and continues to be, a trillion-dollar industry of theology, creeds, magnificence architectural structures, and a great many land holdings, all to glorify a Jesus who led a simple life of demonstrating living in the likeness of God through His ministry to the Jews based on God's love, grace, and forgiveness.

Christianity continues to be based on the belief that Jesus had an inside track to his relationship with God that common people could not have. Evidently, the early leaders of Christianity felt that the opening verses of the Bible could not be taken at face value, that it was unrealistic to think that God gave mankind the gifts of being made in his image, and being given the world of His making, without a manual of instruction.

Each person's concept of God is of that person's own making just as the concept of God and their relationship with Him was of the people who gave us the creation story. The realization that we can be greater than we perceive we can be is indescribable.

No one has seen God, although some people have seen or felt His presence. Each one of us has an image of God. Jesus said that "If you have seen me you have seen God." But for us who never saw Jesus, that is little help, unless you can envision Jesus' spiritual connection to God that He showed in his lifestyle of calm composure in the face of the strong push back from the powerful Jewish religious leadership.

God is infinite, without limits. Any description or definition of God would establish limitations on who and what God is. Yet we have theologies that limit our relationship with God and interject man-made religious stipulations on the relationship with God. While the idea of being made in the image of God may still be part of Christianity, it no longer has the importance that God gave it as His gift to us.

Do we really have the power to limit God's concept of man being made in His image and the magnitude of His creation? Not supporting or allowing man to use his God-given abilities to investigate, study, and analyze his world precludes man's potential for developing a fuller more exciting relationship with God, and limits man's ability to recognize the full extent of God's creation and that His creation is changing and evolving.

RELIGION Vs SCIENCE

Should not science and religion co-exist without getting into each other's way? However, that is not what has happened over the past many years. With science generally being described as the search for, and application of, knowledge, and religion being describe as belief in and worshipping a superhuman controlling power, the conflict comes in the current time, with science using the knowledge of today as the basis for future discoveries and knowledge, and with religion weighing today's knowledge against the past knowledge that has been accepted as being true beyond question. As has been true in other areas, the continuing disagreements from the inability to find a compromise or find common areas of agreement, have caused pain, suffering. and death.

We continually struggle to find common areas of agreement or areas of acceptable disagreement in such areas as defining God's creation. There are several theories and opinions on such things as what caused the Universe to be. Did it begin out of nothing with a sudden expansion of energy and elements known as the Big Bang, or was the universe formed from an unknown source? Was that source God or dark matter or dark energy or a combination of all three? Even with as much formation that is available there is still much that is unknown. It is a case of the more we know the more we do not know.

If that is not enough to think about, think about how life started. There are two competing theories on the beginning of life. One is that God created life and the other is that life evolved over time.

The truth is that, even with the great scientific advances that have been made over the last couple of centuries, we do not know enough to be able to accurately explain what happened at the beginning of life or the universe.

While the research continues to get us closer to answers for these questions, we are still a long way from having the complete answers, and it may be beyond our ability to fully answer these questions. Regardless of what is found out about the beginning of life, the Christian answer remains for many that the seven-day timeline for the beginning of the world and all that is in it is the right and indisputable answer.

Just because we are made in the image of God does not mean that we are God. Some things may be best left to our imagination. I think the best we can do, without naming names or describing processes, is accept that there is something greater than us at work in the world and the universe.

A more compelling question is why in the world is it necessary to pit God against science? What prevents both God and science from being involved with establishing our beginnings? After all, God of the first creation story made the world and saw that it was very good. What about that story says that the science of creation was not part of what God made and saw was good? Would it really be disastrous if both sides agreed that it is more important to accept that we can do better than continuing the unending battles over how the world and life were created? And as we continue to increase our knowledge of our world and who we are, the only criteria need is to live to our fullest and leave the world better than it is.

Regardless of how the universe and the world began and what God's role and the natural processes, neither the universe nor the world was created to remain stagnate. Rather, we live in a dynamic active world and a small part of a dynamic active universe both of which can be explored, and both of which continue to present unending questions and unending opportunities for man to fully use his God-given abilities.

So, What Is Our Relationship With God?

We continue today to have no idea of what these gods are, what they look like, or how they function. Is the God of Abraham a physical being or a spirit, a he or she, or is God an entity that combines all forms of being? And how can we define God without limiting God?

We cannot prove unequivocally that there is or is not a God. The best we can do is accept the first creation story, or if you rather, the second creation story, as the story developed by the ancient people to explain their belief there are forces or entities that affect our lives that are beyond our control. Abraham's God of the mountain is the force or entity that is the God of the Jews and Christians.

There are Christians who have gone beyond religious requirements and have lived as God intended. Unfortunately, today many Christians are in the same boat as Jews were in Jesus' time. They are busy following religious dictates rather than living in God's blessing.

Living in the blessing of God or in the kingdom of God is not something that one can achieve by paying money, nor can it be achieved as an award for long and faithful service, or by belonging to a particular organization, or by reading and studying Bible passages, or religious theology and manuscripts, or being involved in humanitarian activities. While these are pathways to receiving God's blessing, they, in and of themselves, do not result in receiving God's blessing.

The issue is simply this; how can one receive God's blessing if he or she is not paying attention to God? Rather, God's blessing is achieved within oneself, by having a connection with God through one's heart and soul that provides the ensuing support one receives from God that excels all else. It provides comfort and support in the face of despair and hopelessness. When all seems lost God gives new life and strength.

It is applying Jesus' ministry to all mankind, regardless of what level of turmoil and uncertainty one encounters in the world of today. God's promise to Abraham, that Abraham's descendants would bless all the families of the earth is still available to all mankind.

Christianity apparently does not believe God's promise to Abraham because our efforts that have turned people's lives into a living hell far outweighs our efforts that have people live in God's likeness.

I think that it is reasonable to think that when God made us in His image, He did so with the expectation that we would live in His likeness. It is a good thing that God included His grace and forgiveness in our creation, for we have certainly made a mess of living in his world. Even with our failure to live up His expectations, God continues to extend to us His unencumbered grace and blessing. Can Christians do less?

God keeps short accounts. He does not hold grudges or keep score. Every time Abraham broke loose from his spiritual relationship with God, God would welcome him back without harping on his failures. Jesus' Prodigal Son story is a strong story about forgiveness and acceptance. Accepting the message of the Prodigal Son story is key to understanding God's grace. God does not require penitence for previous mistakes to receive His blessing and grace, just a heartfelt desire to live a God-centered life.

While both Jews and Christians have wandered away from God and lived outside the reach of God's love, God's response to our prodigal ways has been to accept us back into a relationship with Him. Living in a relationship with God is the basis for living in the likeness of God.

It is through our relationship with God that each one of us can find peace with ourselves and our world.

Through all the ups and downs I have had with my relationship with Christianity, this story has been the one constant that I have retained. It is central to my belief in a friendly God I can trust and count on for support and guidance.

It would have been well if my parents' church members would have followed God's example. Years ago, when I was in the Air Force and I was home on leave for Christmas, I went to the annual meeting of mother and dad's church. Dad was upset and nervous. As soon as the meeting started, I knew why Dad was upset. The meeting quickly devolved into an unruly shouting, name-calling meeting with nasty language. These people I known and had respected had turned into warring factions who were bent on destroying each other, supposedly in the name of following Jesus. The disagreements were about such things as the minister not paying enough attention to the youth programs and some elders were unhappy about how things were being done while other elders thought things were fine. It seemed to me that the issues were ones that, in a nonreligious setting, would be solved through discussion, agreement, and compromise. I was taken back by what I had observed.

God does not want committee meetings. He wants a separate relationship with each person. A God-centered relationship is a one-on-one relationship. For God, each person is worth God's personal attention. God does not choose sides in church disagreements or any disagreement for that matter. He gave us what we need to resolve our differences without the chaos that hatred causes.

Group relationships, such as God had with the apostles on Pentecost, affected each apostle differently. God was OK with that, for continuing their relationship with God was not a joint effort. It was up to each apostle to continue his relationship with God, just as it was up to each church member in mother and dad's church to have their own relationship with God.

Jesus' ministry came from the ancient Israelite writings including those in the Old Testament. Jesus was strongly opposed to the Judaism leaders using these writings as the vehicle for maintaining control of the Jews and to become wealthy at the expense of the Jews. It is unfortunate that Christianity has turned Jesus' demonstration of living in the likeness of God into a religion driven by rules rituals and theology and the acquiring of great wealth rather than emulating Jesus' life.

It would be hard to summarize Jesus' ministry any better than His answers to the three temptations and His Sermon on the Mount.

If one can strip away all the religious information about what one ought to do and what rituals to follow to become a Christian and concentrate on Jesus' ministry, he or she can find the spiritual relationship Jesus had with God. Paul thought Jesus' relationship was uniquely spiritual; however, he did not think the Gentiles would accept Jesus' ministry without Jesus being divine, even though there were Gentiles who related to Jesus' ministry just as Jews did, without Paul's idea that Jesus was divine.

Based on the idea that we can live in the likeness of God, who, other than ourselves, will save us from our failures? Several years ago, there was a comic strip called Pogo. In one of its strips the main character, Pogo, made a profound observation. He said, "We have found the enemy and it is us." It would serve Christianity well to take the observation of Pogo to heart.

Accepting God's forgiveness and grace, which is always available to us, can take the sting out of our failures. We do not have to be without faults be to receive God's love and acceptance. So, what more do we need than to decide to live in harmony with God? You will not find a better offer than God's. We need to be willing to accept responsibility for our own actions and develop the ability to forgive ourselves, regardless of what we have done, and accept God's forgiveness that is freely given.

To live in the likeness of God is to live in a spiritual relationship with God. Then, God's guidance becomes an integral part of who one is and how one lives. God's presence will be evident in what a person does and how that person lives.

What one does is forgiven by God's grace but not by the church. God set no rules, but Catholic and Protestant religions have. The lack of tolerance is in the need for everyone to read the Bible the same, worship the same, and think the same. *My way or the highway* is a strong statement of intolerance. People can be like-minded; however, the hard question is can they allow others to be differently like-minded.

As we continue to struggle to get out of our own way, the good news is that God does still believe in us and believes that someday we will fully live in his blessing. Until that day comes, we continue to receive God's forgiveness and grace for our failures.

The core failure of Christianity is that Jesus' life and ministry is not the top priority over and above Jesus' birth and death. While Jesus' birth and death are important, the lessons a person can receive from these two events pale in comparison to the lessons one can receive from Jesus' ministry.

Christians would do well to remember that the message of Jesus' life in his ministry is just as true today as it was in Jesus' time.

It is up to us whether we keep the world a wonderful place to live or make it a hell on earth. Although God believed we could figure out how to live in his likeness, God did not instruct us or direct us on how to do that. He left it to us to receive guidance through our spiritual relationship with Him. God is always available; however, He does not go looking for people to help. It is incumbent on each person to have a relationship with God and to request God's help.

So, what would get Christianity back to being God-centered? Christianity can start by going back to the basics. That mankind is made in the image of God and can live in the likeness of God. The rich young ruler's requirement to give up all that he had to follow Jesus was no more daunting than what Christians must do today?

Chapter 12

CONCLUSIONS

W hat conclusions can be drawn from all that has happened in the 4,000 plus years beginning with an ancient people's idea about God that is told in the first verses of the Bible through the stories of the Christians today?

From the arrival of early mankind, eons ago, we have felt that we were not alone living on earth. That there were spiritual things and forces to which we were, and are, beholding. Over the centuries the effort of mankind to relate to the unseen spiritual things and forces has resulted in many religions that have tried to relate to the unseen spiritual things and forces.

There is a constant theme that threads through biblical stories. It starts with God making us in His image and offering us the ability to live in His likeness. From this beginning, the biblical stories in both the Old and New Testaments describe God showing His love for us through His forgiveness of our failures, and His welcoming us back, no matter how large or how small our failure has been.

The simple idea that we are on earth because God wanted us to be on earth is not well received by many of us. Some say that there must be more to it than that. Others say there is no unseen entity, with whom we can be spiritually connected. All we have is the natural sequence of being born, living, and dying. That the mystery that surrounds us is not from God but, is from naturally occurring activities that we are yet to discover such as dark matter and dark energy which when found will have a plausible explanation.

Some two thousand years ago there was a man named Jesus, a carpenter, who saw the simple message that all mankind was made in God's image and could live in the likeness of God. The Jews of his time thought of him as a man who took God's message to heart and based his life and ministry on his understanding of God's relationship with the Jews.

Jesus' primary concern was for the Jews to break away from their dependence on living in the stifling environment of the misuse of the Jewish religion by the Jewish priests' and the control imposed by the conquering Romans and live with God's guidance and blessing. Although the number of Jews who heard and followed Jesus was small, the positive impact of his three-year ministry on those who followed him led to the religion called Christianity.

There were men who lived before Jesus began his ministry and men who lived after Jesus' death that provided positive guidance and direction to the Jews; however, none had the overall impact of Jesus' ministry. Jesus' message filled a void in Jews and Gentiles which led to groups of Jesus' followers, which were called the Way. The different Way groups had different interpretations of Jesus' ministry.

During the early time of Christianity, when Christianity was struggling and in danger of being overtaken by the existing pagan religions Paul, a Pharisee, converted to being a member and became a leader of Christianity. Paul has been called, "the second founder of Christianity." There is no question of the strong impact Paul had on Christianity. A divide had developed in Christianity between the Jerusalem Church that retained Mosaic Law and Jewish practices, and the more liberal Greek speaking, or Gentile, Church. Paul became a leader of the liberal Church and was able to relieve the liberal church members of the requirement to adhere to Jewish Law.

Paul brought to the Gentile Church his Pharisee thinking, which included organization and structure which were helpful to the Church;

however, he also brought his Pharisee thinking about the relationship between God and the Jews which led to his decision that Jesus was divine. Having a divine Jesus rather than a Jesus living in the likeness of God totally changed Jesus' relationship with God and Jesus' relationship with people.

Whatever Paul thought would come out of Jesus being divine, it certainly was not the chaos and destruction that has happened within Christianity. Instead of following Jesus' example of living in the likeness of God, the Christians' set about establishing and following the theologies of the various Christian denominations, with their intolerance of each other. Surely, Christianity and the world would have been better off if we would accept living with the guidance of God in the chaos of our time as Jesus had in the chaos of His time.

Regardless of who we are, our station in life, the language we speak, or the color of our skin, or what religion or theology each one of us may follow, or where we live, or the political belief each one may have, God loves each one of us. Yes, God gets disgusted with us from time to time, and we certainly give him just cause for that, but He never takes away His forgiveness or His belief in each one of us or our ability to accept His invitation to live in His likeness. The stupid things we do will not change who He is or His relationship with us, they only change who we are and our relationship with Him.

So really, what does God want from each one of us? God wants each one of us to live in a simple, spiritual personal relationship with Him. He wants us to follow and trust His guidance and support in all that we do. He wants us to accept His love for us. To accept that His guidance comes from His love for each one of us.

The relationship each one of us has with God is just between God and each one of us. Our individual relationship with God is not part of the relationship a religious group, denomination, or organization has with God.

The strength of our relationship with God rests solely on the strength of our part of the relationship. God's part of the relationship will always be strong enough to support our part of the relationship. It is up to us to keep the relationship clear and uncluttered and not sidetracked with doubts, concerns, or our loss of belief.

The impediments of obtaining a relationship with God do not come from God, they came from us. The writers of the stories in the Bible recognized that God could only help those who believed in Him and accepted His guidance.

Jesus' ministry centered on people, nothing else. His answers to the three temptations and His sermon on the Mount provide the direction and purpose of His ministry, but His ministry was always about people and their relationship with God.

I end this book with three statements that are my favorites. They are:

- He has showed you, O man, what is good; and what does the Lord require of you but to do justice and to love kindness (or steadfast love) and to walk humbly with your God? Micah 6:6-8

- The declaration by Pogo that, "We have found the enemy and it is us."

- God believes in each one of us, that we can live in His likeness. The question each one of us must ask ourselves, do we believe in *us*?